for Maurice
with gratitude for your help
& challenging dialogue
on "epiphany"!

Robin

Shakespeare's Tragic Form

Shakespeare's Tragic Form

Spirit in the Wheel

Robert Lanier Reid

DELAWARE

Newark: University of Delaware Press
London: Associated University Presses

Associated University Presses
440 Forsgate Drive
Cranbury, NJ 08512

Associated University Presses
16 Barter Street
London WC1A 2AH, England

Associated University Presses
P.O. Box 338, Port Credit
Mississauga, Ontario
Canada L5G 4L8

The paper used in this publication meets the requirements of the American National Standard for Permanence of Paper for Printed Library Materials Z39.48-1984

Library of Congress Cataloging-in-Publication Data

Reid, Robert Lanier, 1943–
    Shakespeare's tragic form : spirit in the wheel / Robert Lanier Reid,
        p. cm.
    Includes bibliographical references (p.) and index.
    ISBN 0-87413-725-X (alk. paper)
    1. Shakespeare, William, 1564–1616—Tragedies. 2. Shakespeare, William, 1564–1616—Technique. 3. Literary form. 4. Tragedy. I. Title.

PR2983 .R39 2000
822.3′3—dc21   00-028623

In loving memory of
Ralph Connor Reid, Sr.,
and
Nancy Campbell Lanier Reid

and for Suzanne

Contents

Acknowledgments   9
List of Abbreviations   11
Introduction   13

Part I: Shakespearean Dramaturgy

1. The Dramaturgical and Psychological Structure of
Shakespeare's Plays   23

   Debating Shakespeare's Dramaturgy: Five Acts,
   Three Cycles   24
   Shakespeare's Dramatic Form: 2-1-2   31
   Adapting Source Materials to Dramatic Form   38
   Shakespeare's Compositional Process   44

2. Multiple Plots and Protagonists in Shakespeare's
Tragedies: A Problem of Dramatic Form   48

   Tragic Form and Social Diversity   49
   Shakespeare's *Sprecher-Magus:* Orchestrating Diversity   52
   Tragedies of Insularity, or of Mutuality   55
   Doubling Tragedy in *Hamlet* and *King Lear*   58
   Multiplicity vs. Mutuality in *King Lear:* Chaos
   Shaped by Love   62

Part II: Shakespearean Epiphany

3. Epiphanal Encounters in Shakespearean Dramaturgy   69

   The Sources of Shakespearean Epiphany   70
   The Evolution of Epiphany in Shakespeare's Plays   74
   Shakespearean Epiphany vs. Modern Epiphanies   81

4. Shakespeare's Immanent Epiphanies: Soul and
Spirit in the Works of Spenser and Shakespeare   89

   Human Essence as "Soul" and "Spirit": The Rival
   Traditions   91
   Spenser's Houses, Shakespeare's Clouds   93

Fulfillment as Rational Ecstasy or Passional Ripeness:
     Contrary Views of Passion, Woman, and
     Commoners   96
Shakespeare's Changing Use of "Soul"   100
The Soul at Death: Spenser and Shakespeare   103
"Spirit" in Spenser and Shakespeare   104

Part III: Shaping Psyche's Tragic Quest:
Contrary Faces of Nothing

5. Macbeth's Three Murders   111

Killing Duncan: Usurping and Dismantling
     Superego   114
Killing Banquo: Envying the Ego Ideal   116
Killing Lady Macduff and Her Children: Annihilating
     the Id, and All Otherness   120

6. Lear's Three Shamings   123

Seeing Goneril: Superego Disabled by False
     Sublimation   126
Seeing Poor Tom: Reconstituting Ego by Projection   129
Seeing Cordelia: Restoring Id by Introjection   138

Notes   145
Bibliography   171
Index   185

Acknowledgments

Eleven years ago in a lively NEH seminar I became intrigued with the "inner plot" of *Macbeth*. Psychologically, what happens to the protagonists? Is the regicide, their first kill, the only one that counts? After examining many theories of human nature, both ancient and modern (especially the developmental schemes of Freud, Klein, various Object Relations psychologists, and Kohut's Self Psychology), I published "Macbeth's Three Murders: Shakespearean Psychology and Tragic Form" (*Renaissance Papers 1991*). Finding the same pattern (though psychologically inverted) in the companion-tragedy of *King Lear*, I devised a sequel, "Lear's Three Shamings: Shakespearean Psychology and Tragic Form" (*Renaissance Papers 1996*). These essays, revised, provide this book's culminating chapters.

The dramaturgic impact of this tragic form derives partly from the stunning confrontation Shakespeare places at the heart of each of the three cycles of action. Hence my analysis of "Epiphanal Encounters in Shakespearean Dramaturgy" (*Comparative Drama*, 1998). That essay, together with a meditation on Shakespeare's use of the words "soul" and "spirit," forms the heart of this book.

The most recent component of my study, chapters 1 and 2, looks more broadly at Shakespeare's dramaturgical form and his frequent use of multiple plots and protagonists. Does the three-cycle pattern inform only the two great tragedies, or all of Shakespeare's plays? For supporting this final, arduous project—analyzing plot structure throughout the canon—I am grateful to my institution, Emory & Henry College, and to the Appalachian College Association. They jointly provided the sabbatical funding that enabled me to undertake this final study and shape the manuscript into a coherent whole. During the decade in which this book was written, Emory & Henry in fact provided several sabbatical leaves and funds for summer research.

I am grateful to the Virginia Foundation for the Humanities for a residency fellowship in Charlottesville which initiated this study; to the National Humanities Center in Durham, North Carolina, for a residency which further advanced it; and to the Mednick, Mellon, and NEH foundations for funding five summers of research at the Folger Shakespeare Library and at the libraries of Oxford and Cambridge.

My life has been richly blessed by intelligent, generous-spirited librarians—especially at the Folger, the Bodleian, and Emory & Henry. I am particularly obliged to Thelma Hutchins, Jane Caldwell, Patty Greany, Claudine Daniel, Janet Kirby, Pat Norris, Tonya White, Sherry Lyttle, Jeanine Yarber, Deborah Ratliff, and Juanita Ratliff (all quite familiar with my scholarly obsessions, technical problems, and endless requests) who have my full endorsement for canonization.

Special thanks to the many scholars who encouraged me during the years of this project, giving astute commentary and advice at various stages, especially Mark Taylor, Arthur Kirsch, John Shawcross, Joe Bryant, John Drakakis, Kent Cartwright, Naomi Liebler, John Lang, and Maurice Luker. To Darryl Gless I am grateful for much assistance and friendship during my sabbatical year. And to George Williams, whose generosity regarding this project is impossible to assess fully, I bow the head.

Thanks also to *Renaissance Papers* and *Comparative Drama* for allowing me to reprint in revised form the essays on *Macbeth, King Lear,* and Shakespearean epiphany.

I am specially appreciative of those close to home, the many students in "Shakespeare," "Great Books," and other classes who challenge and enliven me in more ways than they know.

Of course I am most grateful to Suzanne, Jenny, and Tristan for their endless support and bright surprises, their deep reactions and intellectual candor, their affectionate companionship.

Abbreviations

AI	*American Imago*
CahiersE	*Cahiers Elisabethains*
CompD	*Comparative Drama*
CL	*Comparative Literature*
ELN	*English Language Notes*
ELH	*English Literary History*
ELR	*English Literary Renaissance*
ES	*English Studies*
HLQ	*Huntington Library Quarterly*
IJP	*International Journal of Psychoanalysis*
JAPA	*Journal of the American Psychoanalytic Association*
L&P	*Literature and Psychology*
MRTS	*Medieval and Renaissance Studies*
MLN	*Modern Language Notes*
MLR	*Modern Language Review*
MP	*Modern Philology*
NLH	*New Literary History*
N&Q	*Notes and Queries*
PQ	*Philological Quarterly*
PMLA	*Publications of the Modern Language Association*
PsyQ	*Psychoanalytic Quarterly*

PsyR	*Psychoanalytic Review*
PSOC	*Psychoanalytic Study of the Child*
RenD	*Renaissance Drama*
RenP	*Renaissance Papers*
REL	*Review of English Literature*
RES	*Review of English Studies*
SE	*Standard Edition of the Complete Psychological Works of Sigmund Freud,* trans. and ed. by James Strachey. London: Hogarth Press, 1953–74. 24 vols
SEL	*Studies in English Literature*
SR	*Sewanee Review*
ShAB	*Shakespeare Association Bulletin*
ShJE	*Shakespeare Jahrbuch*
SQ	*Shakespeare Quarterly*
ShakS	*Shakespeare Studies*
ShS	*Shakespeare Survey*
SAQ	*South Atlantic Quarterly*
SoAR	*South Atlantic Review*
SpEncy	*The Spenser Encyclopedia.* Ed. A. C. Hamilton *et al.* Toronto: University of Toronto Press, 1990
SP	*Studies in Philology*
UCrow	*The Upstart Crow: A Shakespeare Journal*

Biblical quotations are taken from *The Geneva Bible: Facsimile of the 1560 Edition.* Madison: University of Wisconsin Press, 1969.

Shakespeare quotations and titles are taken from David Bevington's updated 4th edition of *The Complete Works of Shakespeare.* New York: Longman, 1997. I follow his modernized spelling, including the omission of "u" in many names.

Introduction

The fingers of the powers above do tune
The harmony of this peace.
. . . let our crooked smokes climb to their nostrils.
Cymbeline 5.5.470–71, 481

To SEEK A SIMPLE, SINGULAR FORM IN SHAKESPEARE'S PLAYS IS TO court frustration. As Bullough's *Narrative and Dramatic Sources* attest, Shakespeare draws from radically disparate texts and social cultures—British chronicle histories, lives of Greek and Roman worthies, Ovidian myths, romance anthologies, folk tales, and anecdotal gossip—stories that elicit quite different cultural values and ritual patterns. His dramaturgy exploits an equally broad heritage—Seneca, Plautus, and Terence; medieval mysteries and moralities; Lyly's courtly allegories; and Greene's, Kyd's, and Marlowe's staging of lovers, revengers, and overreachers with a bold new eloquence in their drive toward fulfillment.

Shakespeare shapes these varied tales and psyches into the full gamut of dramatic genres—sometimes rendering the same tale in contrary modes: "Pyramus and Thisbe" as tragedy *(Romeo and Juliet)* or comedy *(A Midsummer Night's Dream);* "the maiden falsely slandered" as comedy *(Much Ado about Nothing)*, tragedy *(Othello)*, or romance *(The Winter's Tale)*. In the final plays the diversity broadens, with tragic-comic-pastoral-historical facets mingled in the inclusive cycle of "romance," yet each play quite singular. Though scholars like Frye and Barber have described the prominent mythic and festive patterns of each genre, or like Holland, Wheeler, Schwartz, Adelman, Skura, and Sprengnether have traced psychological patterns within each genre, finally one wishes to agree with Kenneth Muir that "there is no single Shakespearean dramaturgy; each play is unique."[1]

Yet despite Shakespeare's evident delight in multiplicity, his restless, playful experimentation with diverse materials, I believe a common pattern *does* inform his plays. Indeed, the pattern is precisely what makes it possible for him to engage in such different genres, to draw stories, characters, and ideas from virtually anywhere—integrating them as needed to fulfil one main highly effective pattern, which must have become part of his way of "reading" life, history, and literary fictions as he coped with competitive deadline pressure.

This study will ultimately focus on the sophisticated form of that dramaturgical pattern as found in *King Lear* and *Macbeth,* the pair Harold Bloom describes as central both to Shakespeare's canon and to Western literature.[2] In these partner plays Shakespeare presents contrary perspectives on the same psychic scenario—the desire to exploit the absolute power of sovereignty.[3] In the concluding chapters I trace these two plays' complementarity, their use of the same progressive sequence of dramatic cycles of action for opposite psychological ends, and their display of a complex dramaturgical format whose main features are shared by Shakespeare's entire canon of plays.

Chapter 1 examines the first of those features, *five-act construction,* and its further arrangement as *three cycles* (acts 1–2, act 3, acts 4–5): this form-within-a-form is Shakespeare's basic dramaturgical model— if we allow three caveats. First, his early plays use the scheme superficially, managing characters of limited conscience, implementing modes of discovery-and-reversal without the psychological depth or inner plot of the mature plays. Unlike Hamlet and Prospero, Titus Andronicus shows no restraint or reflection in seeking revenge; unlike Lear, he experiences no "epiphany," learns little from suffering. Second, Shakespearean dramaturgy is complicated by a bent for profusion: multiple plots and multiple centers of consciousness, which pervade the comedies, histories, and romances, persist even in the individualized focusing of the tragedies. Finally, some late plays—notably *Antony and Cleopatra, Pericles,* and *Cymbeline*—display what Barbara Mowat describes as "open form,"[4] a seemingly limitless fluidity that perpetuates surprise in both characters and audience. Even more than in the earlier comedies our attention is diversified among varied groups, and heroic protagonists are reduced to frail playthings, as if Shakespeare wished to flaunt his providential ability to subject them to continual delusions and shocking reversals: such dazzling manipulation obscures the customary plot format at first viewing.

Chapter 2 treats the evolution of multiple plotting in Shakespeare's plays, his preference for a polyphonal vision that activates diverse centers of consciousness and alternating plots. Dramaturgical form is greatly complicated by such diversity—including frequent highlighting of the uneducated mind (Bottom, Dogberry, tavern idlers, gravediggers, drunken porter, bawd and Bolt, shepherd and clown). Such proliferation of points of view sometimes overwhelms the partner-impulse that seeks to unify the mirroring strands of consciousness and plot development. Shakespeare controls and shapes the diversity in many ways—all encouraging interactive levels of consciousness, involving both characters and audience in conceptual, metadramatic participation in the unfolding action: (a) the *sprecher-magus*,[5] either detached from the action or varyingly involved, provides an overview of moral issues or makes festive narrative connections that extend the stage-world so all time, space, and human change may be imaginatively compassed; (b) framing scenes enforce closure, and embedded scenes, or embedded plots[6] (plays within the play), expand characters into self-conscious players-watchers-directors, making a sophisticated web of analogy, a wondrous hall of distorting mirrors, as in *A Midsummer Night's Dream;* (c) alternating plots[7] mimic, contrast, or complement each other throughout the play, deepening the metaphysical implications of seriously attending to a multiplicity of souls; and, above all, (d) a multilevel hierarchy of plots[8] presents Shakespeare's fullest vision of human society (clowns, naive ingenues, sophisticates, spiritual magi), the lower levels serving as functionaries, vulgar foils, or complementary analogues for the more educated and spiritually aware but always capable of upstaging them. This four-level hierarchy of plots, which embraces the other three organizing principles, appears fully only in *A Midsummer Night's Dream* and *The Tempest* but is implicit, *in potentia*, in many other plays. The presence of a spiritual magus (Oberon, Vincentio, and Prospero are only the most obvious examples of a figure that pervades the plays) evokes the full range of less-sophisticated beings and plots.

Contrarily, a subordinated character may rise to claim a share of center-stage and a role in bringing about the communal resolution, strengthening tragedy's substance and structure—as in *Romeo and Juliet* (the nurse), *Hamlet* (guards, players, gravediggers), *King Lear* (Fool, servants, Poor Tom), and *Antony and Cleopatra* (numerous servants and attending officers in both Rome and Egypt). This interplay with otherness is central to Shakespeare's struggle to exemplify true kingship (the *Henriad, King Lear*); and it is what Macbeth and Coriolanus increasingly scorn in their quest for a power based on absolute autonomy.

King Lear, like *Antony and Cleopatra*, consummately exemplifies the proliferating dramaturgy of the *tragedy of mutuality*, which promotes multiple plots and consciousnesses. Contrarily, *Macbeth,* like *Cori-olanus,* exhibits the compacting dramaturgy of the *tragedy of insular-ity,* where the main figure, increasingly alienated from self and oth-ers, reduces life to a more singular, streamlined dramatic form.[9]

Whereas chapters 1 and 2 explore Shakespeare's management of *form,* the next two chapters examine his revelatory exposure of *being*—the ontological mystery that, in the mature dramaturgy, ani-mates each cycle of action. Chapter 3 argues that, building on a deep-ening awareness of the soul's spiritual reality, Shakespeare increas-ingly masters the art of epiphany—the effective showing-forth of a kind of divinity in human faces and actions. Each of Shakespeare's mature plays (beginning with *Hamlet, Othello, Measure for Measure,* and *King Lear*) presents a series of three "epiphanal encounters," focus-ing the protagonist's psychological development by providing a pow-erful "axis" for each of the three main cycles of action. Each cycle is centrally animated by an encounter with otherness, manifested in three figures who exemplify the three main types of human bonding and identification. Central to the first phase (acts 1–2) is confronta-tion with a figure representing parental power and social authority, a persona greater-than-oneself, the conscience of the race, or, in Freudian terms, the superego. Central to the second phase (act 3 [and thus central to the play as a whole]) is confrontation with a fig-ure representing others seen as comparable to oneself, a universal siblinghood, an endless supply of mirroring selves, doubles, envious and threatening rivals—and insofar as this figure reflects repressed elements, the shadow self. Central to the final phase (acts 4–5) is con-frontation with a figure, usually female, who embodies the highest spiritual aspirations of the protagonist—one who inspires or gives love, fulfilling a craving for the absolute love bestowed by nurturing parents, especially the mother. Only gradually in his career does Shakespeare evolve this scheme of progressive encounters, endowing each with "epiphanal" meaning—incipiently in *Hamlet* and *All's Well That Ends Well,* then overwhelmingly in *Othello, Measure for Measure,* and subsequent plays. In the romances, epiphany proliferates into many facets, reuniting all parts of the psyche and the human family; here access to spiritual vision is like a nuclear reaction, resembling but technically surpassing the revelatory dramaturgy of the mystery plays.

Chapter 4 takes a broader look at Shakespeare's awareness and treatment of spiritual realities by comparing Spenser's and Shake-speare's use of the words "soul" and "spirit." Spenser's reverent and relatively unchanging use of the two terms throughout the six books of *The Faerie Queene* derives from his Christian-Platonic privileging of spiritual ideality, including a careful effort to avoid or to control the material body and its demeaning modes of experience. In contrast, Shakespeare's works consistently privilege bodily and passional experience, as indicated in his increasing use of "spirit" to designate passional human nature and his use of "spirits" to embrace a wide spectrum of meanings that included heavy emphasis on "bodily spirits," but allying that meaning with at least three more ethereal levels of being. Shakespeare's skeptical views during the period of the tragedies, especially in *King Lear,* led to a sudden severe restraint toward the word "soul"—using it very rarely, only in momentous crises that evoke the profound interchangeability of essential being and nothingness.

Chapter 5 traces the dark mode of this dramaturgical pattern in *Macbeth:* its three cycles of action are animated by increasingly evasive anti-epiphanies, showing the protagonist's commitment to demonic powers as he annihilates each component of the human family. Chapter 6 compares the analogous structure of *King Lear,* whose three shamings, or self-mortifications, bring progressively enlightening epiphanies—though only amid "storms" of anger, madness, and shame. These tragedies' similarity in dramaturgical form highlights their striking difference in psychological development.

Shakespeare's Tragic Form

I
Shakespearean Dramaturgy

The wheel is come full circle.
King Lear 5.3.177

1

The Dramaturgical and Psychological Structure of Shakespeare's Plays

Shakespeare has had no higher task . . . than . . .
revolutionising our ideas of Plot, until the old
critical conceptions of it completely broke down when
applied to his dramas.
   —Richard G. Moulton, *Shakespeare as a Dramatic Artist*

ONE MARVELS AT HIS FECUNDITY—NEARLY FORTY MAJOR PRODUC-
tions in two decades. While no one can account for feats of genius,
many have examined Shakespeare's plots for a "pattern in the car-
pet," divulging the moral and psychological implications of his evolving design and resolving the mystery of how he created stageable
scripts at such a pace.[1] When he selected a French or Italian narrative to stage as romantic comedy, a reign from Holinshed to fashion
as history-play, a life from Plutarch or an ancient English legend to
remold as tragedy, did he have in mind a dramaturgical blueprint to
aid the selection/composition process? Does his revising of sources,
especially dramatic *(Menaechmi, The Troublesome Reign of King John, The
Famous Victories of Henry V, Gl'Ingannati, Epitia* and *Promos and Cassandra, King Leir)*, disclose his version's superior dramaturgical plan?

    That plan, I believe, has three main structural features: a con-
frontational climax for each of the five acts; arrangement of the acts
in three cycles, with the beginning, middle, and end of each cycle ac-
cented by an intense, repetitive encounter; and at the play's center,
a major soul-changing event. The concentric pattern is thus *1 within
3 within 5.*[2] This sequence of deepening disclosure is far more complicated than *Oedipus Rex,* which crowned Aristotle's hierarchy of
plots (episodic, simple, and complex—the latter with a deep reversal
based on recognition).[3] Finding the main reversal in a Shakespearean play is difficult, for he includes three-times-three such dis-

coveries: in *King Lear* is it the initial divestiture scene, the blow-up at Goneril (1.4), or the public face-off that ends Act 2; in the intense sequence of act 3 is it Lear's initial fury, his encounter with Tom, or Gloucester's blinding; in the final, resolutional sequence of action is it the "blind reunion" of Edgar and Gloucester (4.1), the reunion of Lear and Cordelia (4.7), or the final trial-by-combat and reunion-of-living-and-dead? Most of these have been proposed as the play's main discovery-reversal. As psychogenetic myth *King Lear* rivals the *Oedipus*, but as an incremental series of *anagnorises* it is far more complex in form.

As this dramatic format evolved along with his vision of human nature, Shakespeare increasingly rendered the three cycles as stages of moral-psychological development: the opening two-act cycle probes ever more deeply and in diverse perspectives the question of *Authority* and its abuses; the central one-act cycle brings a varied engagement with *Otherness* as a result of that questioning; the final cycle, to resolve this psychic upheaval, discloses a vulnerable *Communion* at the core of human life and identity. Together these cycles enforce an archetypal transformation of consciousness. What then, in the fullest sense, is the "form" of a mature Shakespearean play?

DEBATING SHAKESPEARE'S DRAMATURGY: FIVE ACTS, THREE CYCLES

Until about 1960 the beginning, middle, and end of a Shakespearean play were defined by Bradley, Baldwin, and others partly in accordance with Donatus's and Evanthius's comments on Terence's comedies, especially as elaborated by fifteenth and sixteenth century humanists. The beginning *(protasis)* exposes the main characters and problem; the middle *(epitasis)* rises to a central turbulence, usually with a major discovery causing a reversal; the final section *(catastrophe)* resolves the problem. Erasmus noted that "every plot, as Donatus shows, is divided into three parts. . . . The *protasis* is the first excitement, swelling as it goes on. The *epitasis* is a flurry of complications. The *catastrophe* is a sudden transformation of the whole thing."[4] But commentators differed in assigning five acts to the three segments, and in explaining the three parts' functioning in a way that embraces all plays. Granville-Barker's championship of continuous performance also fostered dispute over Horace's "law of five acts":[5] was this scheme imposed retrospectively, aiding critical analysis but of little use to playwrights or actors?

Bradley generalized a *1–3–1 pattern:* act 1 as exposition; acts 2–4 as complications, with stress on 3 as central crisis; and act 5 as catastrophe.[6] Bradley hedged on the purpose of acts 2 and 4: does each present a phase as distinct as acts 1, 3, and 5?—or do 2 and 4 form sequential adjuncts to other acts?

Bradley's description of act 1, matching the humanists' rhetorical bias, is quite misleading, for Shakespeare avoids abstract "exposition." He rarely presents all personae in act 1 but withholds major characters to distinguish subsequent acts. In *The Comedy of Errors,* for example, act 1 presents Egeon and the Syracusan Antipholus, act 2 Adriana and Luciana, act 3 the Ephesian Antipholus, act 4 Dr. Pinch, act 5 Emilia. Moreover, the "conflicts" or "complications," which Bradley deferred to acts 2–4, in fact begin immediately. Except for choric prologues like Egeon's long recount, *Romeo and Juliet's* brief sonnet-choruses, and the epic-romance choruses of *Henry V* and *Pericles,* Shakespeare's plays all begin in medias res as protagonists or secondary characters react with considerable tension to a prior crisis: war in *Titus Andronicus* and *Macbeth,* feuding in *Romeo and Juliet,* famine in *Coriolanus,* elopement in *Othello,* changing governance in *Julius Caesar, Hamlet,* and *King Lear.* To heighten that tension, secondary characters may enact a microcosmic lead-in (Christopher Sly wakes, servants brawl, a ghost hovers, witches chant, shipmen resist a tempest), and act 1 continues this highly symbolic conflictual action, as in folk tales.

Act 2, instead of beginning the complications, answers the action already afoot. Here Shakespeare introduces an alternate authority-figure and worldview to "answer" the situation of act 1: in *Love's Labors Lost* act 2 is initiated by the French princess and her ladies; in *Midsummer Night* by fairies in their enchanted forest; in *As You Like It* by Duke Senior in the pastoral; in *Twelfth Night* by the other twin, Sebastian; in *Merry Wives* by Mistress Page and Mistress Ford; in *All's Well* by the French king. Likewise in the other genres a complementary authority usually initiates act 2, graduating the conflicts of act 1 into an alternate dimension. In the histories, act 2 in *Richard III* is initiated by King Edward, in *King John* by King Philip of France, in *Richard II* by John of Gaunt. In the tragedies, act 2 of *Titus Andronicus* is initiated by Aaron, in *Romeo and Juliet* by lovestruck Romeo (answering the family feud which initiates act 1), in *King Lear* by Edmund, in *Mac-*

beth by Banquo, in *Timon of Athens* by the senator calling in Timon's debts, in *Antony and Cleopatra* by Pompey and Roman *realpolitik,* in *Coriolanus* by the tribunes. In the romances, act 2 of *Pericles* is initiated by the hero washing up naked in Simonides' kingdom (countering the incestuous realm of act 1), in *The Winter's Tale* by Hermione, in *The Tempest* by Alonso's party.

Equally problematic for Bradley was act 4. Does its absent protagonist, deep pathos, and misleading climax simply extend the turbulent chaos of act 3 (the central "knot," or "*nodus*"), or does it begin the final resolutional sequence, completed in act 5?[7]

T. W. Baldwin, by opting for the former, misconstrued act 4. In *William Shakspere's Five-Act Structure* (1947) he described the fifteenth–sixteenth century humanists' model as a *2–2–1 sequence:* acts 1–2 as *protasis;* acts 3–4 as *epitasis* (with act 4 as *summa epitasis* or *extrema epitasis,* magnifying the central turbulence); and act 5 as *catastrophe.*[8] Linking acts 3–4, however, fits only one play, *Henry V,*[9] and it violates one of the most prominent features of Shakespearean dramaturgy, the break after act 3, as noted by Emrys Jones.[10] Baldwin discounted the view that act 4 begins the resolution by introducing a "cure." Scaliger called it the *catastasis,* Willichius the *paraskeue* (the preparation for Passover), initiating the *catastrophe* which is completed in act 5.[11] The emotional impasse of act 4 matched with the climactic finale of act 5 produces the effect noted by Robert Wilcher of a complex "double-ending" in Shakespeare's plays.[12]

In "Shakespeare's Use of a Five-Act Structure" (1957) Clifford Leech properly revised Baldwin's summary of the humanist model: for Landino, act 1 "unfolds the argument," and act 2 "seeks to bring to an end the things which already have been begun"; act 3 "brings on the perturbation and the impediments and despair of the desired thing"; act 4 initiates "a remedy for the impending evil," and act 5 "brings the whole to the desired outcome."[13] Willichius concurred.[14] This *2–1–2 pattern,* which Leech briefly traced in many English Renaissance plays, is the basic skeleton Shakespeare endlessly refleshed.

Leech's discovery, however, was obscured by an assault on the "law of five acts." Wilfred Jewkes (1958), elaborating W. W. Greg's earlier survey, found no act-divisions in quarto editions of Shakespeare's plays nor in most public playhouse scripts.[15] The notable exception is Ben Jonson, who paraded his awareness of Classical drama's five-act, three-part structure and whose plays all show act division.[16] Jonson's influence is evident in the rising number of five-act scripts in the early 1600s. But for Shakespeare, Jewkes argued, only the Blackfriars plays after 1607 used act divisions with music or interludes to amuse aristocrats: public playhouse productions were continuous performance.

Since 1970 most dramaturgical studies have avoided Bradleyan concern for five-act structure and holistic form, turning to the intricacy of the scene and its relation to neighboring scenes. In *The Structure of Shakespearean Scenes* (1981) James Hirsh urged that we discard act-division, number scenes sequentially, and examine them by size (monologue, duet, larger public groupings), comparing similar types of scenes[17]—advice parlayed by Rose, Cartwright, Howard, Brennan, and others into astute commentaries.

G. K. Hunter resisted this trend. In "Were There Act-Pauses on Shakespeare's Stage?" (1976) he affirmed five-act structure after examining the use of choruses, references to "acts," directions for music or other stage business, and plot development. He concluded that neither the quartos' omission nor the folios' inclusion of act-division is as important as plot development in defining the nature of Shakespearean dramaturgy.[18]

Expanding Hunter's inquiry, Gary Taylor, in "The Structure of Performance: Act-Intervals in the London Theatres, 1576–1642" (1993), exhaustively surveyed act and scene headings, choruses, music directions, marginal notes, contemporary gossip, and folio revisions to attain the following summary:

> *During 1591–1607,* of 75 extant manuscripts of plays written for adult companies, none has act-division except for the five by Jonson. In contrast, plays written for children's companies—from at least 1599, and perhaps in the 1570s and 1580s—used act-intervals, often with entre-act music and songs. Of 61 extant plays for children's companies, only two have no act-divisions.[19]
>
> *During 1609–1616,* over half the plays written for adult companies have act-divisions, which appear more frequently.
>
> *During 1616–1642,* all 245 extant plays written for London companies have five-act division, many noting long intervals and musical interludes. Eyewitness accounts of act-intervals date from after 1616.

Taylor concludes that "before c. 1607–10, the adult companies did not perform plays with intervals between the acts."[20]

Shakespeare's formative period (1591–1607) thus offers contrary evidence. He was surely influenced by the five-act dramaturgy and symmetrical structuring of Lyly and other coterie playwrights, especially in the early comedies, as Feuillerat, Baldwin, Hunter, and Beaur-

line observe.[21] But until Jonson's insistence, scripts for public theaters omitted such notations, which would have been unneeded,
even distracting, for continuous performance.

On two crucial issues Taylor's analysis finally concurs with
Hunter's. First, the use of choruses: that they emphasize act structure
(though not always *five* acts) in 10 of 155 extant plays before 1610
(and almost none thereafter) shows that, until displaced by act-intervals, the chorus sometimes served—as noted in *Venus and Adonis*
(ll.359–60)—to make "acts . . . plain."[22] The irregularities of the choruses in *Romeo and Juliet, Henry V,* and *Pericles,* however, make this argument inconclusive. Second, the main issue: how did the practice
of continuous-performance in public theaters prior to 1607 affect
Shakespeare's dramaturgical conception during composition? Taylor
insists that if an author "intends a division and wants it to be any way
recognized on the stage, it is essential that he should indicate it in the
manuscript."[23] But if continuous performance was the rule, *why*
should five-act structure be noted? Does the quartos' omission of act
divisions prove Shakespeare composed only in scene-units?

I believe Shakespeare consistently used the five-act, three-cycle format to shape plays of power; but prior to 1607 he distinguished each
act dramaturgically, *as a coherent sequence of action building to climax.*
This coherence includes orchestration of entrances and exits, the traditional means of determining "scenes" and "acts";[24] but it also builds
on consistency of time, place, and mood;[25] and sometimes the sequence is unified by counterpointed scenes or parodic scenes.[26] Always it achieves some degree of closure, partly by building to climax,
partly by repeating an earlier event with radical and ironic alteration,
and partly by some spectacular and definitive gesture. Finally, each
act invites comparison with the buildup and climax of other acts, including the cyclic linking of acts 1–2 and the similar linking (and par-
allelism) of acts 4–5, so that together they form a holistic 2–1–2 act
structure.

Even in quarto scripts this form is evident, despite linking-material
that partly obscures act structure. As Taylor astutely observes, the
quarto *King Lear* includes connector-chats to accommodate the
needs of continuous performance.[27] The servants' dialogue that
ends act 3 (urging divine retribution on Cornwall and Regan, vowing
to comfort Gloucester) is not easily omitted—either by Marxists or
Christians. Similarly encoded with caste value, and supporting both
spiritual and materialist readings, is the contrary bridge-dialogue at
the end of act 4: Kent and a gentleman laud Cordelia in aristocratic

voice, though Kent remains in servant dress. Thus the peasants' revulsion at Regan's and Cornwall's abuse of privilege is counterpointed by the courtiers' praise for Cordelia's humble service. These
comments by secondary figures not only enable continuous action
but enforce central themes, giving choric emphasis to the play's most
heinous and admirable deeds. With the installation of act-intervals,
however, these dialogues, no matter how thematically effective, were
deemed expendable and omitted in folio. As Taylor notes, these
choric remarks have impeded awareness of Shakespeare's counterpointed finales: Gloucester's vicious disfigurement and lonely expul-
sion at the end of act 3, Lear and Cordelia's tender reunion and communal exit at the end of act 4, and (we might add) the final complex
reversal of act 5: Lear's howls at Cordelia's murder give way to strange
rapture (in folio) as he dies watching her face. If to these three climactic finales we add Lear's fiery encounter with Goneril near the
end of act 1 and his humiliation by both daughters at the end of 2,
we can see even in the play's earliest form its development in five acts,
each act building to a climactic encounter which elaborately coun-
terpoints the previous act.

A remarkable symmetry is also exposed: acts 1 and 2 each rise to
fierce contention with cruel daughters; acts 4 and 5 each rise to rapt
reunion with a loving daughter. Act 3, the nexus cycle, shows its own
symmetry of alternating scenes, centered on Lear's encounter with
Tom and ending with Gloucester's similar revelation-through-suffer-
ing. The intricately symmetrical 2–1–2 structure of the five acts is
made explicit by the folio's overt designation of acts and its omission
of the bridge-dialogues.[28]

Considering the conflicting evidence for act-division in quarto and
folio editions, we must explore other textual and dramaturgical cues
for the play's form. Several critics suggest principles for such a study.
Maynard Mack's "The Jacobean Shakespeare: Some Observations on
the Construction of the Tragedies" (1960) established the crux of
Shakespearean tragic form: *contrast between a grandiose heroic voice and
a pragmatic or deflating voice, consummated in a central encounter where the
protagonist becomes his/her antithesis.*[29] Fortune's wheel is thus internalized. This axial encounter brings to crisis the confused soul, which
has been obstructed by occluded empathy (Hamlet, Othello, Lear,
Timon, Antony and Cleopatra) or by egoistic dominion and alienation (Macbeth, Coriolanus). Radical encounter with otherness thus
becomes an axis for the process of self-discovery and change (or for
expressing paralyzing self-idolatry and contempt). This dialectic of

opposites is parodied in Titania's affair with Bottom, suggesting that comedy too revolves around the mystery of antithesis, though comedy makes central a hilariously distorted and misconceived relation to the other.[30]

The importance of the center was observed by Mark Rose in *Shakespearean Design* (1972). Rose stressed *linked scenes,* with a dynamic symmetry informing each of these sequences and the play as a whole: *concentric segments of action are arranged around a central encounter.*[31] Despite Rose's bias against act-division, his diptich and triptych scenes generally occur in the same traditional "act." Moreover, he tended to locate each play's turning point at the center of act 3. When he ignored that scene as the play's axis, as in *1 Henry IV,* where he preferred the long tavern scene of 2.4, he misconstrued the play's form.[32] As many have noted, the turning-point of *1 Henry IV* is Hal and Henry's central encounter (3.2), around which the rest of the play forms a perfect symmetry. On either side is a parody reckoning (the rebels' contentious realm-division in 3.1, Falstaff's tavern reckoning in 3.3) that together define the central cycle of act 3. Similarly counterpointed are the two-act cycles that begin and end the play. Acts 1–2 emphasize Hal's ascendancy over the tavern's idle allure (the cycle begins as Falstaff awakes, ends with his relapse into sleep).[33] The balancing cycle of acts 4–5, the Battle of Shrewsbury, shows Hal's ascendancy over Hotspur's complementary drive for self-preening glory. The central cycle of act 3 coordinates the three skeins of plot and perfectly divides *1 Henry IV* into 2–1–2 act structure.[34]

Building on Rose's study, Jean Howard, in *Shakespeare's Art of Orchestration: Stage Technique and Audience Response* (1984), by viewing the play as both text and stage production, provided a more comprehensive, dramaturgical basis for linking scenes. A scene or a longer sequential unit is established not just by clearing the stage but by orchestrating many performance strategies—the same strategies that enforce continuity or purposeful contrast between scenes: management of symbolic setting, tone, thematic impact, and audience engagement by means of acting, blocking, and stage business, by modes of speech-making and uses of silence, by costuming and use of props, by music and other sound effects.[35] Howard discouraged slavish adherence to acts but also lamented the atomizing of the play into disparate scenes. Her analysis gives ambivalent evidence about traditional acts: one group of linked scenes crosses an act division (*Julius Caesar* 1.3, 2.1, 2.2), but her most prominent examples (*King Lear*'s counterpointed seven scenes of act 3, the progression and closure of the seven scenes of act 4) confirm the integrity of traditional act-divisions.[36]

Whereas Emrys Jones in *Scenic Form in Shakespeare* (1971) noted Shakespeare's reworking of scenes from his earlier works,[37] Anthony Brennan in *Shakespeare's Dramatic Structures* (1986) observed how Shakespeare enforced character and plot development by means of varied repetition of scenes within each play. Though Brennan rejected the search for a common holistic pattern, his astute directorial suggestions for highlighting the echoing scenes—especially the lengthy ceremonious climactic public encounters involving many characters at the play's beginning, middle, and end (the central one serving as turning-point)—suggests that these scenes are a key to Shakespeare's basic dramatic form.[38]

SHAKESPEARE'S DRAMATIC FORM: 2–1–2

Shakespeare's mature dramaturgic form is evident in the great tragedies: Macbeth's three murders neatly fit a 2–1–2 pattern of acts, Lear's three shamings are exactly parallel.[39] From his earliest plays Shakespeare used this protasis-epitasis-catastrophe format, which he, like Jonson, could have learned in public school while studying Terence with Donatus's commentary[40] —a scheme also prominent in Plautus's and Lyly's concentric five-act dramaturgy.[41]

Only five Shakespearean plays diverge from 2–1–2 act structure, and only one significantly. (a) Though the traditional act-division of *Love's Labor's Lost* is a jumble, the simple emendation of Ruth Nevo brings it neatly into the 2–1–2 pattern: scene 3.1 should be 2.2, renumbering all subsequent scenes; scene 5.1 divides at line 310, the former part becoming 4.2, the latter, act 5. Boyet remains on stage to enforce the continuity of acts 4–5, as Aaron had done between acts 1 and 2 of *Titus*. (b) In *Henry V* the Battle of Agincourt in acts 3–4 surges past the usual break after 3, but otherwise the play conforms to the pattern with its five distinct acts, and three cycles of action. (c) Though *Pericles* distinctly follows the 2–1–2 pattern (in cycles of action, in changes of time and place, and in the stages of the protagonist's development), Gower adds two "inter-act" choruses at 4.4 and 5.2.[42] (d) *Cymbeline* likewise fits the 2–1–2 pattern (in acts 1–2 Posthumus shifts from love to hate; in act 3 Imogen discovers Posthumus's hate, then reunites with her brothers in the pastoral; acts 4–5 move from warfare to universal settlement), but the play lacks a consistent protagonist: in acts 3–4 Posthumus is displaced by ludicrous Cloten (in Posthumus's clothes) and by the idealized innocence of Arviragus and Guiderius; Imogen, though present throughout, becomes increasingly passive in acts 3–5. (e) The most striking divergence from the 2–1–2 format is *Much Ado about Nothing*, where Shakespeare seems torn between Beatrice-Benedick and Hero-Claudio as central; the two plots overlap the usual divisions, and neither courtship endures a turbulent epitasis in act 3. The strongly linked scenes in which Benedick and then Beatrice are duped, the first ending act 2, the second beginning act 3, thwart the usual closure after act 2. Hero's public shaming, instead of being act 3's central "turbation," begins act 4. At the center of the play Dogberry and the watch materialize out of nowhere (unmentioned until 3.3!), as if to distract us from the rival courtships.

Aside from these deviations all Shakespeare's plays conform neatly to the 2–1–2 format, and in his mature tragedies the three plot segments disclose three moral-psychological stages of change, each animated by an epiphanic encounter at its center.

In the opening cycle (Acts 1–2) the arc of act 2 reverses and/or intensifies that of act 1.[43] In act 1 Titus's consummate abuse of patriarchal privilege (ritual vengeance, urging his daughter to wed a tyrant, killing his protesting son) ends in deluding festivity; act 2 ends in the gruesome spectacle of his raped and butchered daughter. In *Romeo and Juliet* acts 1–2 turn from feuding (1.1) to kisses (1.5) and finally to elopement (2.6). Act 1 of *Julius Caesar* builds conspiratorial passion to a fiery storm; act 2 shows the resultant anxieties in Brutus, Calpurnia, and Portia. In act 1 of *Hamlet* night-terror culminates in a vow of vengeance; act 2, defusing urgency in cagey surveillance, ends in a soliloquy of frustration ("O what a rogue and peasant slave am I!" 2.2.550), showing the wheel has spun contrary to his vow. In *Othello* the first act rises to joyful public affirmation of the lovers' union, the second declines to Cassio's public shaming; and each concludes with the villain's vengeful soliloquy. Acts 1–2 of *Lear* lead to public humiliations that reverse Lear's shaming of Cordelia and Kent. Act 1 of *Timon* culminates in Cupid's flattery, act 2 in the revelation of flattery's hollowness. In *Macbeth* act 1 shows witchcraft's fruition in regicidal lust, act 2 finishes the cycle in horrified reactions and cosmic portents. In *Coriolanus* act 1 concludes with battle deification, act 2 with political trivialization.

At the end of act 1 an epiphanal encounter, often with supernatural overtones, serves as axis for the two-act cycle:[44] in the magic of Romeo and

Juliet's initial communion of spirits their first dialogue forms a perfect sonnet, punctuated with kisses; in *Julius Caesar* a "tempest dropping fire" terrifies Rome; Hamlet encounters his father's ghost; Othello and Desdemona publicly reveal their transfiguring love; Lear witnesses the fiendish lovelessness of Goneril; the Macbeths mutually possess each other with demonic desires; Timon is flattered by Cupid; Cleopatra reveals the depth of her bond with Antony at their parting;[45] soldiers apotheosize bloody Coriolanus.

While this climactic event provides partial closure, it also propels the protagonist breathlessly into act 2. *Shakespeare often stresses the linkage of acts 1 and 2,* by a choric figure who remains on stage (Aaron in *Titus Andronicus*),[46] by ongoing atmosphere (the storm of 1.3, 2.1, 2.2 in *Julius Caesar*),[47] or by impetuous ongoing action, though often reversing its momentum: Romeo and Juliet surge toward communion; the growing passion to kill Caesar draws even the reflective Brutus into its vortex, but increasingly wakens anxieties; the aroused mutual suspicions of Hamlet and Claudius (and Polonius's family) provoke act 2's web of surveillances;[48] Lear, frustrated by Goneril, flies to Regan; Macbeth paces raptly to murder; Antony's fantasy of deifying love shifts to a lust for political power; Coriolanus, seeking to extend his combat glory, finds only shameful compromise in the political arena. *This two-act cycle usually ends in a large public event—in tragedy, a maimed (or displaced) ritual which lays the basis for shameful anagnorisis:* Marcus meets butchered Lavinia, Romeo and Juliet furtively wed, Hamlet directs the players, Othello quells the drunken mayhem and demotes Cassio, Lear is publicly humiliated, Macbeth's thanes survey unnnatural acts as he goes to inauguration,[49] Antony inspires an orgy, Coriolanus refusing to show his wounds ignites an insurrection.

Act 3, the central cycle, is often framed by a striking symbolic action at the end of act 2 which recurs at the end of 3: characters remain asleep on stage before and after act 3 in *Midsummer Night* (stressing that the central action is a "dream"); a door slams to exclude an aged father before and after act 3 in *King Lear;* a prayer invokes divine aid before and after act 3 in *Macbeth;* Antony publicly revels before and after act 3; tribunes and commoners conspire against Coriolanus before and after act 3. *Act 3 builds to a central crisis—the only act with its major disclosure and peripety in the middle:* Hamlet's "Mousetrap" play, Othello's temptation by Iago, Lear's stormy gathering of outcasts, Timon's false feast, Macbeth's foiled inaugural banquet, Antony and Cleopatra's embarrassing battle, Coriolanus's demeaning forum for public approval. *At the core of that crisis the protagonist faces his/her antithesis, an impassioned encounter (often with supernatural ambience)[50] that serves as axis for act 3's cycle.* This encounter assumes quite different forms: a stand-off of "mighty opposites" (Romeo and Juliet's unifying love vs. Tybalt's divisive hatred, Hamlet's innocence vs. Claudius's corruption, Antony and Cleopatra's passion vs. Octavius's stoicism), or magnanimity rebuking pettiness (Timon vs. parasites, Coriolanus vs. plebeians), or greatness of heart acknowledging its own capacity for shameful lowness (Romeo lamenting to Juliet his murderous errancy, Lear identifying with Tom, Antony and Cleopatra mutually admitting their mistakes at Actium), or greatness compacted with a dark double (Othello with Iago—"I am your own forever") or recoiling at having abused his noble double (Macbeth with Banquo's spirit).

The psychic antithesis at the center of Shakespearean tragedy is predominantly a male version of the polarity between idealized self and earthy double (Titus–Aaron, Romeo–Tybalt, Brutus–Anthony, Hamlet–Claudius, Othello–Iago, Lear–Tom, Banquo–Macbeth, Timon–flatterers, Octavius–Antony, Coriolanus–plebeians). But the love-tragedies disclose an alternate mode of psychic antithesis at the center, one based on sexual difference: male and female consummate their love (Romeo and Juliet's reconciliation in the balcony-bedroom, 3.3–5; Troilus and Cressida's more ambivalent liaison, 3.3), or they endure shame that strengthens love (Antony and Cleopatra's reconciliation after Actium, 3.7–13); or, subverting mutuality, the male embraces ruthless narcissism through a tempter's guile or his own ambition (Othello, 3.3; Macbeth, 3.4). This antithetical encounter, with its climactic turn toward self-discovery or self-actualization (or its turbulent obstruction), is complicated and enhanced when experienced as gender difference. Hamlet's resistance to epiphany springs from his central obsession with Claudius's evil (which he symbolically duplicates in the "Mousetrap"), causing estrangement from Ophelia; likewise Othello's preoccupation with Iago's evil distracts him from Desdemona; and Lear, whose central mirror is a poor, mad, demon-distracted male, does not recover fullness of being until he is reunited with Cordelia—the loving female other whom he has identified with weakness and death.

This central crisis is either a maimed public ceremony (inaugural assassination, interrupted play-within-the-play, interrupted banquet, forum riot) *or a chaotic disruption of nature* (enduring a duel, battle, storm—or, in comedy and romance, erotic chases in a dark forest, stormy childbirth at sea, abandoning a babe to wilderness). In all genres, act 3 brings the intensest display of Fortune's twists, the intensest

display of human conniving, and/or the essential moment of reckoning: the mind working at top speed tries to match the freakish
turnings of the wheel. The sequence in act 3 is central to the action:
it fully exposes the antagonists' intentions and confusions; it enforces
total reversal; and thus it heightens conscience. In comedy, home-
body Antipholus is locked out as stranger Antipholus is feasted and
wooed; exiles from court enjoy pastoral romance; the fairy queen
adores an ass. In tragedy, great-hearted Othello is estranged, kingly
Lear maddened, brave Macbeth frenzied, herculean Antony and
venusean Cleopatra shamed and disunited, martian Coriolanus triv-
ialized.

The soul-altering cycle of act 3 is a defining transaction for the play,
its central encounter revealing the profound relationality of human
identity. In comedy, act 3 is an epiphany of love, with multiple pro-
fessions of desire *(Labor's, Shrew, Merchant, As You Like It)* or love-vows
hilariously/anxiously misdirected *(Errors, Midsummer Night, Merry
Wives, Twelfth Night, All's Well, Measure)* or love-vows inverted into slander *(Two Gentlemen, Much Ado)*. In the history-play, act 3 brings an
epiphany of power: Richard III attains kingship, and Richard II loses
it; Prince Hal learns kingly power in facing his father's antithetical
nature *(1 Henry IV 3.2)*. In tragedy, act 3 is an epiphany of self-knowledge through wounding another, a disclosure of evil and guilt that
activates the deepest self, conscience: here Caesar is assassinated and
Antony's oratory fixes the blame; here Hamlet engages in three con-
centrically arranged scenes of entrapment and projected guilt, and
ends by killing Polonius; Lear in act 3 after universally denouncing
sinners sees his own frailty and guilt in Poor Tom, and Gloucester's
blindness is resolved by similarly painful irony; Banquo's ghost makes
Macbeth face his misdeeds; the plebeians eviscerate Coriolanus's fantasy of greatness. "Tragedy is consummated," says Laurence Michel,
"when the dream of innocence is confronted by the fact of guilt, and
acquiesces therein."[51] Of all genres, tragedy, keying on the uncanny
encounter with a "double" (the self's repressed shadow or its disfigured self-ideal), most fully engages the protagonist's and audience's
conscience. In the romances (notably *The Tempest*) act 3 affords a
comprehensive epiphany of selfhood: comedy's exuberant desires,
history's quest for imperium, tragedy's awakening of conscience are
subsumed in romance's discovery of spiritual renewal.[52] In these final plays the diverse trinitarian epiphanies (of power in the history-
plays, knowledge in the tragedies, love in the comedies) become
more coordinated, and fully epiphanal.

Thus act 3, the *epitasis* (with its intense questioning and confused passion, its meeting of moral opposites, its discovery of evil in one striving for ideal selfhood, its subverting of self-control and unleashing of repressed selves), sponsors a momentous inner change. Shakespeare meets Aristotle's premise that discovery should bring *peripety,* transforming both action and protagonist.[53] Gerald Else explains its peculiar potency:

> Its *raison d'être* is its power to concentrate an intense emotional charge upon a single event, a change of awareness; for in that [antithesis] the whole depth of a human tragedy can be "contained."[54]

Act 3's tragic *anagnorisis* is, however, problematic: encounter with evil and impotence brings not clarity and purpose but paralyzing incertitude, even madness—always while craving total love and power. If this is self-knowledge, it is the wisdom of known confusion. Such a "tragedy of total turbulence" (as Arrowsmith says of Euripides) finds consummation in *King Lear.*[55] In connecting this chaos with Jesus' Passion, *King Lear*'s epitasis revisits the central anagnorisis of the mystery plays.

What then of the *catastrophe,* the final two-act cycle? How does it resolve the turbulence of act 3, not only the errant confusion of comedy, but tragedy's intentional malice and guilt? Acts 4–5 form a coherent sequence, a cycle in which act 5 reverses and intensifies the arc of act 4: each act presents a resolution for act 3's psychic chaos, and though the device which climaxes act 4 is inconclusive, it awakens deepest values which precipitate the conclusive resolution of act 5.

From *Hamlet* onward, a dread of defilement[56] disables the male protagonist's sexual-emotional feelings (for Ophelia and Gertrude, Desdemona, Lear's daughters, Lady Macbeth, the mistresses in *Timon,* the nursing mothers in *Coriolanus*), and the "cure" of act 4 directly addresses that problem. *Act 4 brings withdrawal from the chaos and a surge of pathos, building to an epiphanal encounter that concludes the act, serving as axis for the final two-act cycle: either loving reunion* (Lear–Cordelia, Antony–Cleopatra, Timon–Flavius) *or severance by the beloved's death* (Juliet, Portia, Ophelia, Lady Macduff, Antony) *or spiritual estrangement* (Othello).[57] Moving beyond the authoritarian spectre at the end of act 1, and the exposure of the "double" at the center of act 3, the reunion/estrangement at the end of act 4 discloses the epitome of human value, the bond in its clearest form. *Building on that poignant event, act 5 reverses the arc of 4, giving the usual impres-*

sion of a "double ending";[58] the pathos at the end of 4, a fear of fate's impo-
sitions, becomes at the end of 5 an active collusion with fate, consummating
self-actualization. The reunion which, in two much-admired tragedies,
ends act 4 (Lear's reconciliation with Cordelia, Antony's dying thren-
ody with Cleopatra) does *not* complete the protagonist's psychological development or self-discovery. Rather it serves as the final axis that
spins him/her to an impassioned love-death, like the painful ecstatic
rapture Erasmus attributed to holy fools and holy lovers.[59] Instead of
the turbulent intensity of act 3's central cycle, this final cycle brings
a strange serenity, even as the heart swells with sympathy. "The
essence of the tragic result," suggests Laurence Michel, is "a state of
being at rest, of 'being quiet in the face of the mystery brought to
epiphany.'"[60]

That is the pattern. Let us observe it in an early play, *Romeo and Juliet.*
Acts 1–2 as *protasis* introduce the main characters' dilemma and initiate the action with a total cycle of development—a cycle that coun-
terpoints ugly street-fighting with enraptured courtship. Each of the
first two acts begins with a sonnet-chorus; and at the end of act 1, as
"axis" for acts 1–2, Romeo and Juliet's first dialogue forms a perfect
sonnet. Thus in two ways acts 1 and 2 are linked as a sonnet-sequence,
showing young love eagerly surmounting the rival families' enmity,
and the two-act cycle aptly ends in hastily sanctioned marriage.

Act 3 perfectly illustrates the *epitasis,* the crisis and turning point
with its "increment of turbations." Romeo's entanglement in two fatal duels, and Juliet's recommitment to him and deception of her parents, bind the lovers in a web of plots and counterplots. In the duels
Romeo engages not one but two doubles: Tybalt's childish fury
arouses Romeo's brutish instincts, and Mercutio's cynical wit poses a
complementary threat to Romeo's capacity for true love; in trying to
mediate their proud excesses, Romeo ensures his own eventual
doom. To complete the cycle of act 3, reversing the arc, Juliet's angry
grief converts to a deeper romantic ardor. Reconsummating her love
for Romeo as "one flesh" ensures that she will share his fate. As
Romeo quells Tybalt's (and his own) fiendish fury, Juliet severs herself from the nurse's foolish dotage. Thus each lover meets and sur-
mounts an antithetical self—though in neither case is this discovery-
and-reversal very profound. In the two halves of act 3 Shakespeare
thus provides a double anagnorisis-and-peripety, each lover under-
going a soul-crisis that divides and then reunites them, a pattern
recreated with grander scope in act 3 of *Antony and Cleopatra.*

Acts 4–5 are an equally perfect example of the complex two-act *ca-*

tastrophe with its "double-ending"—the false climax of act 4, Juliet's feigned death, providing the epiphanic turning point. Thus, if the axis-event for acts 1–2 is the lovers' first thrilling communion, and if the axis for act 3 is their balcony-bedroom recommitment after the duels, the axis for acts 4–5 is Juliet's feigned death at the end of act 4 (with Friar Laurence's unwitting prophecy of her heavenly bliss) and Romeo's extending the epiphany to himself at the opening of act 5: "I dreamt my lady came and found me dead—. . . And breathed such life with kisses in my lips / That I revived and was an emperor" (5.1.6–9). The lovers' fourth-act withdrawal (Romeo to exile, Juliet to the tomb), with the pathos resulting from this double severance, sets up the conclusive finale of act 5, the lovers' mutual *liebestod*.

Despite *Romeo and Juliet*'s being so masterfully crafted, breathtakingly lyrical and engaging, many critics fault the lovers' superficiality of development, the need of a more substantial, soul-awakening anagnorisis in the cycle of act 3. As a dark double, brutish Tybalt cannot match the clever antagonists of the later love-tragedies. Yet his rash thoughtlessness is archetypal, epitomizing the horrific deviance that exfoliates in gang wars, clan feuds, ethnic genocide; and his impulsiveness precisely addresses the most attractive yet troublesome quality in young lovers. Their love, moreover, is also challenged and obstructed by the quicksilver intellect of Mercutio, an equally problematic double—his proud, lively cynicism forming a worthy prototype for Iago's vengeful envy and Octavius's power-hunger. The impulsive nurse serves as a female blocking double, shadowing Juliet. In coping with such complexity of mirroring psyches, Romeo and Juliet are apt prototypes for the older exemplars of true love: Othello and Desdemona, Antony and Cleopatra.

ADAPTING SOURCE MATERIALS TO DRAMATIC FORM

How did the 2–1–2 format affect Shakespeare's use of source materials, especially dramatic sources—his transformation of Plautus's *Menaechmi* and *Amphitryon* into *The Comedy of Errors*, Whetstone's *Promos and Cassandra 1 and 2* and Cinthio's *Epitia* into *Measure for Measure*, *King Leir* into *King Lear*? Shakespeare draws from source materials in quite different ways yet always uses them to fulfill the 2–1–2 act structure: he elaborates Plautus's masterful five-act pattern into the larger symmetry of *The Comedy of Errors;* he turns to a different source for each of the three cycles in *Measure for Measure;* and in *King Lear* he integrates

a remarkable diversity of dramatic, narrative, and philosophical material in all three cycles—his most creative and comprehensive rendering of the 2–1–2 pattern, especially the central cycle.

The Comedy of Errors: From Menaechmi

Until recently the five-act division of Plautus's *Menaechmi* (and of all
Roman New Comedy) was considered spurious.[61] But in his fine comparison of Plautus's dramaturgy with Shakespeare's, Wolfgang Riehle
affirms the authenticity of Plautus's five-act structure.[62] Though correct in his general thesis, Riehle does not see that *Menaechmi*'s traditional five-act division is faulty.

In act 1 (155 lines)[63] the hungry servant Peniculus, seeking food
from Citizen Menaechmus, watches him flee his shrewish wife after
stealing her cloak for the courtesan Erotium, who is glad to entertain
him and Peniculus for such a gift. Act 2 (212 lines) shifts to Traveller
Menaechmus, who fortuitously enjoys Erotium's fare. In act 3
(strangely unmomentous and brief, 110 lines) Peniculus, furious at
missing the feast and being cold-shouldered by Traveller M, vows to
apprise the wife Mulier, whereas Erotium's servant Ancilla fawns on
the young man who is so lavish with gifts. In act 4 (150 lines) Citizen
M reaps the fury of both wife and courtesan, each locking him out.
The very long act 5 (447 lines) has three parts: Traveller M is accosted
by Mulier and her father Senex (186 lines); Citizen M, waylaid for
madness by Senex, Medicus, and four porters, is defended by Messenio the servant of Traveller M (150 lines); finally the twins meet, clar-
ify errors, and plan to leave Epidamnum, abandoning the wife as well
(111 lines).

The act division is clearly erroneous.[64] Each act should focus on an
alternate Menaechmus: in act 1 (155 lines) Citizen M sets up illicit
pleasures; act 2 should combine acts 2 and 3 (322 lines) to show Traveller M enjoying those pleasures but angering the parasite; act 3
should be the current act 4 (150 lines), showing Citizen M locked out
by both wife and courtesan; act 4 should be the first part of act 5 (186
lines), showing Traveller M questioned by Mulier and her father
Senex; and act 5 should be the rest of act 5 (261 lines), showing
Citizen M thoroughly assaulted by Senex, Medicus, and porters
(150 lines) before the twins reunite and vow to sever all other bonds
(111 lines).

Many factors attest the validity of this division. The twins' alternate
presence defines the five acts (the stage is not cleared between the

current acts 2 and 3, for Traveller M remains to face angry Peniculus). The acts are more equal in length; instead of 110 to 447 lines they now range from 150 to 322 lines.

	Old Division	New Division
Act 1:	155 lines (14%)	155 lines (14%)
Act 2:	212 lines (20%)	322 lines (30%)
Act 3:	110 lines (10%)	150 lines (14%)
Act 4:	150 lines (14%)	186 lines (17%)
Act 5:	447 lines (42%)	261 lines (25%)

This revised scheme is neatly symmetrical: Citizen M featured in acts 1, 3, 5, and Traveller M in acts 2, 4, and the end of 5; the citizen's greedy servant Peniculus emphasized in acts 1–2, and the traveller's loyal servant Messenio in acts 4–5; the courtesan stressed in acts 1–2, the wife in acts 4–5, and both in act 3. Finally, instead of the brief, marginal nature of the current act 3 (Traveller M's surprise at Peniculus's anger and at Ancilla's toadying), the revised act 3 is a far more fitting and suggestive centerpiece: Citizen M's lock-out by wife, then by courtesan.

Locating the center of Plautus's play is in fact a key to realizing Shakespeare's dramaturgical indebtedness. Despite Pius's faulty act-division, which Warner adopts, Shakespeare (who surely read Plautus in Latin) discerned the correct five-act structure, for he too made central the citizen twin's lock-out (3.1),[65] but added a matching panel, the traveller's courtship of an idealistic younger sister (3.2). Shakespeare's central act thus improves on Plautus by depicting complementary reversals in act 3: the citizen's experience of alienating exclusion is "answered" by the traveller's being feasted and bonded.

Shakespeare also revised the concentric material on either side of act 3. Instead of alternating the twins in acts 1–2, Shakespeare presents only the traveller twin: in act 1 Dromio's sarcastic wit fails to get him home to dinner; in act 2 Adriana's impassioned plea succeeds, drawing the bemused stranger toward relationship. Plautus also treats acts 1–2 as a cycle (the citizen sets up truant pleasures, the traveller enjoys them), but where Plautus's sequence is framed by Peniculus's self-interested soliloquys proclaiming clamorous bodily appetites, Shakespeare frames the wandering twin's quest with the father's and wife's communal speeches yearning for lost familial bonds. Plautus's use of act 2 to reverse or answer act 1 becomes for Shakespeare a cycle that not only answers but intensifies and transforms.

Like Plautus, Shakespeare balances this two-act beginning with a two-act cycle of resolution. Plautus in act 4 subjects the traveller twin to questioning by the wife and father-in-law, then in act 5 has the citizen twin thoroughly assaulted and confined by the father-in-law, doctor, and strong-armed men—a cycle of abuse which induces both twins to abandon Epidamnum. Again Shakespeare reforms both action and implicit values: his act 4 (showing the citizen twin apprehended by jailor, wife, Dr. Pinch, and henchmen, and the traveller twin vowing to leave town) mimics Plautus's ending; but act 5 answers that ending with Shakespeare's strikingly different worldview, as all (except Pinch) implicitly enjoy romantic reunion and Christian bonding at the priory.[66] The answering-intensifying pattern of acts 1–2, and then the similar pattern of acts 4–5, becomes Shakespeare's standard technique for beginning and ending his plays.

Measure for Measure: From *Promos and Cassandra* and *Epitia*

Measure for Measure also displays a definitive 2–1–2 act structure, but instead of refining a single play with Classical symmetry, it draws from a different source for each cycle. As J. W. Lever notes in the Arden *Measure for Measure*, acts 1–2 closely follow Whetstone's 1578 comic romance *Promos and Cassandra* (part 1, acts 1.1–3.1)—both in action and tone, exuberantly evoking a range of social types and sentimentally engaging in their personal and political dilemma.[67] Acts 4–5, on the other hand, take their "detailed parallels" from Cinthio's *Epitia* (1583): Cinthio's "high intellectual tone" and "serious treatment of judicial issues" make him closest to Shakespeare in eliciting universal themes to resolve the near-tragedy.[68] Act 3, the heart of the story, is basically Shakespeare's own creation: this continuous scene, with the Duke-as-friar remaining on stage throughout to advise characters as they expose their deepest conscience, sets up a resolution far more optimistic than the sources.[69]

Each of these three parts forms a coherent cycle of action; and in this play, composed near the height of Shakespeare's powers, each cycle discloses a psychological basis, a soul-change that moves from abuse of *Authority* (acts 1–2), to encounter with *Otherness* (act 3), to a ritual of *Communion* (acts 4–5), an affirmation of human relationship. In acts 1–2, the first act begins with the Duke commissioning Angelo and ends with Lucio coaxing Isabella from the convent to appeal Angelo's verdict; act 2 intensifies that sequence, beginning with Angelo's insistence on severity and ending with his proposition to Isabella. As

Angelo increasingly abuses Godlike authority, both he and Isabella are increasingly forced to acknowledge bodily desires. Her poignant soliloquy at the end of act 2 definitively concludes the cycle.

As a result of the abuse of authority in acts 1–2, act 3 draws the characters into a central encounter with Otherness, as the disguised duke asserts authority more effectively than he ever did in office. Each principal is in act 3 exposed to a dark "double," and as with Romeo and Juliet the deepest psychological doubling they experience in this central act is each other. In 3.1 Isabella endures her brother's moral reversal, urging her prostitution to save his life; in 3.2 Vincentio endures the cynical Lucio's lurid portrait of his kingdom and of himself. As a result both Vincentio and Isabella are drawn to acknowledge sympathetically the realm's and their own relational and bodily being. More fully than Prince Hal, Vincentio learns the complexity of evil, the conflictedness of human desire, the impossibility of full and "pure" justice for embodied and impassioned souls.

Acts 4–5 form a half-satisfactory resolutional cycle: act 4 lacks a deeply sympathetic character with energizing pathos, giving us only Barnardine, and it fails to exploit Isabella's grief in thinking her brother has been killed; but act 5's long judgment scene is dramaturgically masterful. Together the two acts form the characteristic resolutional cycle: in act 4 Duke Vincentio engages in proliferating private compromises to cope with quirks of fortune and with deepening villainy; in contrast, act 5 is all public ritual as Vincentio gradually resumes sovereignty to expose Angelo's proud hypocrisy, celebrate Isabella's new confirmation in humble charity, and affirm his involvement in sensuality by offering his hand in marriage.

King Lear: From King Leir

Like *The Comedy of Errors* and *Measure for Measure*, *King Lear* exhibits five distinct acts, each building to a climactic encounter and arranged in 2–1–2 sequence, a pattern evident in both quarto and folio versions. Again Shakespeare consults varied versions of the story, as well as an unrelated tale from *Arcadia;* but there is no single source for his extraordinary dramaturgical synthesis. Moreover, in contrast to his sequential use of source material for the three cycles of *Measure for Measure,* in *King Lear* he masterfully coalesces the disparate sources, utterly reshaping them in each of the three cycles of action in order to form his dramatic parable of the humbled monarch.

His main debt to the maudlin *King Leir* is the long introductory divestiture scene *(King Lear* 1.1), which distills the entire first third of *Leir* (seven scenes involving the love-test, marriages, and division of the kingdom) but transforms its tone and scope. Thereafter Shakespeare used the bathetic melodrama only reactively, inverting its personae and events, notably the complex reunion of Lear and Cordelia that ends acts 4 and 5.[70]

To complete the cycle of acts 1–2, Shakespeare turned to Geoffrey of Monmouth's *Historia regium Britanniae* (c.1135) for the account of Gonorilla and Regan's whittling down Leir's attendants to one man— a series of events that occurred much later, after Leir became infirm, inducing Cordeilla's husband Aganippus, King of Gaul, to return with Leir to England, rout the sons-in-law, and restore Leir to the throne.[71] Thus in beginning with *King Leir's* mythic love-test and immediately answering it with Geoffrey's story of the humiliating withdrawal of attendants, Shakespeare in his opening two-act sequence embraces the entire ironic cycle of Lear's personal and political life. The ensuing cycles (act 3, acts 4–5) subject Lear to anagnorisis in deepening psychological dimensions, displaying Shakespeare's inventiveness as he imagines first a mad ahistorical encounter with Poor Tom, then the poignant and deeply-resisted reunions with Gloucester, Kent, and Cordelia.

Drawing from *Arcadia* Shakespeare inserted at the outset (in Gloucester's dialogue with Kent and Edmund) the second tragedy of father and children, increasingly integrating it in each of the three cycles (notably at the center of act 3, where the two plots fully merge)—his most brilliant coalescing of analogous tales.[72]

As in *Measure for Measure* act 3 of *King Lear* is again basically Shakespeare's own creation (perhaps the finest *epitasis* ever conceived—a complete psychological turning point), confirming Lear's complete difference from Leir: Shakespeare adds a storm, a babbling fool, a demon-haunted beggar, and "madness"; and he alternates scenes of escalating compassionate shame on the heath with scenes of escalating Machiavellian ruthlessness (ultimately, demonism) in the castle. Shakespeare's main source material for this remarkable central cycle is not a single literary narrative but a medley of religious and philosophical treatises: Harsnett's *Declaration of Egregious Popish Impostures*, Erasmus's *In Praise of Folly*, Montaigne's *Essays*, Boethius's *Consolation of Philosophy:* each provides richly allusive details and a deep current of subtextual implication and questioning of human nature—its failure to sustain companionable relationships, its submission to the unfathomable quirks of divine providence.[73] This brilliantly inventive epitasis in act 3—matching the old king's empathy for Poor Tom, the Fool, and "naked wretches" with the new rulers' savagery toward their host Gloucester—greatly deepens the meaning and impact of the Lear tale. Having comprehensively outlined in acts 1–2 the tale's negative message (the proud king's humiliation), Shakespeare then fully integrates the parallel agon of Gloucester's family to provide the distraught monarch with a positive means of self-discovery: Poor Tom.

Acts 4–5 continue the inventive coalescing of historical, fictive, and original material, as Lear and his audiences "see feelingly" the fluid fastness of the human core: souls-in-process provide mutual mirroring as each matches the nothingness of death with the nothingness of love. Blind Gloucester's ongoing conversional "fall," Kent's recovery and rejection of privileged authority, Albany's awakening to evil and humbling by fellowship, Edgar's progressive disguises ending in sovereign self-abasement, Lear's sensational display of multiple personalities (offshoots of kingship and long life)—all prepare for the two concluding reunions with Cordelia's spirit, she who remains the same.

Shakespeare's Compositional Process

How then did Shakespeare construct a play with the help of this formulaic pattern?

Phase 1

He chose a tale with a dynamic and symbolically suggestive problem-situation, one exposing the protagonist to radical soul-change at the center: in the comedies, lovers' identity-confusion (twinship, gender exchange, substitute coupling) or severance (scolding, exile, putative death); in the histories, loss or gain of sovereign power and its impact on personal identity; in the tragedies, the transforming knowledge of errancy and guilt; in the romances, severance and shame followed by reunion and renewal of faith.[74]

Then he arranged the story into scenes, forming three cycles of action. An initial two-act cycle, which begins and ends in a public ritualistic display, establishes a crisis of authority and brings conflicting forces to an initial impasse. At the play's center a chaotic one-act cycle, turning on an antithetical encounter, provokes intense self-awareness.

The final two-act cycle, which again begins and ends in a large public ritual, resolves that central chaotic dilemma of identity and relationship.

*To substantiate thin portions of the script, Shakespeare revised and con-
centrated his sources: either he added sensational material from related texts,
or he invented spectacularly symbolic events.* In the opening of *Macbeth*
Shakespeare coalesced the three great battles of Duncan's reign; he
enlisted witches to initiate the first two-act cycle (as well as the final
two-act cycle), and he invented a drunken porter to enforce the impact of Duncan's murder. In the cycle of act 3 he created Banquo's
spectral visitation as central axial encounter; and for the final cycle's
consummate disillusionment he expanded the witches' display and
imagined Lady Macbeth's hallucinations and suicide. Similarly, in
King Lear Shakespeare added the *Arcadia* tale as a parallel plot to en-
ergize all three cycles; he elaborated Lear's central distress in
provocative symbols of storm, foolery, madness, and demon-possession; and in the final two-act sequence he inserted Gloucester's pilgrimage to Dover, a trial-by-combat, and the piercing display of
Cordelia's body to convey Apocalypse.

PHASE 2

On this framework of scenes Shakespeare performed three forms of
radical revisionary surgery. *He transformed all characters to fit opposi-
tional moral modes.*[75] In *Macbeth* he sanitized Duncan, Banquo, and
Macduff, making them forces of goodness; and he exaggerated the
Macbeths' evil, withholding the historical reasons for murdering
Duncan. He could have mentioned Scotland's unstable tanistry principle that alternated kingship between rival clans, forever exposing
the current king to poisoned food and booby-trapped beds. He could
have shown Duncan's weak and unattractive qualities as ruler:
younger and sturdier than Shakespeare portrays, Duncan relied for
many years on Macbeth's soldiery, then tried to subvert tanistry by
promoting his own child as successor. But Shakespeare wanted a
morality play, not an authentic biography with its irresolute ambigu-
ities. *He concentrated the pace of action into an intense two hours of stage
business*—distilling the long duration of the received tale or chroni-
cle-history, years or even decades, into what seems only a few days.
Macbeth's reign, like Richard III's, seems brief and apocalyptic, mod-
elled on the Antichrist; yet the Chronicles cover twenty-three years—
six of Duncan's reign, seventeen of Macbeth's. Macbeth enjoyed ten

years of stable reign before the seven of unravelling. In the final plays Shakespeare distilled even romance's endless time into two hours. *Finally, as the most typically Shakespearean feature, he duplicated the problem-situation in many forms to mirror and complement it:* doubles for the protagonist (as in *Hamlet, King Lear, The Tempest*), analogue-plots (as in *The Taming of the Shrew, A Midsummer Night's Dream, Twelfth Night, King Lear, Cymbeline, The Tempest*), multiple diction-image-theme patterns to enforce the main plot's moral-psychological impact. *King Lear's* epitasis, for example, is expressed not only as an elderly king in a thunderstorm, but as rhetorical-linguistic breakdown, as madness, as a jester's wise-foolish babbling, as partly feigned survivalist ravings of a demon-haunted beggar, as disappearance of clothes and housing, as proliferation of beasts and bodily wounds.[76] Thus he universalized the central problem-situation, investing it with plenitude. This sophisticated creativity calls for three caveats in invoking the plot-formula for Shakespeare's entire canon.

First, Shakespeare's earliest plays use the 2–1–2 pattern superficially, without attention to "inner plot." Here the plot is not built on the protagonist's inner moral development, so Shakespeare does not formulate comprehensive ironic reversals to assist moral growth in each of the three cycles. What ironic reversals there are (Tamora's tearful kneeling for her son's life [1.1] is answered by Titus's prostrate pleading for his sons [3.1]; Titus's banquet with mutilated Lavinia [3.2] is answered by the gruesome final feast [5.3]) arouse only titillating recognition in the audience, no change in the protagonist's conscience.[77] The Wheel of Fortune is not yet a Wheel of Soul. Nor, in these plays, does Shakespeare shape a definitive epiphanic encounter as axis for each of the three cycles, enforcing the protagonist's moral illumination. *Titus Andronicus* inverts epiphany: instead of arousing moral self-awareness and mutual life, the grotesque sensational horror simply provokes a desire to annihilate.

Second, Shakespeare's 2–1–2 pattern is complicated, especially in the early histories and in many comedies and romances, by his aggressive multiple plotting. The diverse plots of *The Merchant of Venice, Much Ado about Nothing, Twelfth Night,* and *Cymbeline* occasionally overlap the boundaries of the 2–1–2 format. *Cymbeline's* prolific actions crowd the *catastrophe,* and each play's profusion of consciences and wheelings-of-fortune makes it difficult to trace any simplistic line of moral-and-psychic development in the three phases. The first history tetrad is episodic throughout, without strong ongoing coherence.

The problem of not privileging a single psyche shows most clearly in the three parts of *Henry VI,* which focus alternately on Talbot, Somerset, Jack Cade, Joan la Pucelle, the Countess of Auvergne, Margaret d'Anjou, York, Exeter, Richard, and Henry VI. No character has sufficient complexity to show deep awareness, undergo momentous change, and thus unify the plot-development, relegating other characters and plot strands into the role of analogues. Only late in Part 3 does Richard's blossoming ego begin to show such potential. It may be felt, of course, that the absence of a strong, effective protagonist is the whole point of this series; yet the thrilling proliferation of characters in Shakespeare's early plays, as in Dickens's *Pickwick Papers,* seems an end in itself. The over all action is not yet contained in concentric cycles of psychological development, as in the mature tragedies.

Finally, in some late plays *(Antony and Cleopatra, Pericles, Cymbeline)* the 2–1–2 pattern is further complicated by Shakespeare's experiments with "open form."[78] His playfulness with the unities of time, place, and action culminates in *Cymbeline,* where the profusion of events, settings, and times, together with the lack of a dominant protagonist, tends to obscure the customary dramaturgic pattern, especially in act 3. Yet the 2–1–2 scheme is still apparent in *Antony and Cleopatra, Pericles,* and even *Cymbeline,* and it is rigorously evident in *The Winter's Tale* and *The Tempest.*

The 2–1–2 pattern, which Shakespeare ultimately fashions into an intricate and dynamic system of interlocked cycles ("wheels within wheels"), will by the nineteenth century be reduced to the simplistic rise-and-fall of the "well-made play" with its one major climactic discovery, or *"scène à faire"*—a formula that allowed Scribe in the nineteenth century to concoct over 500 melodramas for Paris's boulevard theatres and that, with jazzy lead-ins and codas, underlies Hollywood's modern flood of soap operas and situation comedies.

Such a formula plot stands in sharp contrast to the sophisticated self-conscious development of characters in Shakespeare's mature dramaturgy.[79] Each cycle is energized with irony and paradox, and the three cycles are so ingeniously linked with foreshadowings and reversals, with developing motifs of rhetoric, imagery, and stagecraft, with echoing patterns of character and plot that they appear as a seamless whole—suitable for continuous performance, but also suitable for exploiting a theatrically effective intermission after the climactic buildup of each act, especially before or after the momentous transformative cycle of act 3.

2

Multiple Plots and Protagonists
in Shakespeare's Tragedies:
A Problem of Dramatic Form

Madeleine Doran, matching *KING LEAR* with *OEDIPUS REX*, observed that "a classical play is economical . . . usually concentrated in
its effect; an Elizabethan play, lavish and multiple."[1] Her maxim is
just, though the example misleads, for *King Lear* is the only Shakespearean tragedy with a fully developed second plot, and one of only
three with multiple protagonists. The spirit of diversity—which com-
plicates Shakespeare's festive comedies, histories, and romances with
up to four plotlines—finds in his tragedies less welcome soil. At the
heart of English Renaissance tragedy is a drive for proud singularity
by one extraordinary protagonist (or a loving couple) that strives for
precedence, rising above the jostling interplay of social castes and
surmounting Shakespeare's tendency to endow even clowns and
fools with a vital voice.[2]

If the purpose of multiple plots in the histories and comedies is to
enrich their epic and festive scope, that social expansiveness is partly
curtailed by tragedy's urge for singularity. Particularly absent from
tragedy is a fully developed action for the vulgar clowns; even the sophisticated wit of the cynical consort or jester (Mercutio, Thersites,
Lear's Fool, Apemantus, Enobarbus) tends to disappear midway
through the tragic action. Yet the spirit of generous creativity and
multiplicity that activates so many souls on all social levels, a Shakespearean trademark, persists even in the tragedies—to some degree
in the mirroring subplots of *Hamlet, Othello,* and *Timon of Athens,* and
much more in the fully developed double plot of *King Lear* and in the
multiple centers of consciousness of both *King Lear* and *Antony and
Cleopatra.*

In most of Shakespeare's plays he controls that multiplicity by
means of two main patterns: a *social hierarchy* that ranks the plots of

diverse protagonists, and a *dramaturgical symmetry* that draws the different plots into rhythmic coherence and coalescence. Shakespeare's most comprehensive hierarchy, a four-level scheme which is fully exploited in *A Midsummer Night's Dream* and *The Tempest*, may seem far less pertinent amid the tragedies' insistent elitism; but in Shakespeare's most ambitious tragedy, *King Lear*, we shall find the four-level hierarchy quite relevant, for it defines the cosmic order which that play subverts on every level. As for dramaturgical form, Shakespeare's use of three symmetrical cycles (acts 1–2 as protasis, act 3 as epitasis, acts 4–5 as catastrophe) is clearest in tragedy with its singular psychological coherence. In *King Lear*, however, which embraces multiplicity most bravely, the diversity of plots and protagonists—and of diverse selves within the main protagonist—places a special burden on the three-cycle pattern of Shakespearean dramaturgy. The symmetrical dramaturgy is still evident, giving definitive shape to anarchy, but it is a fearful symmetry, full of surprises and aftershocks.

TRAGIC FORM AND SOCIAL DIVERSITY

Each tragedy's title highlights one or two souls; other characters and plotlines take supporting roles, mirrors for the feature attraction, the *prima donna* or *primo uomo*. This figure, whose "princely privilege" is manifested in every gesture, speech, and relationship, is surrounded by counselors, aides, and servants who reflect or deflect their master's moral bias, and occasionally by commoners who seem limited to social function (guards, players, gravediggers) but whose candid earthy voice often evokes the protagonist's truest self. Indeed, the principal's aspiring heroic voice is often displaced by the jangling dialect of a subordinate: the beguiling loquacity of a nurse, gravedigger, porter, clown; or the more sophisticated antagonism of an Aaron, Mercutio, Thersites, Iago, Lear's Fool, Apemantus, or Enobarbus. How much of the action is devoted to these obstreperous subordinates? And how is the protagonist's central development affected by their subversive and at times digressive antics?

Consider the role of the clown in Shakespearean tragedy. Before each mortal crisis an awkward and uncouth commoner appears, a "poor player" who boldly struts and fearfully frets about the whirligig of time. Response to this figure divides protagonists into two camps. Some are proudly insular—not just intent on revenge, love, power, fame, or absoluteness (as are all tragic heroes) but contemptuously self-enclosed, thus allowing no genuine discourse with commoners: Titus commissions a "clown" only to forward his revenge (4.3); Macbeth ridicules his hired assassins (3.3) and fearful servant (5.3); Coriolanus exchanges insults with Aufidius's servants (4.5) as scornfully as earlier with Roman plebeians. In five other tragedies, however, the brush with vulgar commonness is more attentive, perpetual, and fruitful; the protagonist engages warmly with servants and clowns, heartened by their workaday routine, earthy humor, and bodily desires—heartened too by their awareness, though quaintly mangled, of spiritual realities. Brutus shows tender care for the sleepy Lucius (2.1), and another servant, Strato, assists Brutus's suicide (5.5); Hamlet chats winningly with guards, players, gravediggers, even pirates; Lear banters with the Fool, Kent-as-Caius, and Edgar-as-Tom, and in the mirror plot Gloucester's conversion is confirmed by his sudden engagement in genial discourse, and indeed his identification, with Tom and the poor; Timon treats servants as generously as nobility, and during his nihilistic rage acknowledges only Flavius as an honest man (4.3); Antony shares bounteously with Enobarbus, Eros, and common soldiers, as does Cleopatra with Iras, Charmian, Mardian, and the Clown, and both Antony and Cleopatra are not only assisted but joined (and even preceded) in dying by one or more servants after being abandoned by nobler colleagues.

As Maynard Mack has shown, these lively commoners form the "opposing voice"[3]—earthy and bawdy, practical and efficient, skeptical and subversive—counteracting the protagonist's polished eloquence and hyperbolic self-idealization. The clowns serve a range of functions, at times vulgarly subverting but at other times spiritually affirming, providing a basis and source for epiphanal vision. Those protagonists who contemn commoners deny themselves an essential means of growth and vision.

As a brief *parodic foil* (Macbeth's porter or Hamlet's gravedigger) or as an ongoing *complementary contrast* (Lear's Fool or the serving women of Desdemona and Cleopatra), these figures also channel and defuse audience skepticism, which, especially in crisis, waits for an inauthentic word or action to explode pretentiousness. Wagnerian protagonists, lacking such foils, never attain generous largesse toward others or a broad-based ironic vision. In Shakespearean tragedy, the fool's sensible simplicity widens the psychic scene, exemplifying much that the protagonist tries to ignore or transcend—especially physical shortcomings and relational needs that have been lost in the

rush for power and autonomy. Thus, as many have noted,[4] the awkward clown, the bawdy servant, or the cynical jester is a *totemic meas-
uring-stick,* gauging and proving human nature: Hamlet's gravedigger
initiates final reflections on life and afterlife; Macbeth's drunken
porter reverses the usual eschatology (those who ignored the knocking of conscience now must knock for admission to hell); a clown cau-
tions Cleopatra on the "immortal" consequences of playing with "the
worm." Most fully developed and integral to the action are the highly
symbolic, self-conscious portrayals of both the fool and commoner in
King Lear. In enacting Poor Tom, Edgar vacillates between self-pity for
the abuses he has suffered and, increasingly, self-criticism for his
courtly indulgences, thus providing Lear a complex mirror for his
own psyche, a discovery assisted by the Fool's reversibility principle
that sees kingship and beggary, wisdom and foolery, greatness and
nothing as interchangeable. Lear's kingship cannot be realized without the defining presence of both the fool and the naked, debased
commoner. Partly through internalizing their loyal folly and acknowledged humiliation, Lear is enabled to apprehend Cordelia's
nature in epiphanal fullness. Equally important to the drama's outcome, Edgar himself develops a sovereign persona out of the reductive lineaments of his role as Poor Tom.

Perhaps as a result of the remarkable social-psychological reversal
in *King Lear,* most of the final romances involve a large group of vulgar commoners in the achievement of epiphany, which is portrayed
with notable diversity: Pericles' conversion involves commoners of
both country (fishermen) and city (bawds and prostitutes); *Cymbeline*
paradoxically shows the crudest vulgarity in the courtier Cloten, and
gentle refinement in the pastoral foundlings Guiderius and Arviragus; *The Winter's Tale* enmeshes a royal foundling in a populace of
coarse but gentle shepherds; and *The Tempest* joins city/court clowns
with a country primitive whom Prospero's teachings have not yet
managed to refine. The disturbing but laughable lewdness of these
figures is vital to each play's psychological development and vision.
In *Pericles* Marina's revelation would be impossible without the earthy
display of Bolt, Bawd, and Pander. Their dialect gives voice to the
worker's desperation to survive, the soldier's subjection to princely
ambition and neglect when he is dismembered, the prostitute's total
debilitation and disposal by aristocrats. Even Marina's truly royal nature, her innocence and charity, is put in jeopardy by such treatment.
The Winter's Tale consummates the connection with earthiness:

Perdita's simple goodness springs among the shepherds not just as a regal foundling against a parodic foil but as an outgrowth of their community's alliance with "great creating nature."

SHAKESPEARE'S *SPRECHER-MAGUS:*
ORCHESTRATING DIVERSITY

Only in tragedy does the vulgar commoner operate so singly as Lear's Fool, Macbeth's porter, or Cleopatra's clown. Costard, Bottom, Dogberry, Pompey, Bolt, and Caliban move in a tribe of their kin, generating a distinct action that can usurp center-stage, as in *A Midsummer Night's Dream, Much Ado about Nothing,* and *The Tempest.* Even the cynical jesters of the mature comedies (Touchstone, Feste, Pompey) are drawn by the gregarious instinct, though increasingly they show the skeptical detachment and singularity that culminates in Lear's Fool.

Shakespeare's festive comic spirit ultimately generates four social levels of plot: clownish workmen and servants, ingenuous young lovers, older governors and counselors, and, in some plays, a wise magus with spirit-helpers. He/she integrates this diversity of actions and perspectives in several ways:

1. *The sprecher-magus,*[5] present to some degree in all Shakespeare's plays and increasingly gifted with moral and theatrical craft, tends to create diverse plots and to orchestrate characters within them. This magisterial sage gives a festive, historical, philosophical, or providential overview on characters and events, but from various levels of involvement. Either he/she introduces each act as a detached chorus (as in *Henry V* and *Pericles*); stage manages from the *platea* (Aaron, Puck, Thersites, Apemantus, Autolycus, and in some scenes Oberon and Vincentio);[6] directly engages in the main action, both as provocateur and victim (Mercutio, Falstaff, Iago); or serves as central protagonist (Petruchio, Richard III, Portia, Henry V, Rosalind, Viola, Hamlet, Helena, Vincentio, Macbeth, Prospero). When fully integral to the plot, this figure's importance cannot be overestimated: a lightning rod for the playwright's creative presence, this sophisticate sparks a high audience participation by promoting the fantasy that all time, space, and human endeavor may be imaginatively compassed, yet may also be held at a remove from the self.

Though Shakespeare asserts this eminent power primarily in aristocratic, monarchic, godlike personae, he also activates it through the socially disempowered. In "Comedy and Control: Shakespeare and the Plautine *Poeta*," Douglas Bruster traces the magician-poet-playwright figure of Shakespeare's comedies (Petruchio and Grumio, Oberon and Puck, Prospero and Ariel) to Plautus's wily servant, self-described as a poet or theatrical director, who "magically" resolves each dilemma by inventing a stratagem out of "nothing," figuratively drawing that device from the depths of the sea or from the air—suggesting an alliance between the natural and the supernatural. In keeping with Renaissance social conventions, Shakespeare transfers the cleverness to an aristocratic *magus* joined with an often unreliable servant.[7] To this analysis one might add that the transfer of prowess is variable. Many early servants (the Dromios, Lance, Bottom, Nurse and Peter, Dogberry, Gobbo) are indeed laughable in their pretensions to mastery; but others (Tranio and Grumio, Touchstone and Adam, Feste and Maria, Yorick, Lear's Fool, Macbeth's Porter, Flavius, Enobarbus and Eros, Iras and Charmian, Pisanio, Paulina, Ariel) are increasingly sophisticated, often enlightening their masters.

2. *The framing plot (or framing scenes)*, which encloses the play or encloses actions within the play, involves symbolic "watchers": reunited parents watch the reunion of their twins, a transformed drunkard watches the transformation of a shrew, a royal wedding party keeps watch over errant young lovers, a ruler withdraws and returns to survey and correct the abuses of rule. The framing principle is most apparent at the play's beginning and end, but it may also define smaller cycles within the play. As with the choric *sprecher,* this device in early plays (*The Comedy of Errors, The Taming of the Shrew, A Midsummer Night's Dream*) is detached from the main action. Christopher Sly's duping is thematically related to Katherine's taming, but not directly, and that disjunctiveness adds to the Induction's comic charm. Full integration of the framing principle is achieved by Vincentio in *Measure for Measure* and by Prospero in *The Tempest:* their interventions and revelations aggressively initiate and close each cycle of action. Increasingly in Shakespeare's plays the framing plot highlights the presence and power of the *sprecher-magus,* most notably in *The Tempest.*

3. As prevalent as the framing plot is its inversion, the *embedded plot* (or *embedded scenes*), or plays-within-the-play, which show that each event or character is open to endless improvisational expansion: the pageants in *Love's Labor's Lost,* the elaborately nested scenes of players and watchers in *A Midsummer Night's Dream,*[8] the "Mousetrap" and other entrapment ruses throughout *Hamlet,* Lear's endless cere-

monies of self-judgment, Antony and Cleopatra's self-stagings, Prospero's theatrical productions (storm, banquet, masque). Embedded plots confirm an artful self-consciousness that engages everyone (inside and outside the play) as both actor and audience in an endless cycle of selfhood. Each embedded plot is engineered by a *sprecher-magus,* though with various degrees of skill and fluency.

4. *The alternating (or mirror) plot*[9] parallels the main plot throughout the play: Kate's courtship vs. Bianca's; Hal's aspirations vs. Hotspur's; Lear's enlightenment-by-divestiture vs. Gloucester's; Timon's alienating disillusionment vs. Alcibiades'. In *Much Ado about Nothing* and *Cymbeline,* Shakespeare does not clearly privilege one plot over the other. Usually, however, the main plot provides the moral-spiritual touchstone as its protagonist achieves genuine insight, while the mirror-plot presents a more naive and deluded, or deceitful and treacherous, foil. Shakespeare's parallel plots often involve two or more *sprecher-magi* with conflicting intentions and worldviews, as in *The Taming of the Shrew, 1 Henry IV,* and *King Lear.*

5. *The four-level hierarchy of plots,*[10] Shakespeare's most elaborate dramaturgical form, appears in comedy *(A Midsummer Night's Dream),* history *(1 Henry IV),* and romance *(The Tempest): clownish workmen,* preoccupied with daily sustenance and the whims of masters (Bottom and friends, the *Henriad*'s tavern idlers, Caliban and servants); *young ingenues,* absorbed in love or rivalry (Hermia–Lysander, Helena–Demetrius, Hotspur–Kate, Miranda–Ferdinand); *adult sophisticates,* seeking power or order (Theseus and his wedding party, Henry IV and his counselors, Alonso and his attendants); and *a magus with spirit-helpers,* seeking vision, direction, or atonement (Oberon–Puck, Hal–Falstaff,[11] Prospero–Ariel).

This four-level dramaturgy embraces all the other organizing principles, for when Shakespeare provides, as fully developed *sprecher,* a spiritual *magus* like Oberon, Vincentio, or Prospero (or incipiently, Henry V, Portia, Rosalind, Helena, Lear, Cleopatra)—figures gifted with insight and eloquence who manage others and who address the thunder directly—he shows a mind that images God, the sovereign, the playwright; or, in the case of Aaron, Richard III, and Iago, a mind that images Machiavelli's Prince or a Satanic artificer.[12] Whether angelic or demonic, such an acute and ranging mind insistently discerns the duality of human nature, generating the complementary or mirroring plots of rival siblings, twins, or doubles in virtually every play. Such a mind consciously engenders the concentric cycles of framing and embedded plots, motivating and managing human nature from without and from within. Such a mind ineluctably draws into its ambience the full range of less-sophisticated beings in a hierarchic scale, each with its own plot, and seeks to orchestrate them—indeed, to internalize and integrate them—not always successfully.

These four levels of human nature (subdivided into polarities of naive and sophisticated, good and evil) not only mirror but interact with each other. This comprehensive dramaturgical model is most clearly and fully developed in *A Midsummer Night's Dream* and *The Tempest,* but it is implicit, *in potentia,* in *The Taming of the Shrew,* the *Henriad, Hamlet, All's Well That Ends Well, Measure for Measure, Antony and Cleopatra,* and (with spirited artificers like Portia, Rosalind, Viola, Helena, and Paulina) in all the mature comedies and romances. The key to Shakespeare's management of this scheme lies not simply in the high-minded vision of the *magus,* but in the unpredictable ways in which the *magus*'s drama combines with the plotlines of more naive social castes, especially the clown, who always intrudes in the catastrophe. Rather than weakening the dramaturgy, the digressive pranks of the vulgar commoner strengthen tragedy's substance and structure—as in *Romeo and Juliet* (the nurse), *Hamlet* (guards, players, gravediggers), *King Lear* (Fool, servants, Poor Tom), and *Antony and Cleopatra* (numerous servants and attending officers in both Rome and Egypt). This interplay, which assumes constantly expanding psychological and social-political dimensions, is central to Shakespeare's struggle to exemplify the paradoxes of true sovereignty, particularly in the *Henriad, Hamlet, King Lear,* and *The Tempest;* contrarily, it is what Macbeth and Coriolanus increasingly scorn in a quest for power based on absolute autonomy.

Tragedies of Insularity, or of Mutuality

The quest for greatness, with its frequent consequence of intense isolation, functions quite differently in the diverse Shakespearean tragedies. In *Fools of Time* Northrop Frye distinguishes "tragedies of order" (challenges to paternal authority), "tragedies of passion" (broken relationships), and "tragedies of isolation" (alienation from society).[13] *Macbeth* and *King Lear* comprehensively enact all three dimensions, yet in opposite ways. Macbeth murders paternal order, mangles passion, and utterly isolates himself—methodically severing all bonds by his three assassinations and by estranging himself from his wife. His numerous asides and soliloquies underscore the descent into angry contempt and numbness. Lear suffers the same three tragic debacles but from within anointed kingship: he subverts his own paternal order, unleashes chaotic passions in himself, and severs his deepest familial and communal bonds, enclosing himself in lunacy which the remainder of the play tries to undo and which Cordelia's death makes unendurable.

To Janette Dillon these protagonists' isolation exhibits the growing validation of individuality in Renaissance culture, the rise of a "cult of solitude."[14] Though richly suggestive, this interpretation of Shakespeare's solitary protagonists seems reductive; for although some of his "choice and master spirits" actively promote their isolation, sharply repudiating the rest of humankind (yearning like Coriolanus to be, in Donne's phrase, "an island, entire unto itself"), others strongly affirm social bonds and assert a sovereignty based on mirroring and mutual identity.

Macbeth, like *Coriolanus* and *Timon of Athens,* exhibits the compacting dramaturgy of the *tragedy of insularity,* where the main figure, increasingly contemptuous of others in his urge for absolute autonomy, reduces life to a singular, streamlined dramatic form. Timon of Athens may seem to share Hamlet's thwarted urge for mutuality, yet Timon's capacity for sovereign identity with others is suspect. His cultivation of sycophantic friends by aggressive giving, followed by his retreat into misanthropic solipsism, suggests (as with Macbeth and Coriolanus) a failed attempt to achieve grandiose selfhood, followed by narcissistic rage. The relative disconnectedness of the second plot in *Timon of Athens* underscores the failure of Timon, like Macbeth and Coriolanus, to exercise or inspire a love that is charitable and forgiving. Except for Flavius's brief consolation, Timon in the wilderness does not, like Lear, find communal solidarity and spiritual affirmation among other marginalized, victimized, and disaffected figures (Alcibiades, the courtesans, Apemantus) because Timon rigidly assumes in each a core of self-interest—without acknowledging and accepting it in himself. In the mirroring plot Alcibiades' dalliance with courtesans and his decision not to take vengeance on the ungrateful senators show him to be far less absolute than Timon in repudiating human nature, and his self-indulgence is of a lower cast than Timon's.

In contrast, *King Lear,* like *Antony and Cleopatra,* shows the proliferating dramaturgy of the *tragedy of mutuality,* promoting multiple plots and centers of consciousness as its protagonists (Lear, Edgar, Gloucester) move toward a bonding so profound that death seems less a severance than a consummation of relationship. It cannot be denied that Hamlet, Othello, Lear, Antony, and Cleopatra also aspire narcissistically to grandiose selfhood, but their self-assertion is achieved through object relations. The endings of these tragedies (*Hamlet* is a partial exception) affirm a central bond between the protagonist and a beloved (Hamlet with Ophelia, Gertrude, Horatio; Othello with Desdemona; Lear with Cordelia; Cleopatra with Antony), as well as with social subordinates (Horatio; Kent, Edgar, Albany; Eros, Enobarbus, Iras, Charmian). In these plays the protagonist instinctively bonds both with a significant sexual other and with many social and political associates, fostering in them a reciprocal loyalty. Lear's suffering springs from his growing shame for denying parental and kingly bonds to which he is in fact deeply committed; ironically, like Timon he breaks these bonds by trying to enforce them too absolutely, affecting to give "all" and commanding love as if he were divine—rituals showing his desire to resist and undo mortality. Similarly the suffering of Antony and Cleopatra stems not just from their troubled personal relationship—challenged by perpetually shifting political alliances—but from the persistent threat to their larger communal image of bounteous love and "infinite variety." Both *King Lear* and *Antony and Cleopatra* activate a large cast of characters through a pervasive spirit of mutuality. All the loyal members of Lear's and Gloucester's families, together with faithful retainers, join in compassion for the suffering of the king, and the intensity of his "mad" vision assists others in seeing the suffering of Tom, Gloucester, and Cordelia. Similarly, the antagonistic realms of Rome and Egypt finally join in admiring Antony and Cleopatra's generosity of spirit. The tremendous power of each tragedy's finale springs from affirming a bond: Lear with his faithful child, Cleopatra with her bountiful "husband." The bonding is reinforced by loyal peers and servants who voluntarily die with the protagonists, refuse to replace them in power, or in grief internalize their spirit:[15] Albany, Kent, Edgar, and other "gentlemen"; Enobarbus and Eros, Iras and Charmian, even Caesar, Dolabella, and other soldiers.

Nor is *Hamlet*, for all its soliloquies, a tragedy of insularity. Despite the poisoning of his court relations, Hamlet, like Lear, manifests a royal personality. He habitually consorts with all the body politic, showing an easy affinity with commoners (guards, players, gravediggers, pirates) and profound friendship with the faithful Horatio. Claudius laments

> the great love the general gender bear him,
> Who, dipping all his faults in their affection,
> Work like the spring that turneth wood to stone,
> Convert his gyves to graces.
>
> (4.7.19–22)

As prototype of *King Lear, Hamlet* too has extensive components of a secondary plot—Polonius, Ophelia, and Laertes mirroring Claudius (or the former king), Gertrude, and Hamlet. As with the multiplying actions and consciences of *King Lear* and *Antony and Cleopatra,* where the action often veers into subordinate dramas, Hamlet's revenge is often upstaged: Claudius seeking to repent, Polonius busily managing, Laertes raging, Ophelia deteriorating, the ghost hovering. As in other "tragedies of mutuality," the privileging of multiple souls extends to servants and subordinates: guards, Horatio, Rosencranz and Guildenstern, players, Fortinbras's army, pirates, gravediggers, Osric. In devising the prolific characters and plotlines of these plays, Shakespeare as playwright emulates the sovereign generosity and comprehensiveness of spirit implicit in these central *kulturträger* protagonists—Hamlet, Lear, Antony and Cleopatra.

DOUBLING TRAGEDY IN *HAMLET* AND *KING LEAR*

Despite the proliferation of consciences in *Hamlet, King Lear,* and *Antony and Cleopatra,* few subplots are fully realized in Shakespeare's tragedies as a whole. The mirroring effect of Polonius's family in *Hamlet,* of Cassio and Bianca's courtship in *Othello,* and of Alcibiades' alienation in *Timon of Athens* is in each case truncated; only *King Lear* has a fully developed second plot, with the two plots becoming increasingly interactive in each phase of the three-cycle dramatic pattern. Like Lear, Gloucester is duped by power-hunger in act 1, and by the end of act 2 he shares the dismay over Lear's mistake, but does not yet sense his own. The cycle of act 3 centers on Lear's profound discovery and reversal (with Gloucester ironically trying to dispose of Edgar-as-Tom while Lear seeks to extend charity to him), and this cycle concludes with Gloucester's own bitter discovery and reversal. As with Lear, Gloucester's emotional purgation and purification reaches fullest scope in the final two-act cycle: in act 4 his mortifying shame at Dover cliff prepares for Lear's recovery of sanity and relationship; in act 5 Gloucester's bursting heart prefigures Lear's love-death. The mirroring plot provides an additional psyche as major foil for Lear: Edgar's growth through many disguises, especially the half-feigned madness and demon-possession, parallels Lear's agon, though contrasting and complementing it. It is apt that, at the play's center, Lear identifies with his impoverished godson, that Edgar graduates from self-abusive role-playing to comfort Lear, and that growing compassion for Lear in act 3 prepares Edgar to sympathize and re-bond with his father in acts 4–5. The two plotlines, because of their very distinctness, richly supplement and reinforce each other, and during the play's three phases they become tightly interwoven.

In *King Lear,* even more extensively than in *Hamlet,* Shakespeare greatly enhances the second plot, integrating it as a vital component and mirror of the main plot. In neither play, however, is this use of a second family justified by legend or chronicle history.[16] Why does Shakespeare give such prominence to Polonius's family (especially the spectacular sequence of Ophelia's madness, death, and burial) and to Gloucester's entire family (Edmund's rejection of bastardy, Edgar's riveting frenzy, Gloucester's excruciating anguish)?

The secondary plot in each of these tragedies plays against the main plot on at least three levels. As *parodic foil,* it sets off the mental, emotional, and linguistic maturity of the main characters: Polonius's fussy pomposity, a variation on the *senex* of Roman comedy, highlights the more sophisticated reflections of Claudius and the ghost; Laertes' adolescent parody of *Hercules furens* privileges Hamlet's more mature anger;[17] Ophelia's extravagant lunacy is in many respects still more farcical, setting off Gertrude's motherly self-control and thoughtful eloquence, as in the deeply moving elegy for Ophelia (4.7.167–84) that suggests Gertrude's own loss of innocence, as well as the general silencing of women. As *complementary parallel,* the second plot in *Hamlet* expresses family shame in a more naive but more sincere and outspoken manner than by the three principals. Ophelia's youthful idealism contrasts Gertrude's complacent self-compromises. Laertes as a playful, self-indulgent Parisian student contrasts Hamlet as a religiously aware, philosophically self-reflective Wittenberg student. Polonius, as old-fashioned *pater familias* and as deferential courtly counselor, sharply contrasts Claudius's ruthless drive as a Renaissance "new man," a self-made Machiavellian prince. At the highest level, like God at Judgment, one evaluates the secondary figures as *souls in a moral hierarchy of fulfillment.* If we take Hamlet's view from this level, self-reductive Polonius fades serviceably into oblivion, though the prince's witty ridicule of this "wretched, rash, intruding fool," in contrast to Ophelia's distraught grief, leaves residual distaste; likewise Laertes, after much Tybaltlike ranting, claims only a small memory for penitent friendship. Ophelia, however, in her extended madness and "doubtful" death, becomes—like the ghost—a powerful and disturbing presence, unresolved by the audience or by Hamlet himself.[18] In her mad suffering, with its creative energy and the symbolic suggestiveness of her songs and flowers, she assumes a mysterious life of her own—quite apart from her mirroring of Gertrude or Hamlet. That her madness is more authentic than Hamlet's suggests a missing component or aporia in him, and in the exuberant candor of her sorrow she competes with Hamlet as a prototype for Lear. Her body displaces Yorick's, connecting those who gave pleasance and meaning to Hamlet's life, and he briefly grieves for both. With far deeper feeling, Lear will complete the identification of clown and beloved maiden: "my poor fool is hanged" (5.3.311); instead of Hamlet's skeptical gibes at a skull, Lear gazes raptly at Cordelia's face, internalizing the "fool" in fullness.

The secondary plot of *King Lear* is more intricately and suggestively developed than in any other Shakespearean play. When Lear vacates the stage for nearly seven scenes (3.7–4.6), the spiritual quest of Edgar and Gloucester, culminating at Dover cliff, is sufficiently engaging to distract the audience from Lear's absence; and the metaphoric nuances of Edgar's and Gloucester's acts, speeches, settings—mirroring the condition of the absent protagonist—extend the story's psychological and mythic dimensions in ways that would be impossible for Lear and his daughters to accomplish by themselves.

Was Bradley correct in judging the story of King Lear and his daughters too thin to sustain the play, leading Shakespeare to pad the action with a mirror-plot? And does this double focus become too divisive, weakening the play, as Bradley and Jones suggest?[19] Perhaps Bradley was right about the playwright's initial motive, but in expanding and relating the two tales Shakespeare has made their interdependence a major factor in the play's greatness as artifice and as a vision of spiritual transformation. The double discovery-and-reversal at the center of *King Lear* (when the two fathers exchange children for the discovery process, and induce in the shared child a depth of suffering similar to their own) is more universally suggestive than in any play except *A Midsummer Night's Dream*. Despite the distinctiveness of this achievement, *King Lear* is not radically different as a semiotic and hermeneutic vision, but consummates the interaction of diversely clothed souls, the transformation-of-self that is always central to Shakespeare's dramatic form.

Schlegel, Dowden, and Bradley correctly saw the evils of pride and ingratitude universalized by *King Lear*'s double plot;[20] but the tale is far more than simple duplication. By adding Gloucester's story to Lear's, Shakespeare greatly expands the drama's mythic potential, developing a "father and sons" psychodrama along with that of "father and daughters"—that is, adding the *Oedipus complex* to the "*Lear complex*."[21] The gain in psychic scope is considerable, extending Shakespeare's usual testings and transgressive crossovers of gender boundaries. Lear's daughters experiment with empowerment and sovereignty (and Gloucester's sons cope with disempowerment) in ways that radically challenge tradition. Daughters and sons show revealing parallels, like the jackal techniques of Goneril and Edmund: Goneril slyly uses Oswald to provoke Lear, attacking him and later Gloucester only with the aid of a pack and only when her quarry is defenseless; likewise, Edmund furtively uses Cornwall to abuse his father, and the captain to kill Lear and Cordelia: it is ironic that Goneril taunts *Albany* with cowardice. Contrarily, Cordelia and Edgar gain definitively by their reactions to dispossession: in quite different ways each finds courage and power in nothingness, in love that multiplies amid literal poverty and spiritual humiliation.

Besides achieving this complexity of entwined family romances, Shakespeare's expansive use of the second plot (even including Edgar in the initial title) is a means of addressing the central paradox of kingship—the monarch's relation to the communal body. A similar paradox informs the hilarious central moment in *A Midsummer Night's Dream* when Titania, through love's magical and fantastic wounding, allies with Bottom—literalizing Queen Elizabeth's claim of marriage with all her subjects; and the paradox recurs in the *Henriad* when Hal proclaims himself "of all humors" in associating with tavern idlers and when he later identifies with soldiers at Agincourt. The interlaced stories of Lear and Gloucester explore not only the problem of sharing power with the young but the larger problem of exercising kingship as kinship, especially with the poor.[22] Lear's identification with Edgar-as-Tom suggests a central paradox of selfhood and of sovereignty: *oneself as another*. The cultural myth of the king's two bodies is invoked not merely to undergird the proud claim of divine right but to enforce the humbling lesson of radical commonality.

Edgar's impoverishment, alienation, and subjection to demonic spirit-impulses also assist Lear's discovery of a second and deeper paradox of selfhood and sovereign power: *oneself as nothing*. The king has not two but three bodies, the most important a spiritual one.

MULTIPLICITY VS. MUTUALITY IN *KING LEAR:* CHAOS SHAPED BY LOVE

As noted above, Shakespeare integrates multiple plots by principles of increasing complexity: all are fully operative in *King Lear,* making the two plotlines conspire to fulfill the 2–1–2 pattern of development. As *foil or parody,* Gloucester is more restricted than Lear in thought, feeling, rhetoric, and diction—as in his tactless boast of adultery, his astrological superstition that blames moral errancy on the stars, his impulsive gullibility in repudiating Edgar, his self-pitying and self-important appeals to power (with Kent, Cornwall, and Lear), his body-oriented experience of suffering, his courageless recourse to suicide and despair as an easy way out, his consummate credulity in the Dover cliff sequence. These traits establish him as a simplistic foil (at times almost as comical as Polonius), setting off the greater consciousness, dignity, and eloquence of Lear. Gloucester's simpler nature softens our judgment of Lear for *his* stupid encouragement of hyperbolic flattery, *his* impulsiveness in casting out the wise and loving, *his* self-importance and self-pity, *his* passivity and persistent credulity. Likewise the antics of Edgar-as-Tom deflect laughter from the grotesquerie of Lear's madness; and similar comic irony is evoked by Gloucester's suicidal "fall" at Dover cliff. It is notable that when Edgar and Gloucester have recovered stabler identities—that is, when no one, beggar, fool, or suicide, serves as radical foil for Lear—Shakespeare displays the king's most childish antics. Yet each has endured such folly, and despite Gloucester's new conviction of the soul's capacity for self-change he is still blind and credulous, making him the perfect audience for mad Lear: Gloucester's unthinking deference contributed to Lear's kingly pride; now Gloucester's servility ("Is it the king? . . . let me kiss that hand") provokes Lear to "preach" of privilege's reversibility, the illusion of "office."

As a *complementary contrast* with Lear's agony, Gloucester and his sons expand the story's dimensions. Though Edmund tries to diminish his brother into an untitled, contemptible clown (1.2.137–40, 183–88), evoking a genuine Poor Tom, Edgar eventually achieves a sane and serious identity. Indeed, unless Edgar's evolving roles show him finally on the verge of becoming the legendary King Edgar,[23] nearly half the play's meaning is lost. Gloucester's simplicity achieves a similar spiritual privilege: his eager credulity, absolute affection, and loyalty promote a succession of deep bondings—with Kent and Lear, with servants who give comfort after Cornwall's assault, with Edgar in the series of identities that rise in social confidence until he openly reclaims his role as Gloucester's child. Like Kent and Cordelia, Gloucester seeks the king at risk to his own life and position; he provides shelter for all the exiles on the heath; and after his blinding Gloucester's instinctive charity intensifies, as he confers wealth and blessings on those he believes to have greatest need. In Edgar's recount of Gloucester's end, "his heart burst smilingly" in recovering his son's affection. The story of Gloucester's eager affection, turned from Edgar only through deceit, thus contrasts markedly with Lear's self-generated avoidance of love.[24] More than his comic vanities, Gloucester's large and open heart makes him the best audience for Lear's reflections before reunion with Cordelia: Gloucester's empathetic enthusiasm for loving bonds projects a psychic landscape where Lear can relax his skeptical defenses—where his wit can subconsciously fabricate an extraordinary joke, seemingly at Gloucester's expense, though actually taking as its butt Lear's own shameful fear: "do thy worst, blind Cupid, I'll not love" (4.6.137–38). Thus Gloucester, his loyalty enhanced by blindness, affords a final, major way station (after the Fool and Poor Tom) for Lear's growth toward reunion with Cordelia.

In *King Lear* Shakespeare disturbingly subverts all his major schemes of dramatic order: the controlling power of the *sprecher-magus,* the security of a *framing plot,* the vibrant life of *embedded plots,* and the carefully coordinated and counterpointed *multi-level hierarchy of plots.* One expects the King's actions to subsume those of Gloucester's family, despite Gloucester's speaking before Lear at the outset and Edgar (in folio) speaking after Lear at the end. Both Gloucester and Edgar insist on their subordination to Lear, reverentially privileging Lear throughout, even when he is mad, and this deference is crystallized in Edgar's final speech. As the only Shakespearean tragedy whose title proclaims an anointed sovereign, *King Lear* should invite little debate as to whether the protagonist is privileged over the secondary plot and subordinate characters; yet it is in this play that Shakespeare's paradigmatic four-level hierarchy is most completely subverted. In *King Lear* a host of sophisticated minds (Lear, Edgar,

Kent; Edmund, Goneril, Regan, Oswald) might vie for the *sprecher-magus* role; but instead of privileging a supervisor like Oberon or Prospero who controls life from above, this play focuses on strong wills which are increasingly immersed in chaos. Lear is Shakespeare's most troubled *sprecher*: like Job he questions the thunder, the heart's darkness, and the death of his child, but he receives no direct answer—only Cordelia's nearly wordless forgiveness. Though Edgar finally extricates himself and his father from despair, it is not by imperious magic like Oberon's nor by Vincentio's political mastery, but by a wisdom allied with suffering.[25] Only in shared pain, the play suggests, does a true sovereign evolve. In the midst of that pain, all order, including dramaturgical order, disappears.

Similarly, the masterful framing scenes of *King Lear* (the initial love test and divestiture, the final rapt gaze at Cordelia as Lear divests himself of life) form Shakespeare's most suggestively mythic mating of beginning and end; yet it gives no definitive closure—rather, utter indefinition, as Booth observes.[26] So too, embedded scenes in *King Lear* lack the carefully controlled artifice and stage-management of other plays-within-the-play: Edgar's role as Poor Tom, like his subsequent disguises, is a painfully unpredictable improvisation, walking a windy line of perform-or-die; though coldly calculated, Cornwall's kangaroo court erupts into a similarly instinctive spontaneity we would rather censor than admit; and Lear's lunatic vignettes show the primitive core of human enactment, locking him into a recurrent psychic venue in which he either condemns and executes others or flees from them in terror, the outcome utterly unforeseeable as imagined persons metamorphose into courtiers, daughters, justicers, soldiers, torturers, dogs. In *King Lear* framing plots and embedded plots reinforce, not the securing stage-management of watchers, nor the joyous freedom to exploit life's changing scenarios, but rather the inevitable disintegration and disfigurement of human nature.

Fully developed alternate plots like those of *King Lear* should allow us to evaluate and rank analogous characters, their contrary approaches to power or relationship, and to stress the fulfillment of one special protagonist or group. Shakespeare favors that person who best sustains an outpouring of exuberant energy and desire, combined with effective judgment that attends to all others as well as oneself. The interweaving of Lear's suffering with that of Gloucester and Edgar, counterpointed against the ruthless forays of Goneril, Regan, Cornwall, and Edmund, clearly serves this purpose, distinguishing good from evil, enlightened from self-deceived. But when we turn to particular figures and events, all clarity ends. We witness endless judgment rites that seek to channel and control human passion: Lear's love-test, Gloucester's condemning of Edgar, Goneril and Regan's withdrawing of Lear's retainers, Lear's efforts to organize a series of trials on the heath, the kangaroo court that maims Gloucester, Lear's lunatic advocacy first for universal pardon, then for universal annihilation, his infantile flight from Cordelia and then meek submission to her affection, Edmund's furtive death-sentence on Lear and Cordelia, the trial-by-combat of Edgar and Edmund, Lear's final questionings and howlings at Cordelia's death. These attempts to ritualize human life do *not* clearly privilege one character and plot over another unless we invoke the fullest paradox: Lear rises from the chaos as sovereign only because, more feelingly than Socrates, he senses how little he knows, having identified with the apparition of a "poor bare forked animal" who is wretched, mad, and demon-haunted, and with a "poor fool" who loves too completely.

In *King Lear* Shakespeare's social and dramaturgical master plan, the four-level hierarchy of plots and the three symmetrical cycles for transforming the soul, is ravaged on each level and in each phase. Its one significant clown disappears in midquest, and other servants are stocked or executed if they follow conscience; its paramours are adulterous sisters vying for a selfish opportunist, while those who might conceivably seek true love must struggle for mere survival; its political agenda is so disjunct that English audiences must favor a French invasion; and, unless Edgar (or Albany or Kent) evolves further, there is no effective spiritual *magus*. In the three cycles of action Lear loses his sovereign power in acts 1–2, his sanity in act 3, his loving child in acts 4–5. In reducing his social and dramaturgical program to this shambles, a chaos balanced by those who love despite humiliation, Shakespeare seems to have achieved a strange kind of affirmation.

II
Shakespearean Epiphany

. . . the glory of God is a living person, and in human life is the vision of God.

—Irenaeus, *Adversus Haereses* 4.20.7

3

Epiphanal Encounters in Shakespearean Dramaturgy

But you, O you,
So perfect and so peerless, are created
Of every creature's best.
—*The Tempest* 3.1.46–48

JUST BEFORE PERDITA'S REUNION WITH LEONTES, A COURTLY GENTLE-man announces her presence in evangelical terms:

This is a creature,
Would she begin a sect, might quench the zeal
Of all professors else, make proselytes
Of who she but bid follow.
(*Winter's Tale* 5.1.106–9)

Leontes calls her "princess—goddess!" evoking again her role as "Flora," a part of "great creating nature" (4.4.2, 88). In act 5 she is integrated into the sophistications of courtly Art, which thus claims Nature's wonder as its basis (as in *Revelation*, the jeweled city-court of New Jerusalem finally discloses an Edenic garden at its core).[1] But if, like her precursors (Ophelia, Helena, Isabella, Desdemona, Cordelia, Marina, Imogen), Perdita with her flowers can revitalize the sovereign and his realm, a second recognition scene more conclusively resolves Leontes's abuse of kingship. The awakened statue moves him from generation to regeneration, revealing divinity not only in nature but in grace, the wonder of Hermione's persistent loving forgiveness. These conjoined discoveries, a magical piece of theatre, draw on Shakespeare's most potent dramaturgical device: *epiphany,* a recognition that awakens faith in spiritual identity, arousing the spiritual body.

As a "showing-forth" of reality in its essence and fullness (in Christianity, of Jesus' divinity),[2] epiphany in *The Winter's Tale* occurs not simply in the final recognition scenes but throughout the play. Hermione's gracious love is apparent from the outset, is acutely confirmed in her majestic self-defense during the trial, and achieves fullest impact in her radiant unsilencing and tender attentiveness in the final scene; yet it is perceived by Leontes only after sixteen years of grieved absence, aided by Paulina's stern counsel and consummated in her artful direction of the iconic statue-scene. Epiphany thus depends on the *seer* (and the experiential process and artful management of seeing) as much as on the quality of *what is seen*.[3] The "real presence," Richard Hooker says, "is not . . . to be sought in the sacrament, but in the worthy receiver of the sacrament."[4] To achieve this vision, Lancelot Andrewes in a sermon of 1597 urges continual effort: "look again and again; or . . . 'think upon it over and over again,' . . . to supply the weakness and want of our former lack of attention."[5] The spiritual reality is always there but not always perceived—often it is strangely opposed and obscured.

THE SOURCES OF SHAKESPEAREAN EPIPHANY

In *The Origins of Shakespeare* Emrys Jones finds four features of mystery plays that recur regularly in Shakespeare's plays: stress on the antagonists' "virulent malice"; their "conspiratorial method"; their "legalistic" and "hypocritical speeches," a loquaciousness that contrasts the scapegoat's silence; and the "progressive isolation" and abuse of the victim.[6] Jones's focus on the darkest aspects of the mystery cycle accords with Shakespeare's earliest plays: the first history tetrad highlights the egocentric persecutors (Margaret, Cardinal Beaufort, Richard III); those who are baited (Gloucester, York) seem Christlike only in their subjection to torment. Victims in later plays (Richard II, Desdemona, Lear, Edgar, Cordelia, Timon, Coriolanus) offer richer analogues;[7] but in none of these does Jones treat the positive aspects of the mystery plays: epiphany of the incarnate deity, shown in an outpouring of forgiving love;[8] change from worldliness to spirituality through suffering;[9] and spiritual empowerment of the vulgar and unworthy, evoking empathetic laughter among those who parody the central mystery.[10]

What central mystery informs Shakespearean epiphany? I will consider five New Testament events widely regarded as epiphanal; each, with its drama of obstructing agents, appears with increasing depth of meaning in many Shakespearean scenes.

Most prominent is *Jesus' nativity,* resisted by Herod, deflected by the innkeeper, and celebrated by shepherds and magi. John Donne calls it "a day that consists of twelve days," and all "make up the Epiphany."[11] "Every manifestation of Christ to the world, to the church, to a particular soul, is an Epiphany, a Christmas-day." Priests "who dwell in God's house . . . are most inexcusable, if they have not a continual Epiphany . . . ; and at the sacrament every man is a priest."[12] *Richard III* and *Macbeth* stress the subversion of nativity: deformed birth, violent caesarian birth, and a Herodlike slaughter of innocents.[13] In *All's Well That Ends Well* even nativity from bed-trickery echoes Christ's manifestation: "one that's dead is quick" (5.3.304). In the final plays nativity epiphanies abound, inducing in male protagonists their own empathetic labor as they struggle for spiritual rebirth. Pericles laments the "blustrous birth" of Marina, "as chiding a nativity / As . . . heaven can make / To herald thee from the womb" (3.1.28–34), but is drawn to active participation: "I am great with woe and shall deliver weeping" (5.1.109).[14] In *The Winter's Tale* Leontes repudiates nativity despite Paulina's effort to make him "soften at the sight of the child" (2.2.40): "Behold, my lords, / Although the print be little, the whole matter / And copy of the father" (2.3.98–100). In *The Tempest* the "cherubin" Miranda preserves her father's faith, eliciting another spiritual pregnancy:

> Thou didst smile,
> Infused with a fortitude from heaven,
> When I have decked the sea with drops full salt,
> Under my burden groaned, which raised in me
> An undergoing stomach, to bear up
> Against what should ensue.
>
> (1.2.152–58)

And in *Henry VIII* Cranmer as *magus* holds up a newborn babe to behold ("royal infant—heaven still move about her!") swaddling it in biblical allusions to predict an England where "God shall be truly known" (5.5.16–77).

Almost equally prominent is *Jesus' baptism* with God's approving voice and the Spirit descending as a dove,[15] obstructing agents being those who resist cleansing, making the water destructive, as in Noah's flood and the Red Sea debacle. Lancelot Andrewes plumbs the levels of this second epiphany in a Whit-Sunday sermon: the cleansing bap-

tism of water, atoning baptism of blood, rapturous baptism of fire—
each conferring freedom, power, and love by sacrificing all that im-
pedes vision.[16] With a baptismal allusion Romeo confirms his affection ("Call me but love, and I'll be new baptized" [2.2.50]); Henry V,
his conscientiousness in invading France (1.2.31–32); Iago, his villainy
(2.3.337–38). Baptismal imagery may be negatively inverted (Othello's flood of guilt, Macbeth's and Lady Macbeth's vain washing),[17]
painfully ambivalent (the tempestuous nativities of Marina, Perdita,
Miranda; the steeple-drenching, cock-drowning storm of madness
that transforms Lear's pride),[18] or joyously direct (the national baptism of Elizabeth). Besides watery dissolution, baptism may bring a
change of name (Romeo), clothing (Lear),[19] national identity (*Cymbeline*),[20] or religious faith (Shylock).[21] These cleansing renewals are
parodied by Falstaff's mock-Puritan devotion to sack and his dousing
in the river. Such an inversion is described in Andrewes's Whit-Sunday sermon: "'even soused over head and ears' in their sins, in 'many
foolish and noisome lusts, which drown men in perdition.'"[22]

A third epiphany is *Jesus' transfiguration,* when Peter, James, and
John saw fully his spiritual being,[23] yet were unable to interpret or to
participate in that glory. Transfiguration epiphanies figure prominently in Shakespeare's plays, first as comic parody. The duping of
Christopher Sly—"I am a lord indeed" *(Taming of the Shrew,* Ind.2.72)—
humorously suggests the power of play-acting to transform commoners into aristocrats, and implies humankind's genuine capacity
for deeper transformation: in the finale Katharina's stunning self-
revelatory performance (including the humbling change of name to
"Kate") draws force from the model of epiphanal transfiguration. To
be convincing, however, such "epiphanal" change would have to derive not so much from an enforced humbling (withheld food, clothing, movement) as from Petruchio's frequent complimenting of
Katharina's fiery spirit, implicitly able to match his own, and from his
demonstrating to her the power of play-acting and the paradoxical
power of self-abnegation: these lessons are implicit in the central
wedding epiphany when his self-mockery affirms inner spirit over
outward show, an Erasmian praise of folly—but only a blustery comic
parody of genuine, Christlike holy folly. What keeps Katharina's self-
fashioning from being fully positive (Maslovian self-actualization) is
Petruchio's insistence that she follow only his improvisations. Increasingly Shakespeare's female protagonists—Beatrice, Rosalind,
Helena, Cleopatra—wittily arrange their own plots. The comic parody of a divinely sponsored change is more explicit and sweeping in

A Midsummer Night's Dream.[24] Hippolyta observes in the young lovers' midsummer madness "all their minds transfigured so together" (5.1.24); and to explain his "translation" Bottom alludes not to Ovid or Apuleius but to Paul's Corinthian vision: "eye hathe not sene"; "we shal all be changed" (1 Cor. 2.9, 15.51). Transfiguration by love is affirmed in *Romeo and Juliet* and all the romantic comedies; and in *All's Well That Ends Well* and *Measure for Measure* a deeper change is enforced through humiliating bed-trickery, bringing guilt and gracious forgiveness. In the romances, transfiguration springs from disclosure of an ocean of love, a Nothingness fully accessible to the soul's nothing:

> . . . put me to present pain,
> Lest this great sea of joys rushing upon me
> O'erbear the shores of my mortality,
> And drown me with their sweetness.—O, come hither,
> Thou that begett'st him that did thee beget.
> *(Pericles* 5.1.196–201)

A fourth type of epiphany is *Jesus' resurrection* and then *ascension*[25]—obstructions being Mary Magdalen's sense of unworth, strangers' failure to see, Thomas's doubt. Such risings and wakings from "sleep" recur in many Shakespearean plays, most prominently in the romances but also insistently in the second history tetrad. In keeping with Hal's messianic promise of "redeeming time," Vernon sees him "[r]ise from the ground like feathered Mercury."[26] Falstaff parodies such claims—"we rose both at an instant and fought a long hour by Shrewsbury clock" (*1 Henry IV* 5.4.145–46)—and is resurrected by the Hostess "in Arthur's bosom" (*Henry V* 2.3.9). The romances offer Thaisa's literal resurrection, resuscitation of Imogen from slander's poison and of "Posthumus" from spiritual paralysis,[27] Hermione's climactic reanimation, and Prospero's reawakening of all the ship's "freighting souls" after exposing some to paradisal or penitential dream-visions: King Alonso, in particular, awakes transformed by an oceanic remorse that eluded the Macbeths.

Epiphany takes on fullest meaning amid the desolation of the *crucifixion*.[28] This paradox empowers most of the tragedies, especially *King Lear,* the impoverished venue where epiphany gains full effect. Lear's empathetic defense of Tom, the Bethlehem beggar who is terrified of fiends and obsessed with his sins, matches the allegory of the Passion in Southwell's *Spiritual Exercises:*

[T]hou wert the captive and slave of the devil, bound hand and foot by the chains of sin and at the very gates of hell. Thy king, hearing of this, laid aside His royal majesty, His power, His attendants, and His state, clothed Himself in coarse and torn garments and came into this vale of tears . . . torn by thorns and . . . without protection from the rain and storms.[29]

At first Lear travesties the analogue. In supreme pride, not loving service, he divests himself of "majesty . . . power . . . attendance . . . state," intending to keep all four; and even as suffering awakens sympathy for "naked wretches," he fluctuates from lewd indulgence ("Let copulation thrive") to nihilistic aggression ("kill, kill, kill," 4.6.109, 187). So too, Edgar's imitating a demon-possessed beggar differs markedly from Jesus' Passion. Yet the analogue persists as Edgar and Lear attend to each other's condition, especially when Edgar calls the mad king a "side-piercing sight," forcing Jacobeans and subsequent audiences to recall the crucifixion. For that wound, says Andrewes, consummates the Passion: "the perfection of our knowledge . . . is the knowledge of Christ's piercing," "the deadliest and deepest wound" of "His very heart"; "Christ pierced on the cross is *liber charitatis,* 'the very book of love' laid open before us."[30] Medieval dramas and narratives of Christ's Passion provide prototypes for the tortured body that is central to *King Lear,* though the analogue is continually disfigured by Lear, Edgar, and Gloucester.[31] Cordelia evokes the memory most fully: her silence at Lear's Pilatelike request, France's praise for her honest poverty of spirit (1.1.254–65), her attention to "my father's business" in order to redeem "nature from the general curse / Which twain have brought her to" (4.6.206–7), her "hanged" body in the concluding pieta.[32] Does Shakespeare evoke these powerful epiphanic images of the Passion—which Louis Martz finds central to Renaissance devotions and religious lyrics—only to enforce the most profoundly skeptical nihilism?[33]

THE EVOLUTION OF EPIPHANY IN SHAKESPEARE'S PLAYS

The progressive but conflicted discovery process in *King Lear* will become overtly religious in the romances, but in the early plays it is otherwise. There, recognition is at times a proudly narcissistic self-revelation or cruel exposure of others' vulnerability. In such instances it focuses on body more than soul; it tends to polarize, dividing male from female, master from servant, self from other; it arouses sentimentality or fury rather than complex empathetic awareness; and it brings little learning or growth. In *Titus Andronicus* each "recognition" is sheer anti-epiphany, a Medusan spectacle of savage mutilation which reduces persons to body-parts; it dis-spirits characters and audience, paralyzing us into statuary like Hermione in *The Winter's Tale*.[34] Equally preoccupied with "outward faces" is *The Comedy of Errors,* where the final revelation has virtually no connection with previous moral engagement between the various divided "twins" (three sets of siblings, severed parents, rival cities). The long-awaited disclosure of twins confirms only self-mirroring, not full awakening to otherness and certainly not to the sexual other: the reunion of Emilia and Egeon, reaffirmed marriage of Adriana and Antipholus E, and presumed betrothal of Luciana and Antipholus S are all strangely muted as the virtually unaffianced Dromios finally stress, not fraternity, but undistinguishable sameness:

> Methinks you are my glass and not my brother.
> . . . now let's go hand in hand, not one before the other.
> (5.1.418, 426)

Likewise the moments of spectacular recognition in other early plays—the tamed shrew, the pageants of unworthies in *Love's Labor's Lost,* Proteus's shamed glance at Julia's love—remain partly obscure, opaque, not fully realized.

In the romantic comedies and histories of 1597–1601—with characters who role-play, mirror, and self-parody—recognition increasingly involves a sophisticated, self-determining kind of transfiguration. Hal/Henry V, by baptizing his army in blood *(1 Henry IV* 3.2.132–37), engineers a half convincing epiphany of himself as a prodigal transformed into the "mirror of all Christian kings" *(Henry V* 2.Pr.6). Similarly sophisticated and oblique are the comic epiphanies celebrating undervalued virtues of Hero and Beatrice, Portia, Nerissa, and Jessica, Rosalind and Celia, Viola and Olivia—revelations achieved by humbling male pride and by displaying the women's active wit and artful use of disguise. Here, to some extent, epiphany works both ways, awakening both male and female to spirited and illuminative fullness. The bi-gender twins of *Twelfth Night,* both drawn between homoerotic and heteroerotic loves (neither fully realized), do not entirely escape from courtly Illyria's maskings by means of the final revelation—which occurs, of course, in the context of Twelfth Night, the feast of Epiphany in the liturgical calendar.[35] These disclosures of the soul's reality are complex—interchange of selfhood through love or sufferance, twinship with the sexual other, limited access to Spirit—but none of them, not even the elaborate religious allusiveness of *The Merchant of Venice,* presents a convincing Christian epiphany.

In the problem comedies epiphany is more troubled and thereby more miraculous. Spiritual power is invested in those who must use it indirectly. Helena's self-disclosure must cure the wounded male—the king's body, Bertram's soul—drawing them to acknowledge her goodness; and Vincentio's "second coming" must transform both sensualists and hypocrites. Each play uses a bed-trick to beguile the willful into righteous bonding, as in the biblical story of Tamar and Judah.[36] Epiphany is disturbingly split: a shocking display of shameful guilt, then a stunning revelation of loving forgiveness.[37] Those who engineer the beguilement know it compromises even the well-intentioned—

> . . . wicked meaning in a lawful deed,
> And lawful meaning in a wicked act,
> Where both not sin, and yet a sinful fact
> *(All's Well* 3.7.45–47)

—yet take this sinfulness upon themselves to reclaim the lost.

The tragedies also use epiphany as a dramaturgical axis but with greater impact. Tragic anagnorisis, revealing implacable mortality and profoundest guilt, attains great radiance and power, disclosing a supernatural provenance; yet this intense vision is disfigured by fiendish evil. Hamlet acutely questions the will "to be," yet his vision of being is hampered by troubled relationships. Despite his relatively sensitive dialogues with commoners (guards, players, gravediggers), his efforts to re-bond with Ophelia, Gertrude, and Laertes, his philosophic acceptance of mortality, and Horatio's ethereal eulogy—despite all that fosters admiration for this eloquent everyman, he never attains genuine epiphany. The ghostly encounter, one of Shakespeare's most richly symbolic scenes, suggests how much Hamlet desires such vision; but the ghost—a haunting image of his father as spectral superego—is a subverted epiphany (rightly debated by critics and by Hamlet himself),[38] and the remaining action teases us not just by delaying vengeance but by evading epiphany. At the center of act 3, "The Murder of Gonzago" reenacts the ghostly anti-epiphany, stunning Claudius with a vision of his primal evil: "Give me some light. Away!" This "Mousetrap," baited with queen and crown, is framed by two other entrapments: one baited with Ophelia, one with Gertrude. Social Darwinists might find a paradigm of human nature in this conflict of enemy egos, with love reduced to a deadly lure; but as epiphany it leaves much to be desired. The final cycle of action turns on the dense symbolism of Ophelia's madness, death, and burial, a sequence that should bring enlightenment at the primal scene of the id, the core of self with its craving for absolute love; but her madness lacks focus, missing Hamlet's immediate and genuine responsiveness. Though at the burial Hamlet proclaims (in past tense) his love for Ophelia, the sentiment is quickly displaced by sibling rivalry and self-preening hyperbole:

> I loved Ophelia. Forty thousand brothers
> Could not with all their quantity of love
> Make up my sum.
>
> (5.1.272–74)

Thereafter Ophelia is forgotten, the crowning epiphany voided.[39]

Hamlet's discovery of evil in human nature (though not in himself) activates psychic defenses of denial and projection that cruelly isolate and sacrifice those who might provide access to epiphany. *Hamlet* epitomizes the problem of tragic epiphany, which in radically exposing human guilt obscures the soul's divine mystery. The play's main revelations focus its three cycles of action: the ghost discloses primal evil at the center of acts 1–2; Hamlet's cagey *imitatio* of the regicide (the Mousetrap) at the center of act 3 is a rivalrous manipulation of the vision; and at the center of acts 4–5 Ophelia traumatically, uncontrollably internalizes the evil, her Edenic flowers showing Nature's unused potencies, her bawdy songs showing Reason's disfigurement. Instead of progressive enlightenment these three dark anagnorises render dysfunctional each of the psyche's main object-relational cathexes— that is, its relation to infant-nurturers, rival siblings, and authority figures. These crises appear in reverse order in the three cycles of Shakespearean tragedy, canceling the power of bonding at the sites of superego, ego, and id[40] (or, in Augustine's terms, memory, understanding, and will—the soul's trinitarian powers).[41]

Like the chaos of Lear's escalating madness, Ophelia's disclosures enable neither Hamlet's illumination nor her own. Yet in her dispersed passion lie the seeds of Desdemona's and Cordelia's sacrifice, Cleopatra's and Hermione's passionate transfiguration, and the men's shame-faced recovery of a loving, generative wife or daughter in the romances.

Why does Shakespeare's tragic epiphany conclude with the aggressive sacrifice of women, and his romance epiphany with their recovery? According to David Bakan, *Disease, Pain, and Sacrifice* (1968), in situations involving death-crisis, "that which is 'me' is made into something which is 'not me,' and . . . that 'not me' is sacrificed in order that 'I' might continue to live."[42] Such a psychic scene pervades *Hamlet,* which insistently broods on vulnerability to mortality. The anxiety intensifies in relation to woman, who in many ways is seen as causing the horrid vulnerability. Womb is tomb—once loving source, now feared devourer, of his mortal being. As cause of his vulnerable body, as strange sexual other, as sponsor of dependence, and perhaps above all, as object-relational mirror of his soul, which he suspects of being tainted and attached to evil, she is sacrificed to reassert his power, autonomy, freedom. The lesson of the tragedies, and supremely of *The Winter's Tale,* is that the formulation and exaggeration of that sexual divide—the creation, scapegoating, and sacrificing of a "not me"—completely desecrates the "me."

Second, in moving from the passive victimhood of Lavinia and Ophelia to the more assertive, self-enforced victimhood of Desdemona, Cordelia, and Cleopatra, Shakespeare's tragedies gradually confront and seek to resolve the dismissive scapegoating of woman, which implies the deepest blindness of human nature. Increasingly the tragedies formulate a goal not just of self-discovery but of self-discovery-through-Otherness. The drama of *Othello,* attending more deeply to relationship, refocuses the ontological query: "To love or not to love—*that* is the question." The moving, public epiphany of transfiguring affection at the end of act 1 ("I saw Othello's visage in his mind") is displaced by the contrary revelation Iago engineers at the center of act 3—discrediting Desdemona's love, replacing it with Iago's false devotion ("I am your own forever," 3.3.495), and turning from spiritual communion to obsession with physical sexuality and with the handkerchief (3.3.449ff). The third and final cycle has at its center Desdemona at her death-bed singing "willow" and debating Emilia on the nature of woman (4.3), a scene paralleling that with Ophelia's mad songs, but more overtly spiritual and radiant. The protagonist, murderously absent, does not witness this epiphany; but, as the conclusion reveals, pragmatic vulgar Emilia, who would have considered adultery for the right price, is transformed to imitate Desdemona's spirituality:

> What did thy song bode, lady?
> Hark, canst thou hear me? I will play the swan,
> And die in music. "Willow, willow, willow."
> Moor, she was chaste. She loved thee, cruel Moor.
> So come my soul to bliss as I speak true.
>
> (5.2.255–59)

And in so doing she at last transfers the vision to Othello. In the tragedies such encounters assume great depth by merging self-discovery with awareness of others' consciousness. In *Being and Nothingness* Sartre observes that our identity forms by "seeing others see us."[43] As Prospero notes at Ferdinand and Miranda's first meeting, "They have changed eyes" (1.2.412). In each other he knows they have discovered, despite his insistence on Ferdinand's corporeity, a trace of divinity, the *imago Dei.* Yes, Miranda, it *is* a "spirit" though "it eats and sleeps and hath such senses / As we have" (1.2.416–17).

Third, in each mature tragedy, especially following *Hamlet,* Shakespeare devises a progressive series of epiphanal encounters that systematically illuminate the soul's powers. Increasingly they show the protagonist's success or failure in exhibiting him/herself as perfect, self-knowing, immortal. Recognition is not reserved for the final scene but evolves in a series of encounters that serve as axis and conclusion for each of the play's three cycles. Thus, central to the first two-act cycle of *King Lear* is the face-off with loveless Goneril, in which Lear sees mirrored his own abuse of authority, and the cycle ends with the fuller embarrassment that inverts his initial treatment of Cordelia and Kent. In meeting Poor Tom at the midpoint of act 3 Lear reclaims the vulnerable otherness he has denied in himself and others; and this central cycle ends with Gloucester's analogous insight. In Lear's reunion with Cordelia at the center of acts 4–5, he acknowledges the deepest vulnerability, a childlike dependence on her motherly nurture and love. The tone of the final scene, though poles apart in quarto and folio, focuses on the same phenomenon: Lear's intensely painful devotion that consummately internalizes Cordelia—an event in quarto that stresses nihilistic grief ("O, O, O, O!") and that in folio is transformed to a kind of rapture ("Look there, look there"). Epiphany thus shapes each stage of Shakespeare's dramaturgy, focusing on three individuals who represent the human family's main object-relational bonds, drawing the protagonist toward the primal stage of human development and the core of selfhood.

As prototype for that mature format, consider the matching epiphany-series in two earlier plays. At the center of the first cycle of

Romeo and Juliet (acts 1–2) is their initial encounter when they immediately pledge love in a mutually-devised sonnet ending in kisses, and the two-act cycle concludes with Friar Laurence blessing their secret elopement: "by your leaves, you shall not stay alone / Till Holy Church incorporate two in one" (2.6.36–37). At the center of act 3 is not the duel but the balcony bedroom scene when their union is sexually consummated, a love-epiphany intensified by guilt (his duels before, her family deceptions after). At the center of acts 4–5 is Juliet's feigned death and Romeo's vision of rebirth, the cycle ending in love-deaths that spiritually consummate the marriage. *A Midsummer Night's Dream* parodies that sequence. Central to acts 1–2 is the casting of rustics for "Pyramus and Thisbe" (a hilarious parody of Romeo and Juliet's initial commitment), the cycle ending with Lysander's reversal and Titania's sleep. At the center of act 3 is love's fullest reversal: both young men chase fleeing Helena, Titania dotes on ass-headed Bottom, and the cycle of wayward love again ends in sleep. At the center of acts 4–5 all wake with memories of supernatural metamorphosis; and at the cycle's end, Pyramus and Thisbe perform a feigned love-death. The series of parody-epiphanies (Bottom playing both lovers; Bottom-as-ass enjoying Titania's dotage; Bottom recalling his "rare vision" while garbling I Corinthians, and then thoroughly "disfiguring" the love-death) both celebrates and ironically questions the epiphany-through-love envisioned by Dante, Petrarch, and the romancers—confirming the sophisticated artistic detachment of Shakespeare's mind.[44]

Shakespeare's early plays often satirically disclose the soul's reality, the parody assuming mythic scope in the "translations" and "transfigurations" of *A Midsummer Night's Dream*. Comedies like *The Merchant of Venice, Measure for Measure,* and *The Winter's Tale* adopt the religious idiom more seriously, though always with a parodic analogue, as in the executioner Abhorson's "profession" of his "mystery." Increasingly they expose—in Shylock, Antonio, and Leontes—abuses of judgment and power that require the supervening art of a Portia, Vincentio, or Paulina. Their task is not so much to punish as to prepare the soul for seeing, then to reveal, by effectively managed epiphany, the loving forgiveness that genuinely transfigures.

The deflected symbolic promise of the early comedies is fulfilled in the romances. White calls *The Tempest* "a sustained epiphany," and, with Frye, Kermode, and many others, he points to "recognition" as the goal of each romance:[45] Pericles with Marina and Thaisa, Posthumus with Imogen, Cymbeline with his sons and Belarius, Leontes with

Perdita and Hermione, Prospero even with his enemies, Henry VIII
with his miracle-daughter Elizabeth. In these plays epiphany is progressively and amply realized, culminating in an exhilarating con-
catenation at the end of each play, a chain-reaction of recognitions
like Chinese fireworks. As in Henri Bergson's "*durée*," "ideas and sen-
sations succeed each other with increased rapidity. . . . Finally, in extreme joy, our perceptions and memories acquire an indefinable
quality, . . . and so new, that at certain moments, returning upon ourselves, we experience an astonishment of being."[46]

SHAKESPEAREAN EPIPHANY VS. MODERN EPIPHANIES

Unanswerable questions remain. To what extent does each major reunion and recognition constitute a religious—or more specifically, a
Christian—*epiphany,* directly or subtextually evoking the life and
teachings of Christ as God incarnate? Insofar as they promote what
Robert Hunter calls "the comedy of forgiveness,"[47] the mature comedies—from *The Merchant of Venice* through the romances—suggest a
guardedly positive reply; and the transfigurational parodies in *The
Taming of the Shrew,* in *A Midsummer Night's Dream,* in Falstaff's parody
of puritan divines, and in the romances' vulgar subplots show insistent ironic engagement with the dream of perfecting spiritual empowerment as the greatest and most travestied Christian hope. In the
problem comedies, tragedies, and romances the fuller testings of
love, informing suffering with redemptive purpose, establish a more
comprehensive and religious mode of recognition. Nevertheless, a
wealth of recalcitrant material in each play deters us from making
simplistic generalizations.

Jones has shown how Shakespeare's histories and tragedies adopt
the Passion plays' victimization scenes, especially in *King Lear;* yet the
tragedies, both Roman and Christian, include rituals of violent sacrifice and scapegoating which do not easily evoke the gospel story. Ambitious Caesar and scornful Coriolanus attract violence in a different
way than Jesus,[48] and all the tragedies enact ritual slayings (or threat-
ened slayings) of the three "object relations" that structure familial
and individual identity: *authority figures* (Titus and Saturninus, Julius
Caesar, King Hamlet, King Lear, King Duncan, Coriolanus), *rival siblings or enemy twins* (Hamlet vs. Laertes, Edmund vs. Edgar, Macbeth
vs. Banquo or Macbeth vs. Macduff, Antony/Cleopatra vs. Octavius,
Coriolanus vs. Aufidius), and *nurturing women*—both virginal inno-

cents (Lavinia, Desdemona, Cordelia) and mothers (Lady Macduff, Cleopatra, Volumnia, Virgilia). Such savage rites associate Shakespeare with Aeschylus, Sophocles, and Euripides as easily as with medieval mysteries and martyred saint plays.[49]

Equally disturbing is the epiphanic awareness gained through impassioned, immolative love-death (Romeo and Juliet, Portia, Othello, Antony and Cleopatra, and perhaps implicitly and partially, Ophelia) or through friendship-suicide (Brutus, Enobarbus, Eros). The "high Roman fashion" of noble self-destruction *(Antony and Cleopatra* 4.15.92) joins hands with the medieval allegorizing of romances to present some suicides favorably—not repudiating life but affirming the bond with a beloved. Many Christian critics, however, refuse to see suicide as epiphany.[50]

Though the case for Christian tragedy—and thus "tragic epiphany" —rests most heavily on *Richard II, Richard III, Romeo and Juliet, Hamlet, Othello, Macbeth,* and indirectly *King Lear,*[51] one is awed by Shakespeare's diversity, achieving something like epiphany even in the Roman plays—darkly in Titus's revenge, brightly in Cleopatra's love-death. Unlike some medieval clerics, such as the author of *Ovide moralisé,* who reduced all pagan tales to a narrow salvational masterplot, Shakespeare sustains in part the atmosphere and ethos of Plutarch's Rome or of pre-Christian England; yet he subjects each tale to profound revision, arriving at increasingly epiphanal endings which often differ strikingly from his sources—as, for example, in *Hamlet, Othello, King Lear,* and *Antony and Cleopatra.* As Walter Foreman argues in *The Music of the Close,* those endings brilliantly link visionary insight with passional fullness, embodied in poetic magic or "music" that fully exploits the power of the word.[52]

Does Shakespeare secularize epiphany, recasting the quest for joyous vision in his culture's incipiently materialist ideologies and fictions?[53] Comparison with nineteenth and twentieth century visionary aesthetics offers some perspective on this unsolvable question. Joyce's Stephen Hero, turning from the priesthood to write poetic fictions, explains his new vocation as an openness to moments of "epiphany," both in life and language:

> a sudden spiritual manifestation, whether in the vulgarity of speech or of gesture or in a memorable phrase of the mind itself. He believed that it was for the man of letters to record these epiphanies with extreme care, seeing that they themselves are the most delicate and evanescent of moments.[54]

Whereas the epiphanies of Shakespeare's late plays increasingly serve both artistry and religious faith, Morris Beja in *Epiphany in the Modern Novel* stresses that for modern poets like the Imagists and for novelists like Joyce, Proust, Faulkner, Woolf, and Wolfe, this "spiritual manifestation" is basically secular.[55] Joyce himself insists that this momentous visionary experience is not a "manifestation of godhead, the showing forth of Christ to the Magi, although that is a useful metaphor," but rather "the sudden 'revelation of the whatness of a thing,' the moment in which 'the soul of the commonest object . . . seems to us radiant.'"[56] Ellmann notes Joyce's brash secularization of the mystery's source and meaning: some epiphanies, says Stephen, are "eucharistic," moments of fullness and passion; but "I must wait for the Eucharist to come to me," and then set about "translating it into common sense"[57]—that is, into everyday pragmatism and demystified materialism.

What then is secularization: substantial or only nominal change? If Dante, Shakespeare, and Joyce offer distinct modes of epiphany, does this difference alter the complexities of being (world, body and soul, God) that each experiences? Does it distinguish their inner conditions, or the meaning and impact of their fictions? Do the realities of God, Christ, and Spirit—and devotional or philosophic quests to know this spiritual reality—steadily lose bearing on literary works? The question of epiphany is surely as complex for Joyce as for Shakespeare—each reared in a divided and embattled Christian culture, each a sophisticated master of metaphoric evasiveness, indirectness, irony, reversibility. Let us evaluate some apparent differences between Shakespeare's epiphanies (especially in the romances) and those of Joyce and other moderns.

First, Shakespearean epiphany, evoked by momentous relational crisis, discloses the supreme value and miraculousness of human life. The comedies present epiphanies of love, keying on the magic of twinship, especially twinship of souls, and sometimes deflecting and parodying that transfiguring relationality in embarrassing disclosures of folly. At the same axial points of dramaturgical form, the histories show epiphanies of sovereign power. The tragedies offer mesmerizing anti-epiphanies of violent domination (Titus, Aaron, Richard III, Cornwell, Coriolanus) and, contrarily, epiphanies of spiritual power through self-sacrifice or love-death (Desdemona, Cordelia, Lear, Kent, Edgar, Gloucester, Macduff and family—consummating the earlier intimations of such sacrifice in Talbot, Henry V, Orlando, Viola, Helena).[58] The romances integrate all three modes of epiphanic recognition, combined with disclosures of spiritual rebirth—Pericles hearing music of the spheres, Posthumus's dream of gods and ancestors, Polyxenes' court viewing Perdita as Flora amid "great creating nature," Leontes' court witnessing Hermione's reanimation as "grace," kings/lovers/clowns seeing their spiritual reflections in Prospero's potent visions. *In striking contrast, for many modern artists these illuminations focus on vulgar events and speeches of everyday life, with seemingly trivial, arbitrary causes:* Proust eating a tea-soaked pastry; Joyce reliving a Dublin day—cooking a sausage, drinking at the pub, flushing the commode. Joyce keenly distinguished his special, "radiant" insights from ordinary processes of moral judgment. In his journals he often designated epiphanies by using the "Criterion of Incongruity" (Irrelevance) and the "Criterion of Insignificance."[59] Throughout *Ulysses* both Leopold and Molly Bloom derive epiphanic illumination and passion from the most commonplace, trivial events—with no easily reasoned connection between life's random ordinariness and the rich interplay of sense perception, memory, fantasy, and "spiritual manifestation" springing from that circumstantial flux. Langbaum, Nichols, and Bidney trace these aspects of modern epiphany—its common naturalistic basis, its sudden passionate overflow that defies rational prediction—to Wordsworth's "spots of time."[60]

Modern artists' privileging the "trivial" does not, however, prevent imaginative access to the sublime: the Blooms' quotidian routines and imaginings assume an allusiveness to all human history and to all poetic fictions—making us wonder whether the trivial is, in itself, the substance of epiphany. Joyce's stress on "insignificant" recognitions (of the "whatness" of material and bodily things, of unheroic feelings and commonplace visions of life) seems ironic and disingenuous: disallowing reason's value in such illuminations, he inevitably reasserts intellectual prowess by subjecting those "moments" to rigorous evaluation. Contrarily, Shakespeare's privileging of miraculous spirit-powers does not prevent his embracing the colorfully crude and common. *The Winter's Tale* and *The Tempest,* though admired for sublime spectacle, also delight in vulgar dialect and homely detail—vulgarity that does not desacramentalize the romance vision but substantiates it by making "wonder seem familiar."[61]

Second, Shakespearean epiphany is most prominently experienced by an aristocratic elite—the royal, heroic, and eventually almost saintly—especially those who, after betraying their royal heritage, atone with courage, long-suffering, and humility (Pericles, Posthumus, Florizel, Ferdinand, Leontes, Alonso, Prospero) or whose purity of heart brings sympathetic suffering (Marina and Thaisa, Imogen, Perdita and Hermione, Miranda) or whose imaginative prowess makes wonder of their very foibles (Falstaff, Cleopatra). Falstaff's mock-transfigurations include mirthful role-playing as a great Warrior and King (*1 Henry IV* 2.4.156–427), but then, in a drunken euphoria just before his fall, a serious projection of himself as God incarnate: "Blessed are they that have been my friends" (*2 Henry IV* 5.3.124–40). Cleopatra's capacity for regal transfiguration is repeatedly evident, especially in Enobarbus's account of the barge scene and in her majestic death; but always her apotheosis is based on, or rises out of, "riggish" self-change. *Modern fictions, on the other hand, stress democratization of epiphany:* illuminations may come to anyone, no matter what social caste, no matter how unworthy—indeed almost because of the struggle with self-esteem: Swann and Odette, Leopold and Molly Bloom, or the grotesque protagonists of Flannery O'Connor's "Revelation" and *Wise Blood*. Despite this apparent privileging of the vulgar and unworthy, however, most modern "epiphanies" are perceived and recorded by a sophisticated elite: the well-bred, well-educated Swann (and Proust) whose deeply moral *aperçus* surpass the awareness of most of the aristocrats; the epiphanal insights of Leopold Bloom (and Joyce) revealing a deep intellectual allusiveness, painfully sensitive to the moral failures of self and others. Molly Bloom's and Mrs. Ramsey's empathic, discerning overflow of observations, feelings, and intuitions—intricately recorded by the Bohemian Joyce and the Bloomsburyan Woolf—display an ongoing epiphany of "great creating nature" from the inside.

Contrarily, though Shakespeare continually gives obeisance to "princely privilege" (*1 Henry IV* 3.2.86), he also surpasses most poets in attributing intense consciousness to the common mind: Bottom's "rare vision" and persistent stealing of center-stage; the gravedigger's daunting presence (like the remembered Yorick) that, besides grounding Hamlet in the spry humor and insightfulness of his workman's soul, momentarily *displaces* Hamlet as a source of epiphanal vision; Caliban's irresistible centrality, delighting in the heavenly music and dreams most courtiers neglect (3.2.137–45) and provoking Prospero's admission of relationship (5.1.278–79). Other unruly servants (Lance, Grumio, Puck, Dogberry, Touchstone, Parolles, Pompey) are, often against or beyond their will, similarly instrumental in bringing epiphany to the aristocrats. In their center-stage disclosures audiences see themselves no less than in Hamlet, Lear, and Cleopatra. Each claims a kind of supreme value in the mere act of being. Parolles, even

after complete shameful exposure, affirms, "Simply the thing I am /
Shall make me live. . . . / There's place and means for every man alive"
(*All's Well* 4.3.335–36, 341); and more positively, Bottom represents
humankind both in his energetic good nature and in his inadequacy
to the revelation bestowed on him. Thus persistently and improbably
does Shakespeare engender epiphany out of simplest clay.

Not only does revelation visit the vulgar and literal-minded, but
even the woefully hard-hearted and devious. In such cases Shakespeare tests the limits of the human capacity for epiphany, for in Jewish and Christian tradition the essential requirement for this vision is
cleanness of heart: "I wil beholde thy face in righteousnes" (Ps.
17.15); "Blessed are the pure in heart: for they shal se God" (Matt.
5.8). Shylock, Malvolio, and Iago demonstrate enormous obstacles to
such perception; yet materialistic, vengeful Shylock can poignantly
depict his own humanity ("Hath not a Jew eyes?" *The Merchant of Venice*
3.1.61), and in *Measure for Measure* hypocritical Antonio senses the
depth of his turpitude as he casuistically converts epiphany to nefar-
ious effect:

> What dost thou, or what art thou, Angelo? . . .
> O cunning enemy that, to catch a saint,
> With saints dost bait thy hook!
> (2.2.180, 187–88)

Likewise proudly jealous Lear, Posthumus, and Leontes, as well as
willfully sensual Falstaff and Cleopatra, achieve insights about the human essence despite the great tide of passion that encompasses it.
Most remarkably Macbeth, learning of his wife's untimely death,
voices the darkest anti-epiphany with the most compelling eloquence
("Tomorrow, and tomorrow . . .")—a testament both to residual marital affection and to the resilience of his self-judging conscience. Few
writers (Chaucer, Faulkner) rival Shakespeare in the outrageous un-
worthiness of characters who provoke and receive, in some measure,
epiphany.

*Finally, Shakespearean epiphany, especially in the romances, is caused by
supernatural spirit-power, immanent in nature and human nature yet allied
with transcendent reality:* either by elemental spirits (Puck, Ariel); by
magi using the spiritual force of wit to manage the power of herbs,
words, and human psyches (Oberon, Portia, Helena, Vincentio, Ce-
rimon, Cornelius, Paulina, Prospero); or by deities, who appear in
spiritual crises to enlighten royals who have been humbled, thus en-

suring providential justice. Since the 1606 Act of Abuses had banned reference to Christian deity, Shakespeare enlisted appropriate pagan gods: virginal Diana resolves Pericles' fear of sexual defilement; Jupiter rejoins ancestral bonds in *Cymbeline;* Apollo restores reason in *The Winter's Tale;* Juno, Iris, Ceres ensure generative bonding in *The Tempest.*[62] Still, each romance alludes prominently to Christianity: *Pericles* recreates the nativity and resurrection; Cymbeline reigns during the advent of Christ; *The Winter's Tale* emphasizes grace that brings spiritual rebirth; the transfiguring storm of *The Tempest* ends with Prospero's prayer. *In contrast, the origin of epiphany in modern art is rarely identified.*[63] For many modern artists one assumes "natural" causes: bodily and material circumstances, with tempers, defenses, and fantasies generated by the Freudian "bodily ego." But there is a mysteriously wide suggestiveness in the provenance of modern illuminations: in Faulkner's "The Bear" Ike McCaslin finds the depths of his own nature in a weaponless meeting with a bear ("no more but such a poor bare forked animal"), in ledgers of his slave-owning family ("the dark backward and abysm of time"), and in the apparition of Boon Hogganbeck cursing and banging his jammed gun under a tree alive with squirrels ("some monster of the isle. . . . Where the devil should he learn our language?").[64]

For Renaissance divines and allegorists like Andrewes and Spenser, as for Aquinas and Dante, rational *Ideality* seems the noblest highway to the vision of *God;* thus they privilege the formal cause, mainly as a means to the final cause. Wordsworth's epiphanies stress the efficient cause, or psychic *Existence* ("feeling," "imagination"); and Joyce's epiphanies stress the material cause or *Actuality* ("the 'whatness' of things").[65] These four modes of being and of vision—Actuality, Ideality, Existence, and God—must endure, like the four corresponding "zoas" Blake perceived in human nature; but cultures (and individuals) tend to privilege one over the rest. These diverse epiphanies, says Lancelot Andrewes, affirm the plural manifestation of "the [Lord] of Lights" (James 1.17), who offers to humankind both "the light of nature" and the multifold "light of God's Law": prophecy and the Gospel, "the inward light of grace," "the light of comfort of [the] Holy Spirit," and "the light of glory . . . where we shall dwell with [God] . . . , the sun whereof never sets."[66]

Shakespeare balances these worldviews. Material sensation and bodily drives do not claim full allegiance, though he remains deeply attentive to bodily appearances. Nor does the ineffable vision of God swallow up lesser realities, like the "great sea of joys" Pericles feared might "O'erbear the shores of my mortality, And drown me with their sweetness" (5.1.197–99). Shakespeare's broad humanist focus is on personal encounter, the human face, and all the natural and divine reality it can reflect. The loving, suffering visages of Othello, Desdemona, Cordelia, Marina, Hermione, Miranda, and the questing visages of Rosalind, Lear, Cleopatra, Pericles, and Leontes, finally suggest a creature that in human bonding yearns to mirror and merge with its source:

> Do you see this? Look on her, look, her lips,
> Look there, look there!
> > *(King Lear* 5.3.316–17)

> It is required
> You do awake your faith.
> > *(Winter's Tale* 5.3.94–95)

4

Shakespeare's Immanent Epiphanies: Soul and Spirit in the Works of Spenser and Shakespeare

He letteth in, he letteth out to wend,
  All that to come into the world desire;
  A thousand thousand naked babes attend
  About him day and night, which doe require,
  That he with fleshly weedes would them attire;
  Such as them list, such as eternall fate
  Ordained hath, he clothes with sinfull mire,
  And sendeth forth to liue in mortall state,
Till they againe returne backe by the hinder gate.
                                    The Faerie Queene 3.6.32

What is 't? A spirit?
                    Miranda, *The Tempest* 1.2.413

Aᴛ ᴛʜᴇ ʜᴇᴀʀᴛ ᴏꜰ ᴇᴀᴄʜ ᴅᴇꜰɪɴɪᴛɪᴠᴇ ꜱᴇɢᴍᴇɴᴛ ᴏꜰ ᴀ ꜱʜᴀᴋᴇꜱᴘᴇᴀʀᴇᴀɴ play is a startling transaction. The protagonist's changing nature is revealed in three dynamic encounters, each like a preternatural or supernatural invasion of one being by another, an influence often described as demonic or divine. Shakespeare portrayed this inner being, the fundamental ontology of human nature, in mysterious images of "cloud" and "dream." He stressed its capacity for radical change in metaphors of ocean voyage and storm, masking and play-acting, fatal illness and madness, demonism and bestiality, miraculous cure and transfiguration.

The Middle Ages and Renaissance designated this central self as "soul" or "spirit." Socio-linguistic evolution from biblical and classical antiquity has made both words, especially "spirit," so complex as to invite multivolume analyses.[1] This diversity is richly apparent in

89

Spenser's and Shakespeare's contrary views (and metaphoric renderings) of the human essence to which these terms refer. Shakespeare treats this "knot intrinsicate" with increasing ambivalence and finally with reserve. Midway through the tragedies, in *King Lear,* Shakespeare suddenly curtails use of the word "soul," as if questioning its nature and permanence. In subsequent plays he never again exploits the word with the persistence of the early plays. His use of "spirit" gathers an increasing range of jarring nuances, dominated by the natural (bodily spirits, and passional spirits) but never omitting the supernatural (soul as spirit, and demonic or divine spirits).

Comparing Shakespeare's naturalistic bent with Spenser's Platonism is instructive. Shakespeare's use of "soul" and "spirit" should be understood within the broadest purview of intellectual history; but modern treatments of Renaissance psychology are reductively slanted toward naturalism.[2] They grant almost exclusive hegemony to Aristotelean faculty psychology and Galenic humoralism, a view matching Shakespeare's affinity for bodily experience and prefiguring modern positivism, which takes sensation as the sole basis for truth. Shakespeare's humanist skepticism (like that of Erasmus, Rabelais, Montaigne) might seem prophetic of modern materialism; yet holistic evaluation shows Shakespeare (and most Renaissance thought) teetering between natural and supernatural allegiances. From antiquity to the Renaissance these rival perspectives kept a steady if varying tension—Plato vs. Aristotle, Bonaventure vs. Aquinas, Ficino vs. Bacon, Spenser vs. Shakespeare; yet each of these minds, while privileging one extreme, actually wavers between both worldviews.

In seeking to understand Shakespearean epiphany—the stunning disclosure of essential human nature that serves as axis in his dramatic form—we might profit by comparing Spenser's contrary psychology and artistic mode: Shakespeare's empirical, experiential naturalism inverts Spenser's idealizing intellectual supernaturalism. Spenser's allegorical art, drawing from the Pythagorean-Platonic tripartism of *Timaeus* (as transmitted by Chalcidius, Cicero, Macrobius, Martianus Cappelanus) and from its partner strain of Christian-Platonic trinitarianism (Augustine, Eriugena, Bernard, Bonaventure, Ficino, de Mornay), exploits the often-neglected half of Renaissance psychology.[3] Shakespeare's aesthetic landscape grew by a quantum leap when he discovered the implications of Spenser's complementary vision, a Christian-Platonic view of England as an idealized fairyland, ruled with virginal perfection by a fairy queen. The result was a sublime parody, *A Midsummer Night's Dream* (and its later refinement, *The Tempest*).[4] Shakespeare's art reaches its fullest scope partly by internalizing and revising Spenser's art, expanding the scope of his plays and animating them with a tension between both realms.

HUMAN ESSENCE AS "SOUL" AND "SPIRIT": THE RIVAL TRADITIONS

Privileging transcendent Reality, Augustine desired "to know God and my soul. . . . Nothing else."[5] Treating the body and worldly experience as mere contexts for psyche's functioning, he described them as intellectualized projections of the soul's idealized hierarchic form and powers. Platonists like Philo, Origen, and Augustine subjected not only body to soul, but soul to spirit. As designators of the God-force, the two words are often used interchangeably, but Northrop Frye in *Words with Power* sees a sharp distinction between them, as they appear in Jewish and Christian scriptures.[6] "Soul" is the numinous entity in embodied form, its nature shown in hierarchic ordering of bodily powers and in mirroring God and other souls. "Spirit" connotes that essence as a nature-transcending force, playing freely and actively through the body (and through the social world and cosmos) but not ultimately constrained or defined by these settings. Often symbolized by fire, it could fully activate or transform body and soul, as at Pentecost and the Transfiguration, thereby revealing more vigorously and directly its divine source.

"Spirit" ultimately signifies a divine power and mystery in relation to human nature. But as Verbeke shows in his study of *pneuma* from Stoicism to Augustine, "spirit" drew not only from Platonic-Pauline-Augustinian transcendentalism, in which it reflected the Spirit of God, but from Aristotelian-Stoic-Galenic naturalism, which viewed "bodily spirits" as *materia subtilis,* increasingly refined motive powers in the ensouled body: natural spirits assist digestion, vital spirits move the passions, animal spirits implement ideas and intentions.[7] To Donne such ambivalent "fingers" can connect the incommensurate parts of human being, can "knit / That subtile knot, which makes us man."[8] Many modern studies, however, stress the Aristotelian view of "spirit" for Renaissance culture: it is "a corporeal substance and serves as a vehicle for the senses":[9] "the bodily spirits . . . differed fundamentally from the soul," for "spirit . . . was not itself immortal and would eventually decay into its elements."[10]

Such a view belies the complexity of "spirit" in the Renaissance. In La Primaudaye's influential *The French Academie,* part 2, which Hankins views as the richest source for Shakespeare's concepts of physiology and psychology, "spirit" usually connotes divinity.[11] The treatise affirms Medieval Christianity (and chides Aristotle and Galen) by minimizing attention to materialistic bodily spirits as the basis of human nature and by exalting spirit as a divine power perpetually infused into the soul. In his tripartite model of human nature as spirit-soul-body (divine spirit as first principle of all action and being), La Primaudaye, like Spenser, gives primacy to the Christian-Platonic model developed by Augustine (building on Plato, Plotinus, Origen) and adopted by Erasmus.[12] Many Renaissance *nosce teipsum* treatises imitate *The French Academie*'s structure: they begin by praising divine spirit; they observe the trinitarian Creator's investing the human microcosm with trinitarian "order and number and measure," noting the soul's ultimate imperviousness to bodily contingencies and limitations; and they end by celebrating the soul's immortal reunion with God, the goal of such treatises.[13] La Primaudaye's encyclopedia replaced Bartholomaeus's medieval compendium as the single most important synthesis of Christian-Platonic and Aristotelian-Galenic schemes of human nature, and his synthesis distinctly favors Christian Platonism.

A more troubled effort to reconcile the two realms of "spirit" is found in Timothy Bright's *A Treatise of Melancholie,* long accepted as an influence on *Hamlet.*[14] As both physician and minister, Bright vacillates wildly in explaining the causes of melancholia. Chapters 1–8 trace it to humoral spirits and animal/vegetable diet; but chapter 9, "How the body affecteth the soule," suddenly veers into a six-chapter digression on the hierarchy of body-soul-spirit, stressing that soul remains "one simple faculty" despite the body's mutable multiplicity. Chapters 15–31 return to pragmatic and naturalistic concerns: "How perturbations [(chaps. 15–18)—and passions (chaps. 23–31)] arise from humours"; but again Bright inserts four chapters (19–22) stressing that melancholy's impact on body and mind does not necessarily affect the soul. The final two sequences epitomize Bright's failure to integrate the two psychologies. Chapters 32–36 offer consolation for religious melancholy and despair, treating "Spirit" as transcendent and closely linked with conscience, and mentioning bodily spirits as secondary causes, acknowledged only as a means of easing the burden of conscience. Then chapters 37–42, starkly anticlimactic, list physical-environmental influences: Galen's "six non-natural factors" (climate, diet, sleep, exercise, digestion, passion), social factors (vocation, reputation), and a final pragmatic list of dietary remedies and herbal purgatives.

Bright's disjunctive treatise offers conspicuous evidence of the growing tension between natural and spiritual gnosis. Shakespeare and others must have been moved by Bright's poignant effort to draw from both realms to console and cure his suicidal friend. At one moment "spirits" are material forces ("bodily spirits") moving through the humors, conditioned by the blood's humoral balance and other bodily-environmental factors; then they are spiritual forces, either aspects of the Godlike soul or demonic spirits playing through the body's humors and passions in ways that may exceed human control, as in demon-possession. Half a century later Burton's *Anatomy of Melancholy* would survey similarly diverse causation. His six expanding revisions (1621–55), collating 2000 years of religious-medical-philosophic-literary reflections, enabled Burton to avoid Bright's inelegant wavering by obsessively cataloging the full range of causes and effects—all the modes of "spirit"—into neat hierarchic order.[15]

Like his contemporary Bright, Shakespeare was torn between opposing models for the central mystery of human nature, often pitting them against each other, as in *King Lear.* The mystical understanding of soul or spirit, having lost its presumed supremacy, now vied with naturalist questionings, bringing doubts about the soul's nature, hegemony, and immortal destiny—indeed its very existence.[16]

Spenser's Houses, Shakespeare's Clouds

Spenser's Platonic intellectualizing of soul and spirit as a reflection of divinity forms a constant theme of *The Faerie Queene,* the basis of his elaborate allegory. Books 1 through 6 each present the same parable of fall and redemption, but they offer a series of "descending" perspectives on the soul's bodily housing. In Books 1 and 2 the soul's rational power seeks fulfillment first in the transcendent context of Caelia's House of Holiness, then in the complementary immanent context of Alma's Castle. In books 3 and 4 the soul's affective power seeks fulfilment in the same complementary venues of Psyche's Garden of Adonis and Venus's Temple. In books 5 and 6 the sensory power seeks fulfilment in the similarly contrarious settings of Mercilla's Court and Pastorella's countryside. Thus the holistic perspective of book 1 (the soul's quest for *Grace* in New Jerusalem) narrows to the immanent pluralism of book 6 (the soul as 1-within-3-within-100 *graces* unfolding in Nature's multiplicity on Mount Acidale).

This sequence does not suggest Spenser's subscribing to the "new philosophy" that privileged the natural world and brought a crisis of faith regarding God and the soul, despite signs of his discouragement about Elizabeth's ability to approximate Gloriana. By the poem's end Prince Arthur would surely encounter a supreme fiction of the soul's fulfillment. After his descent in books 1–6 into the mutable multiplicity of the central legends of Courtesy and Constancy (the former marked by incompleted quests and interrupted epiphanal visions), books 7–12 would enable Arthur's reascent to a directly transcendent vision of Gloriana: by change "all things . . . their being doe dilate" only to "worke their owne perfection" (*The Faerie Queene* 7.7.58). Each legend exposes the soul's blind impotence as it discards true armor/housing/doctrine and adopts false housing; then power is restored in an iconographic house or garden that affirms access to divine form.

Never does Shakespeare provide his protagonists with the assurance of such educative houses, moralized gardens, or templar visions. One recalls Friar Laurence's equivocal, fruitless efforts to counsel Romeo and Juliet—his easy accommodation of their impetuous passion and his reliance on deceptive and theatrical devices. In the course of Shakespeare's plays, houses increasingly disappear, lose all connotation of secure confinement, and are transformed into tombs or wisps of cloud, most notably in *Hamlet, King Lear,* and *The Tempest.*

Unlike Spenser's constant affirmation of the soul's spiritual nature and immortal destiny by means of iconic enclosures, Shakespeare's more skeptical view of the human essence undergoes complex evolution during his two decades of playwriting. He treats with mistrustful irony all claims of demonic spirit-power, from the Ephesian sorcery in *The Comedy of Errors* and Joan la Pucelle's witchcraft in *Henry VI* to the equivocating Weird Sisters. Beginning with Hamlet, protagonists of the tragedies and romances pointedly question both supernatural spirits and the soul's own Godlike substance and immortality, often comparing the self and its wishful identities to *clouds*. This analogy becomes a signature for the problem of belief: it connects the struggle for personal identity with teleological aspiration, evoking an ascension "in the clouds," but unlike the jeweled fixity of the New Jerusalem, it depicts heaven as a mutable realm of "vapors."[17]

Similar anxiety invests Shakespeare's related image of soul as a *dream* or a *dream-maker,* which gathers increasing complexity as it evolves from *The Taming of the Shrew* and *A Midsummer Night's Dream* to *Measure for Measure, Antony and Cleopatra, Pericles,* and *The Tempest.* Does Prospero's gnomic "such stuff as dreams are made on" stress the generation of deluding fantasies and nightmares, or does it include prophetic oracles and heaven-sent visions?

The questioning of dreams and their "cloudy" provenance by Hamlet, Timon, Antony, and Prospero—always suggesting dubiety about the soul's nature—offers sharp contrast with Spenser's hieratic display of dream-types, each finally revealing its supernatural provenance and illuminative core. The Arch-imager's false fantasy to delude Redcross Knight is eventually displaced by the waking vision of the New Jerusalem and Una unveiled; Britomart's troubling mirror-inspired dream gives way to her quasi-epiphany in Isis's Temple, clarifying her divine nature and destiny; Arthur's dream of Tanaquill, though at first intensely frustrating, leaves vestigial traces of the embodied Glory that inspires his quest.[18]

For Spenser the soul is contained and defined in hierarchy, a central principle in his fashioning of educative houses and paradisal gardens (figures of Reason and Nature) as the soul's secure and fruitful habitats—substantial, definitive, and clearly contrasted with antitypes (House of Pride vs. House of Holiness, Mammon's Cave vs. Alma's House, Busirane's House vs. Gardens of Adonis, Lust's cave vs. Venus' Temple, Radigund's castle vs. Mercilla's palace, brigands' cave vs. Mt. Acidale). By ordering the soul's powers, such structures temperately balance Nature's contraries and disparage absolute evil.

Shakespeare's protagonists have little recourse to such iconic education in ideal selfhood. For him clouds, dreams, or a drop of water lost in the ocean suggest the soul's "airy nothing"; and the mind's architectonic structures are as mutable as those dreams:

> like the baseless fabric of this vision,
> The cloud-capp'd towers, the gorgeous palaces,
> The solemn temples, the great globe itself,
> Yea, all which it inherit, shall dissolve.
> (*The Tempest* 4.1.151–4)

If, for Shakespeare, all bodily housing, artful super-structures, and "cloud-capp'd" aspirations must submit to Time's dissolution, what of the soul itself—the "stuff" that dreams are made on? Is life "*rounded* with a sleep" by the soul's submergence in drowsy *recurrence,* by completing life's *cycle,* or by gaining perfect *circularity*? Or is it rounded in *pregnancy*—a spiritual labor, like that noted by Plato as philosopher and by Sidney, Spenser, and Shakespeare as artists, to deliver a spiritual body?[19] Does "*sleep*" (like the "rest" that succeeds Creation) bring loss of consciousness, or waking to a more total dimension of dream?[20] Whereas Spenser's dreams affirm a desire for definitive truth or falsehood, forcing characters to determine their source and meaning, Shakespeare's dreams (those of Romeo, Hermia, Hamlet, Posthumus, Prospero) suggest a radical changeableness, intriguing complexity, and discomforting transience in human existence. Yet they also affirm the central importance of relationship.

FULFILLMENT AS RATIONAL ECSTASY OR PASSIONAL RIPENESS: CONTRARY VIEWS OF PASSION, WOMAN, AND COMMONERS

In *Mirror of Minds* Geoffrey Bullough coalesces the two disparate psychologies in his list of Renaissance assumptions about human nature, "inherited from Aristotle and Galen, adapted by Augustine and Aquinas, and handed down through the . . . schools": (1) the soul is an immortal entity—derived from God, made in God's image, and returning to God; (2) the embodied soul, having descended into the body at three levels (vegetable, sensitive, rational), has a multiple, hierarchic nature—each level moved by increasingly-refined bodily spirits (natural, vital, animal); (3) the body, made of four elements, with four matching humors and four matching passions, is subject to dynamic contrariety that the soul must balance; (4) this three-powered embodied soul is a microcosm, laying a basis for poets to see human being mirrored in all aspects of Creation.[21] In their poetic fictions Spenser and Shakespeare diverge on all four points, especially the challenging first—the divine origin, nature, and destiny of soul and spirit—to which the other three are subordinate, elaborating conditions of embodiment. Whereas Spenser uses soul and spirit to authorize and privilege transcendent reality, Shakespeare's evolving use of these words shows his delight in immanent, sensory manifestations of the mysterious life force.

Contrary Perspectives: Passion

Spenser's commitment to the hegemony of spirit, conceived as an immortal essence, is best summed up by Joseph Collins, who in *Chris-*

tian Mysticism in the Elizabethan Age uses the Legend of Holiness and *Fowre Hymnes* as consummate examples of a Christian-Platonic view of the soul's quest for perfection.[22] Repeatedly Spenser shows the soul embarrassed by fleshly passions and needful of divine aid; never does he question its Godlike essence. He depicts the soul's divine origin in the Garden of Adonis and *Fowre Hymnes;* often he stresses the soul's immortal destiny, most fully in the Legend of Holiness (hell in canto 5, heaven in canto 10); and throughout *The Faerie Queene* he discloses the soul's spiritual nature. In each legend the hero is graced by a templar vision when pristine clarity arrives, when veils and armor are removed, deceitful demonic artifices are stripped away, and the chaotic passions aroused by false tempters are replaced by desires harmoniously ordered and directed to their proper end. These epiphanies of virtuously beautiful soul-maidens in figurative castles and gardens (Caelia, Alma, Venus, Belphoebe-Amoret, Cambina, Mercilla, Pastorella, Dame Nature) each involve a knight who actively interprets the vision and then defends it. To help the soul attain that clarity of purpose and desire, Spenser's allegorical art intellectualizes experience and passional human nature, re-forming it in analytic, mystically structured stanzas/cantos/books and numerical patterns—the touchstone of Platonism.[23]

Shakespearean drama inverts this vision and artistry. With no interest in mythic depiction of the soul's supernatural origin or destiny, he privileges immediate experience, despite its deceptive appearances and passions, and enlists intellect not for rigid order but for Protean self-fashioning—the dynamic, ever-changing manipulation of bodily appearances. Shakespeare's one venture into cosmic mythography, Oberon's recount of the origin of erotic passion (*Midsummer Night's Dream* 2.1.148), aptly appears in a play that parodies Spenser's art. Shakespeare's protagonists—Richard II, Beatrice, Rosalind, Viola, Helena, Brutus, Hamlet, Troilus, Othello, Lear, Macbeth, Antony and Cleopatra, and Prospero—each test the soul's capacity for self-control; and Hamlet and Lear initiate questionings of the soul's very existence: "to me, what is this quintessence of dust"; "Is man no more than this? . . . no more but such a poor bare forked animal." Each hero is haunted by the self-image of "a poor player," as well as by self-comparisons to vaporous shifting clouds and "such stuff as dreams are made on." Human identity is a series of fleeting projections in a world of passional flux.

For Spenser such passional experience, a labyrinth of confusion, holds no educative value. The soul gains moral maturity and perfection only by an intellectual mode of epiphany, by being lifted out of bodily-passional experience—mainly by supervening grace. For Shakespeare, however, the immersion in bodily passions, intensifying suffering and love, is what refines and "ripens" the soul. To surmount the unending trivializations of soul through subjection to the body and worldly circumstance, one might like Cleopatra meet death with majestic art, an art always focused on bodily passion: she yearns for sexual-spiritual consummation with "the curled Antony" before he can "spend that kiss" on the sensual Iras. Animating Cleopatra's response—like that of Romeo and Juliet, Lear and Cordelia—is submission to love-suffering. Despite the hilarious parody of Pyramus and Thisbe's love-death in *A Midsummer Night's Dream,* such blind faith in the other inspires the quest for Godlikeness and spiritual communion in the love tragedies: Cleopatra's "immortal longings" foster an Olympian dream of Antony deified (5.2.75–99); Juliet envisions Romeo as the sun (3.2.1–31), and Romeo dreams he dies and is revived as emperor by her kisses (5.1.1–11). Most generative of human Godlikeness in Shakespeare's plays is Lear's reunion with Cordelia; with the patient love of 1 Corinthians 13 she inspires Lear's "wheel of fire," and his envisioning her as "a soul in bliss" (4.7.47, 50) presages a changed identity like that described in 1 Corinthians 15.[24]

Contrary Perspectives: Woman

The difference between Spenser's quest for transcendent rationality and Shakespeare's immersion in passional experience is apparent in their treatment of the sexes. Much of the soul's mystery is lodged in gender distinctions, especially in the notion that woman's self-mastery is achieved through submission and procreative nurture, as when woman symbolizes the soul in Spenser's iconographic centers. Initially Spenser guards and veils the soul-maiden's integrity while exposing the soul-warrior to thorough corruption; but with Britomart's arming and Amoret's wound (book 3), culminating in Serena's naked shame (book 6), Spenser subjects both sexes to the full consequences of the fall.

From the outset Shakespeare is far more aggressive: in *Henry VI* the brutal male overreachers are matched by scheming viragos, and the humiliations of weak-willed monarchs are more than matched by the spectacle of Lavinia mutilated and Ophelia mentally undone. Shakespeare assaults and compromises both sexes, stripping away all veils and civilizing commodities, immersing them in sensory and passional experience, especially in the tragedies, where both male and female suffer abuse, death, and moral chaos.[25]

Both poets, though in utterly different ways, disclose the soul's androgyny—Spenser in templar visions of Venus, Nature, and various hermaphroditic couples; Shakespeare in the protean range of some protagonists (Rosalind, Lear, Cleopatra, Falstaff) and in experiments with bi-gender doubling, cross-dressing, mirroring sexes, and psychic transference between lovers.[26] Both poets explore the tension between hierarchic dominion and mystical communion as goal of the sexes' complementarity. The evolution of Shakespeare's comedies, and then of his tragedies, is toward female protagonists of increasing power; yet after the woman (Portia, Beatrice, Rosalind, Viola, Helena; Cordelia, Lady Macbeth, Cleopatra, Volumnia) asserts the prowess of her consciousness and will, each play ends with a laughably hasty reversal that allows the male to deliver a final dictum.

Contrary Perspectives: Commoners

Spenser consistently portrays the soul as *imago Dei,* whereas Shakespeare's disclosures of the human essence range from humorous parody to serious analogue, often entwined; only in the romances does Shakespeare verge on Spenserian art by privileging invisible reality in recognition-scenes that revive the miracle plays' *ecce homo.*[27] Even in the romances, however, Shakespeare's epiphanies occur not in stately, iconographic, hierarchic order but in empirical, experiential indirectness, colored with humorous vulgarity and showing, as Bradley says, Shakespeare's delight in "the uneducated mind, and its tendency to express a sound meaning in an absurd form."[28] In portraying commoners' role in human nature Shakespeare again inverts the vision of his great contemporary. As in Plato's ideal city-state, Spenser restricts commoners to the serving-class base of a three-level hierarchy, restricting their minds to the belly's appetites and sensational literalism.[29] Though Shakespeare is often similarly reductive in portraying commoners (Lance with his dog, Bottom's crew, Lancelot Gobbo, Dogberry's watch, the drawer Francis), he also repeatedly privileges the "clown" as a dynamic exemplar of the soul's power, a touchstone for its flaws and aspirations. Quaintly mirroring the "mystery of . . . God manifest in the flesh," these hard-handed workmen presume to know what Lancelot Andrewes calls "secrets of divinity": "for all men even by nature love to be knowing."[30] In a 1607 nativity sermon on 1 Timothy 3.16 ("great is the mystery of godliness") Andrewes declares that

> [t]he world hath her mysteries in all arts and trades (yea, mechanical, pertaining to this life) which are imparted to none but such as are *filii scientiae,* "apprentices to them." . . . So they delight to style themselves by the name of such and such a mystery.[31]

Hamlet's gravedigger glories in his "profession," parodying priestly judgment on the mystery of one who "willfully seeks her own salvation" (5.1.31); the executioner Abhorson in *Measure for Measure*) is determined to "profess" his "mystery" (4.2.26–53); the Clown pontificates to Cleopatra of the worm's "immortal" bite (5.2.240–78); Bolt and the Bawd "profess" their commitment to unchastity (4.6.1–199); in *The Winter's Tale* the Clown and Shepherd philosophize of "things dying and . . . newborn" (3.3.112–13); and the unlikely Caliban is a conduit for "music" (3.2.133) and "grace" (5.1.295). Of all the festive Lords of Misrule, the most impressively associated with religious mystery is Bottom: his "translation" fails to bring understanding, as shown in his misquoting of 1 Corinthians 2.5, yet it is he of all mortal lovers who enjoys a "rare vision." As in the mystery cycles, whose terms he borrows, Shakespeare evokes laughter at foolish self-assertion even as he recalls and generously affirms the central mystery of human nature.[32]

For Shakespeare as for Spenser, passion must be ruled by reason, woman by familial hierarchy, the monstrous rabblement by aristocratic governance; but for Shakespeare the experience of these turbulent components—passional experience, womanly nurture, and vulgar commonness—is also valued in and for itself, essential for ripening the soul and defining human nature.

Shakespeare's Changing Use of "Soul"

Not only do Shakespeare's protagonists experience profound soul-change through exposure to mutability and frailty, but in his plays the very meaning and frequency of "soul" also undergoes a continual sea-change. The histories use the word most, averaging twenty-four per play, as compared to nine per comedy, thirteen per tragedy, six per romance. The first history tetrad's busy wheel of vengeance sends many stereotyped souls, like those of the Talbots, winging upward from the stage. In *Richard III* this facile invoking of "soul" peaks with sixty usages, nearly twice the number of any other play. The numerous death-crises that provoke so much shallow and undeveloped soul-consciousness are engineered by Richard himself, who reinforces the superficiality by cynical mockery, gloating over his ability to hurry souls to the afterlife—till ghostly spirits awaken his own night-terrors.

In the second tetrad mortality occasions anxiety in killing a deposed king, then festive triumph at the miracle of Agincourt. The abundant references to soul in *Richard II* (35), especially the seven uses in the mirror scene (4.1), bring a deeper questioning of human identity, anticipating the similar self-consciousness in Hamlet and Othello. The awakening of Richard Plantagenet's soul is fittingly echoed in the Lancasters' insomniac soliloquies (*2 Henry IV* 3.1.4–31, *Henry V* 4.1.228–82); but such fretting over regal responsibility for ambitious sins of the commonweal only briefly interrupts their practical agenda and hardly involves soul-consciousness, as is evident in the word's moderate use in the *Henriad* (fourteen in *1 Henry IV*, seven in *2 Henry IV*, nineteen in *Henry V*). Though Henry V's generous engagement in kingship makes him no mere Machiavellian, he is *not* the "mirror of all Christian kings" in a fully spiritual sense.

Hamlet and *Othello* establish a deeper inner dialogue: their explicit and solemn references to "soul" reach a crescendo with forty uses in each play. Hamlet repeatedly appeals to his soul, emphasizing intense self-awareness and engagement in an ultimate cosmic scenario: "Would that the night would come! / Till then sit still, my soul"; "thou, dead corpse . . . shake our disposition / With thoughts beyond the reaches of our souls"; "O, my prophetic soul! My Uncle!"; "O, it offends me to the soul to hear a robustious periwig-pated fellow tear a passion to tatters"; "Since my dear soul was mistress of her choice, . . . / She hath sealed thee for herself."

Nor is Hamlet alone in habitually addressing himself and others as "souls." Polonius holds his duty "as I hold my soul." The Ghost "could a tale unfold whose lightest word / Would harrow up thy soul." Claudius mistrusts "something in [Hamlet's] soul / O'er which his melancholy sits on brood," and worries for his own "limed soul that struggling to be free / Art more engaged!" Gertrude grieves that Hamlet "turn'st mine eyes into my very soul," for "To my sick soul . . . , / Each toy seems prologue to some great amiss." While Laertes urges the devil to "take [Hamlet's] soul!," Ophelia pleads, "God ha' mercy on his soul! / And of all Christian souls, I pray"; and as the gravedigger wishes rest for Ophelia's soul, the priest ungenerously denies it. Central to the play's long brood on human frailty and mortality is insistent reference to self and others as "souls."

Othello is equally persistent in addressing himself as soul, but here the God-image is drawn into a deep maelstrom of decay. He begins by affirming "my parts, my title, and my perfect soul"; takes pride in gaining Desdemona's love by "such fair question / As soul to soul affordeth"; and, in his rapturous greeting ("O my soul's joy!"; "my soul hath her content so absolute"), suggests the delight of a "marriage of true minds," as in Sonnet 116. His descent into jealousy plays out the darker side of marriage's double-identity: "Perdition catch my soul / But I do love thee!" In arming his mind to kill, he swears "by the worth of mine eternal soul," and before the murder he addresses his soul (as conscience) most directly and seriously: "it is the cause, it is the cause, my soul." At his wretched awakening he laments, "This look of thine will hurl my soul from heaven," and demands to know "from this demi-devil / Why he hath thus ensnared my soul."

Though often preoccupied with his own "perfect soul," Othello at best sees Desdemona and himself as mutually responsive essences—"soul to soul"; so too Desdemona, seeing "Othello's visage in his mind" ("the face," Ricoeur says, "is the trace of the Other"[33]), consecrates to him her "soul and fortunes." After abandonment she is isolated as a "poor soul . . . sighing by a sycamore tree"; but regaining confidence in her final defense she swears "by my life and soul!" Just as often, Emilia uses "soul" with sincere piety, and Iago with ironic self-idolatry, as when he feigns holy virtues and urges Roderigo and Othello to "have some soul" by pursuing selfish interests and by the "manly" act of murder. Even more than *Hamlet, Othello* sustains an intense concern for the soul's destiny, not with Hamlet's philosophic mind but with fullness of heart.

In *King Lear* and *Macbeth,* where death, spiritual death, and residual guilt for moral chaos leave deepest scars, one expects a profusion of references to the soul. But in fact the opposite occurs. In neither tragedy does the heightened questioning of the nature of human nature bring much explicit reference to "soul." Instead one senses a distinct withdrawal from the word. In *King Lear* it appears only three times—a stunning contrast with *Hamlet* and *Othello.* Admittedly, *King Lear*'s three meager uses are richly suggestive: blind Gloucester, empathizing with Poor Tom, urges an Old Man to "bring some covering for this naked soul"; Lear, waking from madness, suggests that Cordelia is "a soul in bliss"; and at the final horror Albany appeals to the survivors as "Friends of my soul." In each case the awareness of soul springs from exposure to nothingness and poverty of spirit.

The paucity of references to "soul" in *King Lear* is no aberrant fluke but marks a watershed in Shakespeare's explicit invoking of the elusive human essence, for the word appears no more than four to eight times in any of the remaining tragedies and romances.[34] The word does not disappear but is harder earned, and its value increases with Shakespeare's resistance to naming it. Far more moving than the facile and prolix naming of the soul in the early plays is the theatrical experience of Gloucester's blinding and Lear's mad sufferings, especially his staring at Cordelia's lips and saying, "look there!"[35] During the long awakenings in the romances' reunion scenes, where soul is also fully exposed, the word is again used very sparingly, always with great force: Leontes' "Now piercing to my soul" (*Winter's Tale* 5.3.34); Posthumus's "Hang there like fruit, my soul, / Till the tree die!" (*Cymbeline* 5.5.266–67). Posthumus's cry epitomizes Shakespeare's valuing of passional experience, or "ripeness," over the distancing, idealizing epiphany of Spenser's emblematic visions. This intense remark initiates *Cymbeline*'s extraordinary sequence of climactic recognitions— each enmeshed in ironies that force both characters and audience to make continual uneasy but exciting adjustments to the soul's utterly unpredictable experience, denying simple intellectual clarity.

Such indirection is especially evocative if we note the degree to which Shakespeare's characters favor bodily, sensory, outward experience over the invisible world of spirit. When through momentous crisis this value is reversed (as in the murders of Desdemona and Cordelia, the self-immolations of Ophelia and Cleopatra, the miraculous "resurrections" of Marina, Thaisa, Imogen, Perdita, Hermione, Miranda), one senses the intensity with which earthly garments either are removed or are transformed into spiritual emblems. The attending characters and the theater audience are then led by musical-poetic-dramaturgic magic—perhaps above all by linguistic failure and silence—to train their inner eye toward "nothing": invisible reality becomes momentarily more apparent than what they see, hear, and touch on stage.

THE SOUL AT DEATH: SPENSER AND SHAKESPEARE

Even in confronting Despair (*Faerie Queene* 1.9), Spenser's protagonist does not express fear of mortality.[36] Chivalry disparages such fear, but the Redcross Knight's disregard for death springs mainly from his disdain for bodily-worldly experience. The *contemptus mundi* of the "too sad" Redcross Knight is shared by all of Spenser's Briton protagonists; each epiphany of a soul-maiden in her castle or garden affirms not bodily experience but the spirit that shines through it (or in the Gardens of Adonis, the souls that such sexual activity enfleshes). When Redcross, finally at one with Una unveiled, is "swimming in that sea of blissful joy" *(Faerie Queene* 1.12), one assumes—despite the energetic bodily image—that he shares with her, only momentarily, a *spiritual* body, a primal ocean of essence.

In Shakespeare's world, on the other hand, where such joys enhance the *fleshly* body (the "spirits" of sherris sack that enforce Falstaff's dream of kingship and then deification *[2 Henry IV* 4.3.88–123, 5.3.138–40]; the sexual spirits that animate Cleopatra's dying transfiguration [5.2.226–312)]), one finds deep, explicit regret when the mortal coil is shuffled off. Mistress Quickly uneasily feels Falstaff's legs (and upper parts) "as cold as any stone" *(Henry V* 2.3.25); and, like Hamlet, Claudio gains chilling eloquence at the horrific fantasy—"to die, and go we know not where, / To lie in cold obstruction and to rot" *(Measure for Measure* 3.1.118–33). Such misgivings are so prominent in the history-plays, problem-plays, and tragedies that Elias Schwartz, in *The Mortal Worm: Shakespeare's Master Theme* argues that dread of mortality and a growing intuition of immortality form the central theme of Shakespeare's plays and sonnets.[37] Duke Vincentio urges Claudio—and all in his sensual kingdom—to embrace the tragedy of mortality: "Be absolute for death." His urgent advice, however, to privilege disembodied spirit over embodied passion, is not heeded in *Measure for Measure,* nor in *King Lear,* nor in the romances. While Spenser's heroes do aspire to such absolution from fleshliness, Shakespeare's protagonists, even in the late plays, remain committed to bodily experience and passional intensity: they are *absolute for love—* a love with many levels but always known through embodiment.

Not the soul itself but the ensouled body is the context for Shakespearean epiphany. While Spenser abstracts the body into an iconic templar form, Shakespeare dissolves all such structures within an intense field of passion.

"SPIRIT" IN SPENSER AND SHAKESPEARE

Shakespeare and Spenser are also poles apart in their use of "spirit." Again Spenser privileges transcendent reality, giving it absolute primacy over the natural order. Of 237 uses in *The Faerie Queene*, 5 refer to elemental air or breath, and 36 to bodily spirits: these elemental/bodily usages together form 17 percent of the whole. The majority (83%) refer to higher modes of being: 140 to the human soul, 59 to various supernatural spirits—ghost (7), demon (34), angel or beatified soul (7), daemon (5), and Holy Spirit (6). Thus in *The Faerie Queene* "spirit" usually signifies the immortal Godlike essence—the soul, whether in its embodied or in its freer and more powerful disembodied form. For Spenser, bodily spirits are in short supply and have little share in the derivation, motivation, and exercise of human personality: they are merely consequences, secondary manifestations of divinity.

In contrast to the ease of summarizing Spenser's orderly distinctions among modes of "spirit," studying the word in Shakespeare's plays can lead to a migraine headache and serious questioning about why one would choose this project. If it was tedious evaluating Shakespeare's 533 uses of "soul," it was far more arduous analyzing his 342 uses of "spirit." Interpreting "spirit" in the mature plays is like riding a thoroughbred or bottling an active volcano. Several examples will illustrate how Shakespeare increasingly invests "spirit" with a shimmering multiplicity of intent, an unstable dynamic tension that defies simple assignment of meaning.[38]

First consider the dark connotations of the opening of Sonnet 129:

> Th' expense of spirit in a waste of shame
> Is lust in action.

Here "spirit" is strongly colored by bodily meanings—semen and vital spirits—yet retains its higher meanings as well, so that contrary modes of spirit, as opposing motivators of human nature, seem at war. In this losing struggle with lust, the lower, bodily meanings dominate; yet the sonnet implies that spirit's higher meaning (soul, Godlike essence) is equally present, but is repressed, travestied, imposed upon in the shameful waste, or "expense," of its nature and power.

In Prospero's epilogue a still greater range of meanings is activated; but here the transcendent meanings dominate, partly through the subtle capitalizing of "Spirits" to begin a line:

> Now I want
> Spirits to enforce, art to enchant.

"Spirits" gathers into itself every level of meaning the play has exploited: bodily spirits or vital force, passional spirits or strength of

will, theatrical spirits or actors, and the divine Spirits or guardian angels who provide grace and succor. That the humbled, prayerful
Prospero must "want" such "spirits" suggests both his wishful yearning for such power (on every level of its meaning) and his acknowledgment of personal limitation and need, caused by advancing age
and the more deep-seated frailties of his moral nature.

Whereas only 17 percent of Spenser's usages refer to elemental or
bodily spirits and passions, for Shakespeare the opposite is true. Over
70 percent of his uses of "spirit" refer to bodily passions, and increasingly in the later plays the word also includes punning allusion
to the flow of bodily spirits (often by sexual arousal)—as when
Goneril bawdily offers to "raise [Edmund's] spirits up into the air"
(recalling the "lust in action" of Sonnet 129). Only 7 percent of
Shakespeare's uses of "spirit" refer to the human soul, and 18 percent
to supernatural beings. Shakespeare has reversed Spenser's percent-
ages of bodily and spiritual (immanent and transcendent) meanings.

Three other factors add to this contrast. First, Spenser's references
to supernatural spirits, good and bad, are quite sincere: the demons
that prey on the Redcross Knight's mind and the angels that invite
him heavenward are genuine, as are Mammon's fiend and the
guardian angel that vie for Guyon's soul. Shakespeare, however, persistently invites skepticism about supernatural beings, hinting at
fraudulent delusions and emphasizing the deceptive theatricalism
that forms a major thread in each play's fabric: Hamlet questions the
ghost, Othello projects witchcraft, Edgar half-pretends demon possession. Even the overt supernatural forces in *Macbeth* (Banquo's
ghost, the witches and their demon masters), while asserting an un-
deniable, staged reality, seem ultimately to be projective effluvia of
human evil, the fantastic outgrowth of warfare and the ambitious
heart, lacking definitive reality: "The earth has bubbles, as the water
hath, / And these are of them" (1.3.79–80).[39]

Second, with regard to supernatural "spirits," Spenser includes a
generous number of divine beings (angelic spirits, Holy Spirit): about
25 percent of the whole. Shakespeare's plays include only a couple of
"spirits" who are bona fide angels (less than 1 percent of the whole).
If we acknowledge the 1606 Act of Abuses against use of the name of
God in stage plays,[40] the reference to pagan gods in *King Lear* and in
the romances might indicate a less severe contrast between Spenser
and Shakespeare in this regard. But throughout *The Faerie Queene*
Spenser's prolific and highly sophisticated symbolic use of pagan
deities to represent the immanent virtues of human nature far ex-
ceeds Shakespeare's use even of such figures.[41]

A third distinctive feature in Shakespeare's use of the supernatural is his bias for elemental spirits and natural magic, as in *A Midsummer Night's Dream* and *The Tempest*, suggesting his concern for the spirit's habitation and fulfillment within the natural world. Though Spenser includes many immanent epiphanies of pagan gods (books 2, 4, 6 of *The Faerie Queene*, which focus on "faery" protagonists, whose souls are portrayed *sub specie temporis*), Spenser always privileges the transcendent Christian manifestations of spirit (Books 1, 3, 5, which focus on "Briton" protagonists, whose souls are envisioned *sub specie aeternitatis*). Spenser thus systematically subordinates pagan deities to Christian revelation: in the six legends' descending specula, each set of pagan spirit-powers is carefully formulated to reflect, for its particular level and perspective, the mystery of the *summum bonum*, the ineffable face of Spirit.[42]

In each generic phase of Shakespeare's career one finds a jostling admixture of four disparate attitudes toward supernatural spirits (ghosts, demons, witches, fairies): (1) straightforward supernaturalism *(Midsummer Night, Macbeth, Cymbeline)*; (2) anti-supernaturalism, with characters voicing skepticism about spiritual causation, reinforced by deluded or fraudulent references to spiritual beings *(Comedy of Errors, Taming of the Shrew, Troilus and Cressida)*; (3) both of these contrary attitudes in unresolved tension *(Richard III, Henriad, King John, Hamlet, King Lear, Antony and Cleopatra, Cymbeline)*; (4) natural supernaturalism, in which magic, miracle, and wonder are treated as valid but also as simply a part of ordinary human existence (*Merchant of Venice, Twelfth Night, All's Well, Measure for Measure, Antony and Cleopatra, Pericles, Winter's Tale, Tempest*). Such diversity, expressed in the varied, contrarious, and shifting tempers of his characters, is the keynote of Shakespearean psychology.[43]

Spenser and Shakespeare would respond quite differently to the Delphic maxim "Know thyself." The former would privilege the soul's invisible and eternally unchanging substance, contemning fleshly appearances that enshroud it; the latter would delight in the soul's immersion in Time-and-Fortune's sensory flux and its protean self-fashioning through play-acting.

Imagine the two bards meeting in bliss. Spenser's resurrection body, no doubt, would shine with the changeless numbered perfection described by Augustine in *The City of God*,[44] while Shakespeare's resurrection body would surely assume a different apotheosis—a protean ever-changing force unlimited in its dynamic capacity to assume all forms of being, what Keats called "negative capability." What sort of dialogue could occur between two such psyches? With their access to expanded paradisal powers one might expect an easy and fluent chat; yet their visions of nature, the soul, and God are so distinct that one can hardly picture them in the same communion of saints. Since one of them is chanting Virgilian hosannas to a national soul-maiden sublimely conceived as Gloriana, while the other is rapping out Ovidian dithyrambs to the same maiden disarmingly and ironically conceived as Titania, one suspects that even in heaven the hosts of angelic scholars will organize separate Renaissance conferences to fill timelessness with praise.

III
Shaping Psyche's Tragic Quest: Contrary Faces of Nothing

When I demanded of them, thei answered not a worde . . . : their worke is of nothing, their images are winde & confusion.

Isaiah 41.28–29

[H]e hathe nether forme nor beautie . . . that we shulde desire him. He is despised and reiected of men: . . . we hid as it were our faces from him: . . . we did iudge him, as plagued, and smitten of God, & humbled. But he was wounded for our transgressions, he was broken for our iniquities . . . yet did he open not his mouth . . . though he had done no wickednes. . . . Therefore wil I giue him a portion with the great. . . because he hathe powred out his soule vnto death: and he was counted with the transgressers, and he bare the sinne of many, and praied for the trespassers.

Isaiah 53.2–7, 9, 12

5

Macbeth's Three Murders

Macbeth is a milestone in man's exploration of . . . this "depth of
things" which our age calls the unconscious.
    —Harold Goddard, *The Meaning of Shakespeare*

Shakespeare inherited a five-act dramaturgical pattern that
he refined into a symmetrical 2–1–2 series of cycles, focusing each cycle on a central "epiphanal encounter," a moment of intense recognition. In the mature tragedies, *Macbeth* and *King Lear,* those three cycles (and epiphanal moments) form stages of psychological
development: a comprehensive inner plot. What transpires in the
protagonist's soul during each of the three phases, and how does
each prepare for the next? What holistic psychological development
occurs in the course of each play?

Interpreters of *Macbeth* have focused almost exclusively on the first
murder, the killing of a king in acts 1–2, as the basis for understanding the play—its social, psychological, and metaphysical meanings.
Macbeth's subsequent two assassinations, of Banquo in act 3, and of
Macduff's wife and children in acts 4–5, either are ignored, or are
treated simply as efforts to secure the usurped crown, or perhaps as
a kind of Freudian "repetition compulsion"—the blooded man's first
heinous kill engendering serial slayings.[1] Neither of the subsequent
murders has been accorded its own distinctive meaning and psychological motivation; they are seen as mere shadowy reenactments of
the Oedipal complex which is presumed to underlie the one essential crime, the slaying of the patriarchal king.[2]

As R. A. Foakes puts it, "the murder of Duncan was the equivalent
in mountaineering terms of scaling Everest, and after this [Macbeth]
has no trouble with lower hills."[3] This exclusive highlighting of the
regicide (as the "be-all and end-all" of the play) entails, however, that
the final three acts must dwindle from real theatrical power to melo-

dramatic spectacle[4] —a result of the victims' shrinking symbolic import and, correspondingly, the shrinking spiritual grandeur of the protagonists, who deliver fewer and fewer eloquent soliloquies, consign their villainies to hired thugs, and finally are swept aside by the nobler (but less charismatic) avengers, Macduff and Malcolm. Many astute critics of the play—including Bradley, Rossiter, Heilman, Sanders, Jorgensen, Mack, Kirsch, and Muir—have struggled with this central conundrum: can the playwright sustain great tragedy if the only true kingly spirit is dispatched at the outset?[5]

Like most of these critics, I believe that Macbeth's capacious mind, despite its moral degeneration, remains at center-stage, showing the horrific consequences of a truly heroic spirit embracing evil. But instead of conceiving the tragedy as one great cosmos-shaking act of regicide followed by two subordinate aftershocks, I would characterize the Macbeths' journey into darkness as three equally significant stages of spiritual catastrophe, three distinctive and theatrically potent dimensions of evil as it evolves and festers in the human psyche. Macbeth murders first a politically authoritative *parental ruler,* then a *brotherly friend* (his "chiefest friend" according to Holinshed), and finally a *mother and her children.*[6] His victims thus represent the three fundamental human bonds, together comprising (in reverse order) the three basic stages of human maturation, or the three essential cathexes of the human psyche. Thus, in the course of the three murders Macbeth deconstructs the entire psychological infrastructure of human identity. Shakespeare's awareness of this pattern is underscored by its earlier prototypical appearance in *Richard III,* where that villain-hero similarly kills a king (Henry VI), then a brother (Clarence), then children (the Princes).[7] In *Macbeth,* however, the playwright is far more apprised of the scheme's psychological implications, which he methodically exploits.

The dramaturgical design of *Macbeth* precisely emphasizes this three-phase pattern: acts 1 and 2 present, in a continuous sequence, the regicide and its immediate consequences; act 3 shows the murder of Banquo and then its impact on Macbeth at the banquet; acts 4 and 5, another continuous cycle of action, presents the slaughter of Macduff's family, then its social and psychological consequences.[8] This 2–1–2 structure, the dramaturgic pattern of all of Shakespeare's mature tragedies, perfectly accommodates his treatment of Macbeth's three murders.

To attain this neatly coherent pattern of psychological devolution, Shakespeare has drastically altered Holinshed's *Chronicles*[9] —first, by condensing all the major crises of Duncan's six-year reign and of Macbeth's seventeen-year reign into the two-hour traffic of the stage. The entire battery of wars and assassinations seems to transpire in a matter of days, rather than a quarter of a century, making the three murders (as well as the broader framework of political violence in acts 1 and 5) seem closely and causally connected.

Equally striking is Shakespeare's moral reshaping of the victims, casting them as iconically benevolent members of the human family, in order to accommodate his three-phase tragic pattern. Instead of the chronicles' portrait of a weak, cowardly, and greedy king, about the same age as his cousin Macbeth, Shakespeare portrays Duncan as aged, humble, and generous—an ideal, almost saintly monarch. Though some recent critics, in the radically revisionist spirit of New Historicism, interpret Duncan's "womanliness" as Shakespeare's indication of his unkingly impotence, I believe Wilbur Sanders's view is correct: Duncan's nurturing, fertile, self-mortifying traits contribute positively to Shakespeare's portrait of "a most sainted king" (4.3.109). Duncan begins where Lear and Cymbeline end, as a king who can "see feelingly."[10]

Similarly Banquo, in the chronicles a co-conspirator in regicide, is recast as a devoted friend in life's warfare, modestly resisting each temptation to which his colleague falls prey. Many critics have questioned the probity of Banquo even more than Duncan. Berger's and Calderwood's subtle criticism of Duncan's "aggressive giving" would also pertain to Banquo's lavish praise of his warrior-colleague (1.4.54–58).[11] Yet that Duncan's and Banquo's compliments are essentially benevolent is underscored not only by their repeated association with "royalty" and "grace," but also by the contrast with Macbeth's deceitful, murderous mode of "aggressive giving"—especially his forceful invitation of Banquo to the feast (3.1.11–39) and flattery of the missing guest (3.2.30–31, 4.41–44, 91–92). Though Shakespeare implies political shortcomings in Duncan's aged weakness and in Banquo's Hamletlike inertia after the regicide (thus qualifying the playwright's compliment to James I), nevertheless in revising the chronicles Shakespeare has taken pains to idealize the moral character of both victims; their frailties, like Hamlet's, derive more from warring evils of the world than from their own innate urges.

Likewise Macduff, who in the chronicles enters the story belatedly, mainly seeking personal revenge, is transmuted by Shakespeare into an ever-present touchstone of charitable social compassion. He is the Man of Feeling, who enacts what his wife and babes, those "strong knots of love," have engendered: the most primitive human bond. Adelman and Hunter devalue Macduff's moral character by taking seriously Lady Macduff's anxious but wittily exaggerated accusations of her husband (4.2.6–14, 44–45);[12] yet even the child appreciates the irony of her remarks. In spite of the pointed criticisms leveled at Macduff by his wife, by Malcolm (4.3.26–28), and, most emphatically, by himself (4.3.224–27), it is clear that he is moved by generous compassion for Scotland as a whole, and that his compassion grows out of the intense family feeling manifested by his wife and child. It is Macduff's horrified response to Duncan's murder that initiates the knocking of conscience in the Macbeths; and it is his patriotic opposition to the usurper that galvanizes Scotland and England into a retributive force.

Shakespeare's radical reconstruction of the chronicles, especially his amelioration of the victims' moral character, thus emphasizes the destruction of three primordial human bonds. This three-phase sequence of psychological disintegration (and implicit affirmation of the values destroyed) provides a paradigm of Shakespeare's mature tragic form.

KILLING DUNCAN: USURPING AND DISMANTLING SUPEREGO

In presenting an initial assault on regal or parental authority in acts 1–2, *Macbeth* is comparable to all the tragedies from *Hamlet* to *Coriolanus*. The murder of a parentlike king, reflecting the Macbeths' aspiration to Godlike greatness and power, is an Oedipal repudiation of superego (as commentators since Freud and Jekels have acknowledged). Yet the gender implications of Duncan's rule have been too reductively construed by Oedipal-oriented psychoanalysts. For centuries it has been assumed that Duncan's *fatherliness* forms the basis of his comprehensive social identity (Scotland) and of his Christlike spiritual identity ("The Lord's anointed temple," 2.3.70)—that as *patriarch* he, like Lear and Cymbeline, represents the acme of psychological development, the mature conscience of the race, or, in Freudian terms, "superego."[13] Critics persistently construe the regicidal motive as an Oedipal antagonism, citing Lady Macbeth's distress at Duncan's fatherly appearance during the assault (2.2.12–13), to which one might add Macbeth's condemnation of the murder as a "parricide," projecting his own Oedipal urges onto Malcolm and Donalbain (3.1.31).

Yet the Macbeths envision Duncan not just as a *father*, who "hath been / So clear in his great office" (1.7.17–18), but also as a *mother*, who vies with Lady Macbeth in expressing love for her husband and for the other thanes, and who is cast as Lucrece to Macbeth's "ravishing Tarquin" with his phallic dagger (2.1.33–55). In addition, both Macbeths at critical moments in their soliloquies envision the monarch as a vulnerable and soul-like *child*, the heavenly infant that Lady Macbeth would deny the chance to "peep through the blanket of the dark, / To cry, 'Hold, hold!'" (1.5.53–54), and which Macbeth projects apocalyptically as a "naked new-born babe" of Pity (1.7.21). Thus, in psychoanalytic (or "object-relational") terms Duncan is not just the father, but all aspects of the human family—perhaps most poignantly, mother and child. By their own gender obsessions, the Macbeths have promoted the erroneous and reductive conception of sovereignty as a pure patriarchy. As recent critics have noted, the Macbeths' urge for sovereign greatness is expressed as a fantasy of becoming exclusively "manly" by taking up phallic weaponry to eliminate womanly and childlike characteristics.[14]

Similarly, in acts 1–2 of each mature tragedy Shakespeare portrays an assault on conscience or synteresis (or Freudian superego), not merely as a fatherly or kingly power, but increasingly as a consolidating, androgynous figure of authority: Othello and Desdemona defend themselves conjointly before the Venetian council; Lear's initial attempt to arrogate and then to suppress female nurture confirms the flaw in his sovereignty; Duncan is androgynous; Antony and Cleopatra struggle toward that communion; in contrast, Coriolanus, like Macbeth, seeks a constrictive autonomy and absoluteness through eliminating "female" relationality and compassion. As Stephen Orgel and Louis Montrose have observed, both Elizabeth I and James I promoted the idea of their monarchy as an androgynous consolidation of paternal authority and female nurture.[15]

The Macbeths' notable series of monologues in acts 1–2, fueled by willful hyperbole, confirms their aspiration to a male-oriented version of "greatness" (a word whose variants appear seventeen times in act 1, more than in the other four acts combined). To the extent that we as audience identify with the Macbeths' grand speechmaking, hypnotic role-playing, and cosmic aspiration for greatness in these acts, we must also experience the ironies that emerge in the actual performance of the murder: pettiness, furtiveness, cowardice, and utter deceit.

As the hyperbolic fantasy of these early soliloquies reveals, the ego function informing this regicidal-parenticidal stage of Macbeth's career in villainy is *sublimation* but in its most perverted form. Anna Freud describes sublimation as the highest phase of psychic functioning in the construction of selfhood, the ultimate means of enriching the ego.[16] Ideally, sublimation resolves the Oedipal struggle (a struggle for the final, genital stage of sexual maturation), not by evading bodily consummation of sexual energies, nor by suppressing their female component, but, as Loewald and Kohut have shown, by promoting comprehensive and free interplay between gender-components of the self. Thus the Macbeths' brutish rape of kingly greatness works exactly contrary to authentic sublimation. By furtively killing the king they not only destroy the bond with this androgynous parent, they also violate the illuminating and consolidating powers of their own superego, or conscience, inducing a deeper regression into self-divisive and annihilative ego defenses.

KILLING BANQUO: ENVYING THE EGO IDEAL

The murder of Macbeth's "chiefest friend" in act 3 is motivated not by further aspiration to greatness, but by rivalrous envy of a brotherly alter-ego. In acts 1–2 Macbeth's basic motivation was not envy of Duncan, Banquo, or Malcolm (though the basis for later envy is established): in spite of anxiety over Duncan's appointing his son Prince of Cumberland, Macbeth never considers killing Malcolm along with Duncan (leaving the unappointed Donalbain to shoulder the guilt). In his initial embracing of evil Macbeth is preoccupied with the sublime fantasy of regicide as the "be-all and end-all," conferring inviolable supremacy; only on discovering its failure to provide such aggrandizement does he turn to bitter envy of others, now conceived as rivals. According to Aquinas, "After the sin of pride [whereby Lucifer aspired to be a deity] there followed the evil of envy . . . whereby he grieved over man's good."[17] Macbeth's fury toward Banquo is thus a second stage of evil, resulting from the failure to satisfy the hunger for greatness, just as Cain's envious fratricide stemmed from his parents' frustrated desire to emulate God.[18] Envy, and the rivalrous doubling and splitting that necessitates confronting distasteful mirror-images of the self at the center of each of the tragedies, is secondary to that earlier violent effort to displace divine-regal-parental authority. The regicide-parenticide thus leads to fratricide-amiticide, a chronologically secondary but equally universal phenomenon, which carries its own momentous psychological implications.

This assault on a warrior-friend who is virtually the mirror-image or double of Macbeth ("all hail, Macbeth and Banquo! / Banquo and Macbeth, all hail!" 1.3.68–69) is a direct violation of ego, involving a psychological "splitting" into self and shadow-self, as Macbeth perversely identifies with the darker, more illusory component. Though he rationalizes the murder of Banquo in only one soliloquy, far less grandiose than the monologues of acts 1–2, Macbeth throughout act 3 continues the fiery expression of his inner powers by a number of intense dialogues in which he no longer effectively communicates his deeper meaning either to his auditors or to himself. They can only guess at the dark nuances in his spate of bestial images: serpents and scorpions (3.2.13–15, 36; 3.4.28–30); bat, "shard-bound beetle," and crow (3.2.40–42, 50–53); "greyhounds, mongrels, spaniels, curs" (3.1.92–94); "Russian bear, arm'd rhinoceros, or th'Hyrcan tiger" (3.4.99–100); "magot-pies, and choughs, and rooks" (3.4.121–24). Jorgensen calls these speeches (like the similar ravings of Lear in act 3) "soliloquies made public."[19] Equally important, they are soliloquys made obscure through intense repression, so that neither Macbeth and Lear nor their auditors can easily fathom the profound self-divulgence in their speeches. If acts 1–2 show a perverse mode of hyperbolic aspiration (appropriating sublimation as a means of overthrowing the superego or conscience), this furtive imagery of act 3 shows Macbeth's regression to the prior psychic function of *projection,* the defensive externalization of his depraved and problematic qualities onto others, which enforces a general process of "decomposition" and "splitting" of the ego.[20] At its best, projection (an expulsive psychic function deriving from the anal stage of infancy) plays a key role in the development of selfhood, enabling one to influence others by projecting onto them one's own ego ideals and inadequacies, and also enabling one thereby to experiment with and test those values and identities. But at its worst, as in malicious rituals of murder and scapegoating, projection revises reality so drastically that "nothing is, / But what is not," and the murderer's own selfhood, his "single state of man," is increasingly shaken and disjoined (1.3.134–42).

Envy, and the resultant splitting of selfhood, dictates the entire sequence of act 3: Macbeth's spiteful soliloquy in which he feels "rebuked" by Banquo's "royalty of nature"; his strange ranking of dogs in the abusive hiring of the assassins, humiliating them, even as he claims to raise and "make love" to them; his furtive insecurity even with his wife (rehearsing her part while concealing his full intent); and his "half-participation" in the murder itself, perhaps as the third murderer. In spite of Macbeth's show of surprise at Fleance's survival (3.4.20–24), it is tempting to believe that Macbeth is the mysterious third assassin[21] —so that he only half-participates in the second murder. That Macbeth can hardly admit (even to himself) his involvement suggests the extent of his splitting psyche: for if he *is* the third murderer, it reveals both a deepening insecurity and a growing obsession with rational control (utter self-repression, anal attentiveness to detail, and a host of other defensive mechanisms aimed at sustaining to others and to himself the illusion of kingship, including the pretense of shock on learning of Fleance's escape—which resembles his extravagant show of dismay on learning of Duncan's death). Macbeth's furtive pretense of uninvolvement even for his own cutthroats would thus demonstrate his increasing cowardice, alienation, and lack of a stable central self. Hence, for the second murder Macbeth both is and is not an active participant, owing to his descent into psychic bifurcation.

George Williams notes that performing the play with Macbeth as the third murderer "necessitates a staging that twice violates the 'Law of Reentry.'"[22] Though the assignment of a third murderer may indicate Macbeth's growing anxiety and may vicariously show his grasping for control (attending more closely than the other assassins to the usurper's crucial purposes), stage convention would thus seem to argue against Macbeth's schizoid reappearance as monarch-cutthroat-monarch in such rapid sequence. Yet if we consider the extraordinary liberties and experimentation in the staging of other Shakespearean plays of this period (e.g., the Dover cliff scene in *King Lear*), one wonders at the theatrical ingenuity of having Macbeth immediately reenter, perhaps with a dark cape only thinly disguising his kingly garments, so that the audience would actually be *aware* of his devious schizophrenic "doubling." If so, it is the most stunningly purposeful violation of the Law of Reentry in the Shakespearean canon.

Macbeth's self-division builds to a climax during the banquet when his vacillation between noblemen and assassins, between true and feigned selves, gives way to a deeper vacillation between conscious and unconscious realities. His obscene praise of the missing guest ("And to our dear friend Banquo, whom we miss") serves the psychic function of invoking his double's macabre presence, filling the central seat to which Macbeth himself is inexorably drawn. In "*Macbeth:* King James's Play" George Williams notes that the ghost of Banquo rather than of Duncan holds sway in the drama's central scene, thus inflating the compliment to King James I though it subverts decorum.

Williams also explains the symbolic seating that underlies the doppelgänger effect at the banquet: "Macbeth does not sit in his throne
(the "state" where Lady Macbeth remains)—to which he has no spiritual right; he does expect to sit at the table—a level to which he does
have a right." The "place reserved" for Banquo, to which Macbeth is
drawn as to his own natural place, is centrally located: "Both sides are
even: here I'll sit i' th' midst" (3.4.11).[23] Almost exactly the same
event occurs in Dostoyevsky's *The Double,* and similar psychic dis-
placements occur in James's *The Turn of the Screw* and Conrad's "The
Secret Sharer"; but only Macbeth confronts a double who represents
not his sinister shadow, but the ruination of his better self.[24]

Throughout act 3 Macbeth's insecurity focuses no longer on the
proud aspiration for kingly greatness, but on envious rivalry with his
antithetical friend Banquo, who is to him what Edgar is to Edmund,
Hal to Hotspur, Orlando to Oliver: the child favored with a loving
heart, who thus calls into question the unloving self's entire "being"
and must be utterly eliminated:

> every minute of his being thrusts
> Against my near'st of life: and though I could
> With bare-faced power sweep him from my sight,
> And bid my will avouch it, yet I must not,
> For certain friends that are both his and mine,
> Whose loves I may not drop.
>
> (3.1.116–21)

Instinctively Macbeth envisions the bond with his "chiefest friend" in
the context of a universal siblinghood, making the murder of Banquo as broadly symbolic as that of Duncan: first he eliminates the universal parent or greater self, then the archetypal sibling or mirror-
self. In each of the mature Shakespearean tragedies this shattering
confrontation with an antithetical self-image occurs at the play's center, the middle of act 3: Othello's temptation by Iago (3.3), Lear's discovery of "Poor Tom" (3.4), Macbeth's spectral encounter with Banquo (3.4), Antony's battle with Octavius and (more important) the
interplay with his female alter-ego, Cleopatra (3.7–13). This positing
of an "indissoluble tie" (*Macbeth* 3.1.15–18) between self and shadow-
self (or alter-ego) occurs at the exact center of *Othello* and *Macbeth*
(and, with more benevolent implications, at the center of *King Lear*).
At this moment each protagonist confronts the darkest possibilities
of selfhood: the imputed treachery of Desdemona, the feigned sins

of Poor Tom, the butchery inflicted by Macbeth himself. As in Lear's meeting with the mad beggar, Macbeth's rencontre with his muti-lated alter-ego engages him in full awareness of fraternal Otherness; but while this stunning encounter leads the kingly Lear instinctively to affirm the oneness of human souls, it provokes the usurper Mac-beth to repudiate "that great bond" (3.2.49). In discarding Banquo, Macbeth thus divests himself of brother-love, the homoerotic bond, the second crucial cathexis forming the normative identity of the hu-man psyche.

Killing Lady Macduff and Her Children: Annihilating the Id, and All Otherness

In acts 4 and 5, focusing on the slaughter of a mother and children (and the immediate social and psychological consequences of that deed), Macbeth eliminates the third and most fundamental human bond as he violates the primitive core of selfhood, what Freud called the id. Most critics treat this third assault as mere "fourth-act pathos," as a dim echo of the previous kills, or as a hasty and illogical after-thought testifying to a kind of madness in the tyrant, since these vic-tims offer neither militant opposition nor patrilineal threat to Mac-beth's royal claim.[25]

But Macbeth's essential motive for the third murder is not a reen-actment of the Oedipal struggle (casting Macduff as the new parent-power to be deposed); nor is it another envious rivalry with a mir-roring sibling (seeing Macduff's goodness, like Banquo's, as a galling comparison to his own evil). Rather, building upon and blossoming out of those two previous modes of aggression, Macbeth's "black and deep desires" now enter a third and culminating phase: scornful an-nihilative hatred of the simple passional core, the mother-and-child matrix of selfhood—the healthy "oral-narcissist" bonding which con-trasts the perverse narcissism now unfolding in Macbeth.[26] Mac-beth's contemptuous repudiation and perversion of the affective-cognitive human core (the "id") informs this final sequence of psychic degradation in acts 4 and 5. The ego-function which domi-nates this earliest phase of psychic development (and which most per-tinently informs the final two acts of Shakespeare's mature tragedies) is *introjection,* the ego's incorporation of desired aspects of the nur-turant other in order to construct its own identity.[27] Introjection of the beloved, for the purpose of achieving (or re-achieving) total self-

hood, is the psychological principle that is either violated or em-
braced in the final phase of each of Shakespeare's major tragedies.
Acts 4 and 5 invariably draw their cathartic and transforming energy
not from the killing of a king, but from the heroic male's reaction to
the destruction of a *beloved maiden* (Ophelia, Desdemona, Cordelia)
or, in the final tragedies, a *mother with children* (Lady Macduff and
Lady Macbeth, Cleopatra, Virgilia and Volumnia).[28]

A wholesome mode of introjective bonding informs the poignant
scene of Lady Macduff and her son (4.2), where in the father's absence she frets over the child's continued sustenance. But the boy's
affirmation that Providential if not parental care will feed him, echoing Matthew 6.26, suggests the dignity of what he has thus far intro-
jected from his parents. This humane and spiritual nurture contrasts
the strikingly perverse mode of introjection in the preceding scene:
the witches' materialistic, cannibalistic ritual. Into their womblike
cauldron's mouth (the *vagina dentata*)[29] they fling fragments of poisonous and ravenous beasts (toad, snake, dragon, wolf, shark, tiger)
and parts representing the erotic and sensory powers of non-Chris-
tians (Jew's liver, Turk's nose, Tartar's lips)—including those lower
senses of smell and taste involved in feeding. This travesty of Otherness (like Othello's suicidal reminiscence of killing a Turk in the service of Christianity) is a too-appropriate symbolism for what the
witches and Macbeth himself have come to represent.

The final and focal object in the witches' catalogue of dismembered parts is "Finger of birth-strangled babe / Ditch-deliver'd by a
drab" (4.1.26–31). Thus, from the "pilot's thumb" of the witches'
early scene (1.3.28), symbolizing the perversion of parental guidance
or superego, Macbeth regresses inexorably to the aborted potency of
the child (or id), as symbolized by the foetal "finger" or phallus,
"strangled"-castrated-devoured by the cauldron-womb-mouth of the
Voracious Mother, the "drab" or prostitute. Introjection (an incor-
porative mode of identification deriving from the experience of sucking and swallowing during the oral stage of infancy) is thus material-
ized and brutalized by the witches to secure worldly power.

From the vicious opening ritual of act 4 (which provokes the entire cycle of action in acts 4–5), Macbeth embraces the witches' om-
nivorous perversion of the primal introjective principle. Each of his
three murders has been associated with imagery of feasting, but it is
particularly in his impulsive butchering of mother and babes that
Macbeth has willingly and unhesitatingly "supp'd full with horrors"
(5.5.13). Thus the third murderous assault, a Herodlike massacre of

innocents from which Macbeth completely distances himself, but which Shakespeare exposes to the audience with the most excruciating intimacy, brings us to the peak of horror, the breaking of the deepest taboo, which violates the very rudiment of selfhood and of social bonding.

Far more than King Duncan and Banquo, whose entrammelment in political motivations partly cloaks their essential being, the intimacy of mother and child brings us closest to the core of human nature. In each of Shakespeare's mature tragedies, the final cathartic sequence of acts 4–5 jeopardizes the primal psychic ground of being, the inception of love: the drawing of woman, "fool," or child into the web of deceit and violence promotes in the male authority-figures not merely revulsion against evil, but clear and intense awareness of the rich essence of life which has been lost. Macbeth himself, in his finest show of inner light, envisioned the soul's greatest power in its early innocence and in its affective mode of "pity": "like a naked new-born babe / Striding the blast" (1.7.19–20). As he loses touch with that childlike and woman-nurtured essence in himself, Macbeth also loses his capacity for true sovereignty.

6

Lear's Three Shamings

The face is the trace of the Other. . . . [One] cannot say whether this Other . . . is another person whom I can look in the face or who can stare at me, . . . or my ancestors for whom there is no representation, to so great an extent does my debt to them constitute my very self, . . . or *God . . .* , or *an empty place.*

Paul Ricoeur, *Oneself as Another*

I colde also speake as ye do: (but wolde God your soule were in my soules stead) . . . , I wolde aswage *your sorowe.*

Job 16.4–5

DESPITE *KING LEAR'S* IMPRESSIVE ENLARGEMENT OF THE OEDIPUS-Job-Everyman myth of human sufferance,[1] critics as astute as A. C. Bradley and Emrys Jones find its plot structure lacking. They blame the growing madness and passivity of the king (inadequately causing the action, even retarding it in half-mad reverie) as well as the double plot that further diffuses Lear's agency.[2] For Susan Snyder and Stephen Booth, the audience's shock at watching Lear's loss of control and of certitude is compounded by deliberate undoings of plot: Shakespeare's persistent miscues, reversing generic expectations and denying conventional closure, enforce a moral, teleological indeterminacy.[3]

Yet each of these unsettling features—the protagonist's growing "passivity" and "madness," the various splittings of character and of plot, and the subversion of expectations—has a paradoxical complexity that subsumes the imputed weaknesses into a larger, stronger vision of what it means to be human. Lear is engaged in what Ernest Becker describes as the definitive human quest, the *"causa sui* project." Through the illusion of self-creation Lear asserts his absolute Godlike being and potency against the ultimate human anxiety, the "terror of death," dissolving his powers into non-being, nothingness.[4]

In this struggle against mortality Lear is far from passive: he never ceases to exhibit tremendously willful self-assertion; and—even more than Oedipus, Job, and Everyman—he displays considerable powers of self-obstruction. Lear is a cynosure of repression and all its subordinate defenses. Surely Elton and Berger are right to note the aggressiveness of Lear's apparent yieldings.[5] Each withdrawal (from kingship, from loving bonds, from facing malice) is actively and proudly self-enforced, not just the feeble reactions of a fading old man to the commands of selfish children.

Equally deceptive is Lear's "madness." As he, even more than Edgar and the other exiles, is stripped of civilization's comforting illusions, exposing him to bodily impotence and communal shame, and as he simultaneously sees the reality of human bonding and the pervasiveness of inequity, he begins to demonstrate the indefinition of reason, its alliance with an insightful mode of madness.

Paradox likewise informs *King Lear*'s division of characters into mirroring and conflicting quests. Tragedy's usual focus on a single protagonist (or a single loving couple) here divides into planes of increasing complexity. Many commentators assume that Lear's executive power is utterly displaced by that of Goneril, Regan, their spouses and henchmen, and eventually Edmund; yet their opportunistic and divisive sway does not seriously challenge Lear's centrality since they do not validate their authority. Never do they command the audience's respect, never do they demonstrate true sovereignty—as is evident in their impulsive indictment and blinding of Gloucester and their final hasty self-destruction. Second, Lear's agon is more seriously displaced, though only intermittently, by the suffering consciousness of Edgar and Gloucester; yet ultimately their drama reinforces that of Lear, both as a mirroring analogue and as an intensely realized drama of Otherness by which Lear can resolve his own crisis of identity and selfhood. The third and subtlest form of character-diversification involves Cordelia, who in her silent goodness, her presence-heightened-through-banishment, truly displaces Lear's moral and spiritual authority as sovereign. Instead of diffusing the dramaturgical focus, however, all three modes of splitting/displacement contribute to the play's main action—its revelation of human nature's liability to dispersal and consequent need of communion. For Lear and the audience each alternate drama clarifies the central mystery of monarchy: *the king's two* (or perhaps three) *bodies*. Since the vicious characters who oppose Lear are hollow and envious, and since the compassionate characters (whose moral goodness and suffering might challenge Lear's moral hegemony) all seek to restore and sustain his authority, all three levels of displacement ultimately affirm Lear's central habitation of the problematic role of sovereign.

Similar paradox shapes the play's dramaturgical form. Its cycles of action subtly contain the anxiety of generic reversals by disclosing a deeper plan, a deeper purpose; for the plot of *King Lear* exhibits the same exacting symmetry that informs all Shakespeare's mature plays, a pattern closely resembling that of *Macbeth.* In both tragedies an evolving crisis of kingship and of psyche occurs in three cycles of action: first, acts 1–2, with 2 reversing the arc of 1; next act 3, an action-reaction within itself; and finally acts 4–5, with 5 reversing the arc of 4.[6] Using the same pattern, these plays show obverse sides of human tragedy: the two monarchic crises, springing from Lear's abdication and Macbeth's usurpation, have contrary effects on their souls.

The complementarity of *King Lear* and *Macbeth* is Shakespeare's culminating meditation on this central theme. In each history tetrad he had depicted the contrary monarchic crises in causal conjunction: in the first series, the childish abdication of Henry VI invites Richard III's ruthless usurpation; in the more complex second series, Richard II, though weak and self-indulgent, matures through deposition, as does the usurper Bolingbroke through assuming the tasks of rule. Abdicator and usurper reach full complexity in King Lear and Macbeth: each fully *causes* the personal/monarchic tragedy; and each, despite madness and repression, is conscience-struck by his mistakes.

In both plays, especially *King Lear,* the assertion of monarchic power is impelled by personal relationship, making Lear seem closer to the family romance of Oedipus than to the God-centered dialogues of Prometheus, Job, and Everyman; yet for Lear, as for Hamlet and Prospero, human relationship becomes a mirror and impetus for the relation with divinity.[7] Thus in *King Lear,* as in *Macbeth,* an epiphanic (or anti-epiphanic) human encounter serves as a central axis for each of the three cycles of action. Lear undergoes increasingly illuminative confrontations with the "fiend" Goneril (1.4); with the "spirit" Poor Tom (3.4); and with the "soul in bliss" Cordelia (4.7). Contrarily, in the three powerful scenes involving the "spirit"-possessed Lady Macbeth (1.7), Banquo's ghost (3.4), and Macduff's response to his family's slaughter (4.3), Macbeth increasingly evades epiphany. By having Macbeth command but not join the execution of Macduff's family, and having him assiduously avoid Macduff himself as long as possible, Shakespeare distinctly alters the chronicles (which say that Macbeth led the force to Macduff's castle and only killed the family as an afterthought—in frustration at Macduff's absence).

Each of these encounters has been treated as a crux, especially the three scenes in *King Lear*. Gary Taylor explicates the deep significance of Lear's clash with Goneril (1.4) in *To Analyze Delight*.[8] The central import of Lear's meeting with Tom (3.4), axis of the play, is often noted, for example, by Robert Heilman and Maynard Mack.[9] Lear's reunion with Cordelia (4.7) is commonly viewed as Lear's (and the play's) goal, the essential moment of accession to self-knowledge.[10] Though intensely painful, Lear's epiphanies expand into fuller vision; Macbeth's anti-epiphanies contract into evasion.

In each play the three cycles reverse the sequence of metapsychic development (whether we borrow the terminology of Ego Psychology, Object Relations Psychology, or Self Psychology): building on each other, the three sequences enforce a cathartic regression to primal selfhood. These complementary tragedies draw us back to the two "archaic relational" scenes: in *King Lear* the "nurturant scenario," where anticipated loss of a caring other "awakens the infant to its own dependence, helplessness, and impotent rage"; in *Macbeth* the "antagonistic scenario," where "one is either predator or prey, . . . master or slave."[11] In these contrary psychic processes the protagonists inversely apprehend the spirit world as a direct outgrowth of the recovery or loss of human kinship. Macbeth increasingly seeks and reifies the phantasmic witches, becoming fiendish himself as he massacres loving innocents; Lear, at first obsessed like Tom with "fiends" he has helped to create, turns from their grotesque reality to Cordelia as a "soul in bliss." Thus Macbeth's three murders systematically deconstruct the three cathexes of human identity; Lear's three self-mortifying experiences reestablish those three basic bondings of human, and sovereign, selfhood. Having traced the 2–1–2 pattern of devolution in *Macbeth,* we shall now observe the same pattern in *King Lear* but with inverse psychogenesis and outcome.

SEEING GONERIL: SUPEREGO DISABLED BY FALSE SUBLIMATION

Whereas Macbeth in his initial two-act cycle usurps authority, Lear in acts 1–2 awkwardly relinquishes it. In *King Lear* this cycle opens with the long scene (310 lines) in which Lear asserts godlike power, humiliating and banishing Cordelia and Kent for refusing to confer idolatrous flattery; and it concludes with a closely analogous degenerating ritual of 311 lines (2.4) in which Lear enforces his own humiliation and exile.

Near the end of this two-act sequence Kent and the Fool draw attention to Fortune's ironic cycling. In *Fortune and Elizabethan Tragedy* Frederick Kiefer notes that "in no other of Shakespeare's plays do characters invoke Fortune so insistently," especially "at pivotal points in the action"[12]—that is, near the end of each completed turning. Kent's Stoic, proto-Christian view—"Smile, . . . turn thy wheel" (2.2.175–76)—allows for wisdom through sufferance: "Nothing almost sees miracles but misery" (168–69). The Fool stresses the more humbling lesson of material needs and humankind's willful role in shaping Fortune's cycle (2.4.70–73).

And Lear does shape it. He is Shakespeare's most complex version of the Abdicating King, whose evasion of rule incurs moral decay, usurpation, and civil butchery. Unlike earlier portraits of the withdrawing monarch (meek Henry VI in the first tetralogy of history plays, diffident Richard II in the second), Lear aggressively directs his abdication-deposition and helps enforce each subsequent cycle of shaming. Elton rightly contrasts Leir's passivity in the source-play with Lear's active role.[13] Lear's aggressive abdication parallels Hamlet's occluded kingship and delayed revenge, and Prospero's initial evasion of rule. All three, though capable of extraordinary agency, incline to skeptical detachment and, like Vincentio in *Measure for Measure,* suggestively mirror the *deus absconditas* of Reformation controversy. Yet of all Shakespearean protagonists, Lear experiences the fullest passion, raises the most disturbing questions, dominates plot and audience with the greatest psychic energy, and most fully exemplifies sovereignty—his mad reveries evoking a lifetime of authority and proud accomplishment. It is thus inaccurate to call him passive. A "repetition compulsion" drives Lear's three acts of self-abasement no less than Macbeth's three murders.[14]

Shakespeare's plot structure highlights the centerpiece:[15] in each of Lear's shamings, Fortune's wheel turns on a central encounter. The axis for the initial two-act cycle is his fiery meeting with Goneril near the end of act 1, a scene looking back to his disowning of Cordelia and forward to his total emasculation by the older daughters. When Goneril rebukes Lear's governance and withdraws half of his hundred knights, he endures his first shameful anagnorisis, an anti-epiphany in which the disclosure of Goneril's consummate evil inverts his mood, self-image, and actions. His explosive reaction, a defensive evasion of the distasteful mirror-image of his own selfish will, shivers the glass of his personal, parental, and sovereign identity; and the recoil draws Lear to the cycle's conclusion, the protracted humiliation at the end of act 2.

The face-off with Goneril closely resembles Macbeth's fiery confrontation with Lady Macbeth at the same central turning point of the two-act cycle that begins that play. Each fierce virago, reflecting the protagonist's pitiless urges, is portrayed as a demonic spirit. Lear calls Goneril a "marble-hearted fiend, / More hideous when thou show'st thee in a child / Than the sea monster!" (1.4.257–59).[16] Albany also depicts Goneril as a monstrous fiend, stressing that in turning against her parent she commits herself to a disturbing uncertainty principle, unaware of itself and thus losing true being: "That nature which contemns its origin / Cannot be bordered certain. . . . / Like monsters of the deep. . . . / See thyself, devil!" (4.2.33–34, 51, 60–62). Like Lady Macbeth's fiendish threat of infanticide (1.7.55–59), Goneril's antimaternity draws from Seneca's *Medea*.[17] In both tragedies the abuse of Authority in acts 1–2 is portrayed as an exclusively male dominion: each protagonist suppresses in himself the "female" component of maternal nurture, the "mother" (*King Lear* 2.4.55–57)[18] and "the milk of human kindness" (*Macbeth* 1.5.17); and this self-reduction is enforced through a Medea-figure whom he has helped to create and who mirrors his own willful obduracy.

Though both Lear and Macbeth have partly elicited and sponsored this demonism, their responses are diametrically opposed: Macbeth embraces his spouse's regicidal lust; Lear is repulsed by Goneril's cold, measured lovelessness. The same galling infertility he invokes on Goneril ("Into her womb convey sterility; / Dry up in her the organs of increase," 1.4.277–78) is voluntarily assumed by Lady Macbeth ("Stop up th' access and passage of remorse, / . . . take my milk for gall," 1.5.43–48). The unveiling of Goneril's and of Lady Macbeth's life-denying *weltlust*, mirroring the dark power-hunger of Lear and Macbeth, serves as pivotal experience for the cycle of self-discovery, passional release, and inner change in acts 1–2.

This initial two-act sequence is in each play dominated by the mechanism of *sublimation,* the most refined ego-function in the service of superego. Hans Loewald and Heinz Kohut have explained sublimation's important role in forming superego or conscience (internalized parental authority); and they have also stressed its synthesizing of gender roles into a comprehensive androgynous adulthood, while also learning to resist the lures to false images of what Kohut calls the "grandiose self."[19] The soul's aim in sublimation is self-aggrandizement, seeking through abstraction and spiritualization to achieve the "be-all and end-all"—genuine sovereignty, androgynous wholeness, omnipotence and immortality. The Macbeths' thrilling soliloquies in acts 1–2 voice their aspiration for such "great-ness," though without comprehending its nature. Prior to murdering Duncan the Macbeths refer seventeen times to the "greatness," prom-ised by the Weird sisters, for which they yearn. The long opening rit-ual of *King Lear* demonstrates Lear's assumption that he already pos-sesses, in Godlike fullness, such greatness, which the love-test is designed to confirm. In keeping with the mythic content of the love-test,[20] Lear's ritual demands lavish flattery to affirm his sovereign magnanimity (and implicitly, his immortality): "Which of you . . . doth love us most?" The command to praise proves a devastating test for monarchic absolutism as well as for proud superego: it deflates the "great image of authority" (4.6.158), the integrity of state and self-hood, as effectively as Macbeth's murder of Duncan. Paul Ricoeur ex-plains the signal role of hyperbole in efforts to attain "absolute Oth-erness" through "Elevation" and "Exteriority," producing an utter breakdown in relationship.[21]

Those who do evil, says Boethius, "cease not merely to be power-ful, but simply to be. . . . For that *is*, which keeps its order and pre-serves its nature":

> Those lofty kings you see seated high on thrones, . . .
> Threatening with visage stern . . .—
> If a man strip from those proud kings the cloak of
>   their empty splendour,
> At once he will see these lords within bear closely
>   bound chains;
> . . . anger whips the mind as a whirlwind.[22]

Lear's anger sweeps him from all housing and official community, re-vealing his "mind-forg'd manacles" as well as the hollowness of his love-ritual. Disowning all responsibility for relationship, all truthful mir-roring by others, he ceases "not merely to be powerful, but simply to be": "Who is it that can tell me who I am?" (1.4.227). Contrary to Mac-beth's violent but furtive claimancy, however, Lear's public shaming exposes him to a painful anger which is cleansing and restorative.

SEEING POOR TOM: RECONSTITUTING
EGO BY PROJECTION

The superego's cyclic loss of authority in acts 1–2 leads to the ego's cyclic loss of rational control in act 3, a sequence neatly demarcated by a repeated gesture. *King Lear*'s third act is framed on each side by a slamming door: at each juncture an aged father is expelled but with increase in savagery ("Shut up your doors, my lord," 2.4.310; "Go thrust him out at gates," 3.7.95). Similarly, *Macbeth*'s third act is framed on each side by a prayer for holy succor (2.4.41, 3.6.46–51). In each play this gesture helps to close the cycle of acts 1–2 (Lear's loss of authority, Macbeth's grasp of it), and then the cycle of act 3 (Lear's psychic splitting on the heath, Macbeth's at the banquet).

Act 3 is also set apart by Lear's exposure to contrary characters and setting, outcasts on a barren heath.[23] Unlike the courtly affairs of acts 1–2 which build on elaborate rituals of privilege, the more primitive events of act 3 are dominated by a storm, matched by the exiles' mental anguish. Fortune (in its intensest form as "tempest")[24] wheels on a deeper level as Lear's wits "begin to turn" (3.2.67). Again the cycle opens with Lear assuming Godlike power, commanding the storm to destroy sinners, and Gloucester plotting war against the new order; and it ends, like each of the cycles, with both fathers' deepened impotence: Lear's madness and sleep, Gloucester's blindness and exile.

The axis for this second cycle of psychic divestiture is the meeting with Tom, combining Lear's neglect and Edgar's embodiment of spiritual poverty. Edgar's riveting enactment serves as peripety for Lear's change in act 3: preceded by Lear's care for the suffering Fool and "poor naked wretches," Tom's naked crying "spirit" appears almost magically, as if called forth (or projected) by Lear's evolving consciousness of need. In this central confrontation the two plots meet and join, showing how intrinsic is doubleness of plot to the play's meaning—not only providing complementary analogues of self-abasement but promoting selfhood through relational awareness: *oneself as another.*

Again Lear's epiphany of human Otherness is shown as a supernatural ontology: Tom, whom the Fool perceives as a vexed "spirit" (3.4.39, 42), is haunted by "fiends," though unlike Goneril he fears them and tries to "defy" them (3.4.45, 51, 60, 79, 97, 114, 130, 139, 157; 3.6.8, 17, 29). In act 4, after a brief reprise of such fantasies on becoming Gloucester's guide (4.1.57), Edgar disengages from demonism, spatially distancing it on the cliff of pride, and exaggerating it into farce: "his eyes / Were two full moons; he had a thousand noses, / Horns whelked and waved like the enridged sea" (4.6.69–72). No viewer, however, can easily judge the genuineness of Edgar's obsession with demons.

By echoing Harsnett's exposure of fraudulent exorcisms, Edgar's ghoul-babble seems to parody Gloucester's superstitious credulity; moreover, it stands in sharp contrast to the staged reality of Macbeth's witches.[25] Yet the strenuousness of Edgar's performance makes it more than hoax: "Though we may not believe literally in the devils with outlandish names . . . Flibbertigibbet, Smulkin, Modo and Mahu," still "Poor Tom's rhapsodies bring an intimacy with them and with the natural world through which he is driven."[26] For Edgar, each aspect of otherness (his body, his social connections, his conscience) has become a genuine hellish torment, until Lear's anguish moves Edgar to abandon his nightmarish role in an aside—"My tears begin to take his part so much / They mar my counterfeiting" (59–60)— and then to emerge fully as chorus (102–15). Edgar-as-Tom epitomizes the "poor player" who recurs at the heart of Shakespeare's vision, where duplicity and authenticity persistently mingle. Like Hamlet's use of players to test the veracity of the supernatural, Edgar's survivalist role-playing does not discredit his genuineness, as Lear attests: "Thou art the thing itself." The allusions to Harsnett, instead of demystifying God, providence, and the spirit-world, affirm the potent immanence of spirit: humankind's genuine capacity to fashion itself as deluded fiend, its need of charity to become *imago Dei*.

Nor are the fiends mere fancy. As Gulstad notes, Lear's fantasy-trial of his daughters (3.6) is encoded as witch-trial;[27] and Edgar's persecution fear is reified, starkly contextualized when, at the cycle's end (3.7), Goneril, Regan, and Cornwall "rash boarish fangs" in Gloucester's flesh. The savage blinding, no less than Iago's treachery and Macbeth's blood lust, suggests cloven feet, demons incarnate. The explicit witchcraft of *Macbeth* generalizes the fiendish behavior in all three plays.

Each protagonist's failure to sublimate or exalt himself as omnipotent parent or superego in acts 1–2 gives way to a more primitive functioning in the central cycle, where *projection* accommodates ego's doublings.[28] Macbeth's bloody assertion of omnipotence in acts 1–2 gives way in act 3 to envious rivalry with peers, evoking the mangled Banquo as his double. Lear's failed fantasy of omnipotence in acts 1–2 gives way in act 3 to a contrary form of splitting, empathetically projecting himself in victims: the shivering Fool, naked wretches, and especially Poor Tom. The same psychic division that makes Macbeth waver between public praise and secret murder of his noble double makes Lear waver between indicting his proud children and exalting his wretched double, Tom. Such projective splitting—crucial to the secondary stage of self-composition in early childhood—serves contrary ends in Macbeth's and Lear's central phase. Macbeth's sadistic projections enforce self-alienation; Lear's empathetic projections begin to restore sovereign selfhood.

Some recent critics question Lear's moral probity in act 3, viewing his identification with Tom as irresponsible self-obsession ("Did'st thou give all to thy daughters, and art thou come to this?" 3.4.46–47). According to Berger, Lear's sympathy for "poor naked wretches" vanishes at the sight of an actual wretch. Leggatt sees Lear "losing touch with literal reality—and losing his selflessness as well"; "his pity for Tom is all too obviously a projection of his pity for himself." With Dollimore they see Lear, until the reunion with Cordelia, driven by lunacy and self-concern, generally ignoring his auditors.[29]

I would offer a more optimistic, at least more ambivalent, reading of this central sequence. First, that Lear's pity springs from self-pity is only natural: there is no shame in "loving one's neighbor as one loves oneself." From Augustine to Kohut, healthy self-love is the key to ethics and psychological well-being.[30] Self-love may sponsor blind exercise of power as in the initial love-test, but also genuine (though confused and deflected) sympathy as in the meeting with Poor Tom, and meek gratitude as in the reunion with Cordelia. As Lear learns, self-love may be distorted by excessive privilege and commodities (as also by their absence, wretched poverty). Though act 3 begins with an inner storm of wounded pride and exclusive self-love, these motives form a tension with shame and compassion, beginning with sympathy for the shivering Fool. Lear in his "madness" instinctively extends charity, partly recovering the sovereign nature that originally drew the devoted loyalty of Cordelia, the Fool, Kent, Gloucester, Edgar, and other "gentlemen." Their devotion, especially their pursuit of the king in his madness, seems more than habitual servitude. The "authority" in Lear's countenance which Kent "would fain call master" implies not merely Lear's anointed sovereignty but his effective exercise of that power (1.4.27–30). Berger faults both Lear and his supporters for subverting love;[31] yet plain-speaking Kent and Cordelia do not simply antagonize Lear but express admiration for his lifetime of fatherly/kingly guidance (1.1.95–98, 139–42), and the suffering caused by Lear's shame and compassion, though crude and incomplete, helps bind him and the other exiles into a fellowship of the heath.

Lear's initial response to Poor Tom ("Has his daughters brought him to this pass?" 3.4.48–49, 62–64, 66–67, 69–72), though affirming

Lear's sovereign habit of empathy, does indeed neglect the beggar as an *other;* and this self-indulgence seems an empathetic response to the beggar's initial self-pitying speeches (45–47, 50–61). Then comes Lear's jolting sense of responsibility for "begetting" (congenitally and morally) his unkind daughters:

> Is it the fashion that discarded fathers
> Should have thus little mercy on their flesh?
> Judicious punishment! 'Twas this flesh begot
> Those pelican daughters.
>
> (3.4.71–74)

This self-judgment begins to draw Lear out of himself, leading him to elicit the beggar's identity as an other: "What hast *thou* been?" (83). Then, in a lengthy confession of sins, Tom responds to Lear in kind: whereas his first catalogue was self-pitying, blaming his vexations on the "foul fiend" (45–62), this one is self-judging, listing his vices to forswear them, urging others to avoid sin and "defy" the fiend. Most readers have viewed this extraordinarily long and colorful catalogue of sins, like the pretense of demon-possession, as part of a tour-de-force performance, a disclosure purely theatrical, having nothing to do with Edgar's real life, his moral and psychological self. But consider what a deeper dimension the play assumes if we take the list, at least in part, as Edgar's genuine confession. Has Edgar (like Prince Hal or, more to the point, like the promiscuous Gloucester) led a self-indulgent life of privilege? This reading would give considerably more weight to Edmund's resentment of his "legitimate" half-brother. Tom's lengthy self-indictment provokes Lear's most self-judging remark: "Thou art the thing itself. . . . / Off, off, you lendings!" (100–108). These initial interactions of king and beggar suggest neither mere insanity nor mere selfishness but a significant give-and-take, a complex form of compassion, which deepens in the next sequence.

Gloucester's sudden appearance, provoking Edgar to imagine a cruel fiend who "hurts the poor creature of earth," stresses anew humankind's vulnerability to abuse. In this sequence, however, Gloucester's capacity to reject his child, and the group's capacity to reject Poor Tom, is abated, especially through the influence of Lear's "madness." As Lear continues his "other-directed" frame of mind ("What's he?"), the group erupts into a torrent of identity questions, emphasizing both their unbonded strangeness and their anxious desire to relate:

> *Lear.* What's he?
> *Kent.* Who's there? What is't you seek?
> *Gloucester.* What are you there? Your names?
> (3.4.125–27)

Fearful of being identified by his father, Edgar in his role-playing relapses into self-pity, listing Tom's disgusting habits and society's efforts to punish and marginalize him (128–39):

> Poor Tom . . . that in the fury of his heart, when the foul fiend rages, eats cow dung for salads, that eats the dead rat and the ditch dog, drinks the green mantle of the standing pool; who is whipped from tithing to tithing and stock-punished and imprisoned.
> (3.4.128–34)

Edgar's shift from impersonal to personal pronoun ("that . . . that . . . who . . .") enforces his identity-shift from a bestial predator on vile lower beings to a human who is himself despised by those pious betters who "tithe." Gloucester, one of the self-righteous, would deny the beggar their fellowship ("What, hath your grace no better company?"), and he ignores the beggar's cry, "Poor Tom's a-cold." But Lear refuses refuge without his new acquaintance, insisting that Tom be included in Gloucester's charity: "Come, let's in all"; "With him! I will keep still with my philosopher" (3.4.178–80).

A major sign of Lear's compassion is his addressing the almost-naked, ranting beggar as "noble philosopher" and "learned Theban." Lear's conceit is more than insane confusion, or a selfish enhancing of his own status by raising Tom's. Playing on a Boethian subtext, Shakespeare revises the dream-vision of Lady Philosophy's splendor and measured eloquence into the vulgar reality of a mad-dog Cynic: Lear has good grounds for comparing Tom with the legendary Diogenes (whose contempt for proud artifice led him to wear a blanket and speak bluntly) and his follower Crates (who threw his wealth into the sea and sharply criticized lustful hearts).[32] This demeaning vision of "Philosophy" likewise plays on an Erasmian subtext, reflecting Renaissance sages' praise of folly.[33] It is not just Tom's poverty but his confessional candor, comparable to the Cynics' self-annihilative zeal, that impresses the guilty Lear. His madness thus seems increasingly purposive, and far from passive.

While Lear admires such aggressive, even abusive, self-stripping, his calling Tom "philosopher" also has a constructive purpose: Lear, as part of his subconscious conflictual motives in act 3, seeks to establish the beggar's dignity and worth, making him acceptable to Gloucester and the others, as well as to the beggar himself. Gloucester, while trying to ingratiate himself to Lear in self-pitying terms, treats Tom as a disposable nothing (3.4.140–79); and though Kent-as-Caius assists in persuading Gloucester to accept the beggar, he too (Edgar later recalls) "having seen me in my worst estate, / Shunned my abhorred society" (5.3.213–14). In reaction to their snubbing, Lear addresses the Bethlehem pauper as his better, someone in touch with life's deepest truths. His attributing worth and wisdom to the beggar, a central instance of "reason in madness," carries both symbolic import and characterological impact: it helps Edgar to sever himself from victimization fantasies, and it challenges the caste-bound mindset of Lear's former courtiers. Though Lear does not offer money or clothing (a flaw to Marxist critics),[34] his wish to extend sapient fellowship to Tom serves as catalyst for Gloucester's later generosity (4.1.31–76).

Such charitable communality is hard-won, especially for Tom, who concludes the scene with the bitter vision of a hero who uses the grandiosity of his proud height, his "dark tower," to devour others:

> Child Rowland to the dark tower came;
> His word was still, "Fie, foh, and fum,
> I smell the blood of a British man."
>   (3.4.181–83)

He is a "child" not just as a candidate for knighthood but, like the protagonists of *King Lear,* as the privileged person who is in fact immature, self-obsessed, and fearfully primitive.

In scene 6 Lear at first seeks to consummate the vengeful fantasy that began scenes 2 and 4: "To have a thousand with red burning spits / Come hizzing in upon 'em" (3.6.15–16). Lear begins to arraign his daughters as demons, a psychic hell which Tom fears: "Frateretto calls me . . ."; "The foul fiend bites my back" (3.6.6, 16). But as in scenes 2 and 4, Lear's empathetic impulse gains ascendancy. He empowers the wretched exiles as justicers, and they play along, comforting and enabling him to voice rage without acting on it. Lear's fantasy-trial ends not with an auto-da-fé of burning witches but with images that gently domesticate their identity as he guiltily displaces them in the dock: "The little dogs and all, / Tray, Blanch, and Sweetheart, see, they bark at me" (3.6.61–62); yet he still evades culpability by projecting his power-hunger on others: "Is there any cause in nature that makes these proud hearts?" (3.6.76–77).

To assist Lear's fantasy and "working-through," Edgar—as if sensing his psychic impact on Lear through transference—abandons his demon-obsessed role: "Let us deal justly" (3.6.40). He sings a ballad to solace Lear ("Sleepest or wakest thou, jolly shepherd? . . ." (3.6.41–44) and answers Lear's desperate sadness with a lengthy exorcism of dogs, thus dispelling his own vicious familiars and self-abusive impulses. Lear is enabled to lull his tempestuous conscience ("Make no noise"), veil his pride ("Draw the curtains"), and defer his narcissistic appetites ("We'll go to supper i' the morning" (3.6.82–83). Lear's and Gloucester's judgmental proceedings thus turn back upon themselves. Their attempts to enforce trials of others are transformed into a process of self-discovery through the nurture of exiles and servants, who comfort Lear and carry him from danger, defend Gloucester and tend his wounds—enabling both fathers to turn inward and confront conscience.

Edgar-as-Tom is often described as choric and functional, without Lear's psychic depth, self-consciousness, and capacity for self-discovery; but minimizing Edgar's character, which is richly complex as he undergoes profound psychic change, eviscerates a major component of the play. Near the heart of *King Lear* is the deep psychological exchange transacted between Lear and the protagonists of the mirror plot. The form of *King Lear* cannot be understood without acknowledging the importance of the actions of Gloucester and his sons, both as a suggestive analogue for Lear and his daughters, and as a central factor in Lear's self-discovery. Lear approaches his true self through the otherness of Tom's naked misery and then through Gloucester's blind misery; both humbling confrontations prepare Lear for the deeper epiphanal awareness of Cordelia. Lear's anagnorisis must, to some extent, privilege Edgar and Gloucester: through their experience of the same ultimate death-terror and shame of mortality, they assume a depth and presence that informs Lear's acknowledgment of them.

Enthusiastic Gloucester, like other counselors (Polonius in *Hamlet,* Gonzalo in *The Tempest*) is more gullible in his proud self-insulation than Lear, more vulnerable to deception and abuse; yet he is also more open to emotional expression. Gloucester is less able than Lear to understand and enunciate, less experienced in the self-control, judgment, and authority that one hopes to find in sovereignty; but he is also less hampered by skeptical questioning and detachment, more spontaneously open to love.

The polar opposite foil for Lear is Edgar (and Edmund), whose penetrating intelligence is evident in his quick wit and ironic aphorisms, his cleverness in role-playing, surviving, and eventually conquering; but, traumatized by his brother's treachery and his father's easy abandonment of their bond, Edgar distances himself from all emotional bonds—a condition which makes him extremely similar to both Prince Hal and Hamlet. Traumatized brilliance helps to explain his long delay in revealing his identity to his father, his persistent losing himself in volatile role-playing, his brutal remark to his dying brother ("The dark and vicious place where thee he got . . .," 5.3.175–76). Edgar's consummate defensiveness makes him as much an avoider of love as Lear; and his half-feigned madness, his half-feigned demon-possession, and his genuine impoverishment and humiliation make him an extraordinarily complex and appropriate embodiment of the "otherness" that Lear must centrally acknowledge. Finally, in the extravagance of Lear's "madness"—subjected to the anguish of all passions and all conscientious awareness at once—his agon surpasses that of both Gloucester and Edgar, revealing a poignant childishness inextricably mixed with a truly sovereign sympathy that begins to reconstitute human bonds in the poverty of the heath.

In contrast to Macbeth, who in his central sequence tries to "cancel and tear to pieces" the "great bond" of universal siblinghood by butchering his former best friend,[35] Lear in the cycle of act 3 affirms a radical community of spirit. His sympathetic self-stripping attracts faithful servants who mirror that sense of relatedness, drawn to foolish fellowship with an outcast king. Amid such sensitive souls Lear experiences an inner storm of guilt and charity—more painful than the whirlwind of suffering by which Job perceived the face and voice of God. To enforce a skeptical reading of Lear's experience, Elton cites polar opposite Renaissance views of storm: old-fashioned naifs identify the thunder with divine providence, newfangled skeptics demystify it.[36] But surely a sophisticated mean (Erasmus, Montaigne) is closest to Shakespeare's view. Elton also neglects Renaissance use of paradox in tempest allusions and the metaphoric "inner storm" of madness to awaken God's voice within, conscience.[37]

Again the cycle ends with a choric reflection by one at the wheel's nadir. After surviving act 3's stormy cycle, beggared Edgar, like Kent in the stocks, is detached and hopeful:

> To be worst,
> The lowest and most dejected thing of fortune,
> Stands still in esperance, lives not in fear.
> The lamentable change is from the best,
> The worst returns to laughter.
>
> (4.1.1–7)

That Edgar's resilience is met by Gloucester's despair (Fortune having whirled them contrarily in act 3) underscores the wheel's mysterious interconnectedness, irony, and paradox as they begin the final two-act cycle of reunion.

SEEING CORDELIA: RESTORING ID BY INTROJECTION

In acts 4–5 Lear's development again inverts Macbeth's. Macbeth precipitously initiates his final murderous cycle by seeking out the witches (forcing a false epiphany), but he absents himself from the slaughter of innocents and is also absent as Macduff's English pilgrimage achieves, with Malcolm, the true epiphanic moment (4.3). (We are not moved by Malcolm's ritual temptation, an archaic remnant from chronicle history which most directors cut, but by the poignant moment when Macduff learns of his family's massacre, a revelation that is axis for the cycle of acts 4–5 in that it fixes the resolve of Macduff, Malcolm, the Scottish and English forces, and the audience.) Lear, absent for much of act 4 as Gloucester's Dover-journey wavers from suicide to pilgrimage, appears belatedly for reunion with Gloucester and epiphanic reconciliation with Cordelia. Again the illuminative encounter in the last scene of act 4 is pivotal, the dynamic and defining axis for the final two-act cycle.

Though the outer storm has abated, the inward fiery wheeling of shame and love intensifies as in acts 4–5 Lear incurs humiliating divestiture at the self's most primal stage. In this final cycle the king, like Gloucester, returns to a childlike state of physical and emotional vulnerability, an introjective dependence which vacillates between frustrated despair and ecstatic renewal of bonds. Gloucester in act 4 is a barometer of Lear's direction, but Lear is far prouder, more resistant to recovering childlikeness. His intense dependency-love for Cordelia alternates with cruelty toward others: mockery of Gloucester's (and love's) blindness, an urge to kill the sons-in-law who threaten his sole claim to nurturant love, boasts of slaying Cordelia's executioner and of former battle prowess, spasmodic fury at being distracted from watching her body. These impulses characterize Lear's regression to the primal core of selfhood, the id, and its experience of the most deeply nurturant parental love, usually expressed by the mother. This final sequence activates the memory of absolute affection, so travestied in the opening ritual by presumptions of kingly worth: "Which of you doth love us most?"

In *King Lear* the psychic functions in the three cycles of action parallel the main bondings of human identity, though in reverse order: in acts 1–2, bonds with parental authority (adult-heterosocial strivings to consolidate gender and power); in act 3, homosocial bonds (sibling-love, or envious rivalries); and in acts 4–5, infant bonds (especially mother love). In this final two-act cycle the dominant relational mechanism is *introjection,* the most primitive and powerful ego-function, especially in response to the death of a beloved nurturer.[38]

In acts 4–5 the introjective principle is reformed as Gloucester rebukes his blindness as a "superfluous and lust-dieted man" (4.1.66) and his cannibalistic rage when Edgar was the "food of thy abused father's wrath" (4.1.21–22). Now, wishing Tom the "bounty and the benison of heaven" (4.6.228–29), the changed Gloucester unknowingly lavishes wealth and affection on his child. In turn, he accepts generosity from the poor (from servants, from the good old man, and from Edgar-as-Tom), helping him become, like Lear, a "child-changed father," impassioned by good and evil children, but also restored to childlikeness. Thus Gloucester is fully attuned and receptive to Lear's "mad" reflections: "Thou know'st the first time we smell the air / We wawl and cry." Edgar, "pregnant to good pity," reinforces the primal affection, gaining, as in Macbeth's insight, the Godlike simplicity of "a naked new-born babe" (1.7.21). In acts 4–5 Macbeth destroys children, Lear and Gloucester die for love of them.

Lear, however, proudly resists this deepest bond and its reduction to vulnerable simplicity. He crowns himself with rank, poisonous weeds that infest the "sustaining corn" (4.4.6); he accuses women of "riotous appetite" (4.6.123); and he runs from Cordelia, becoming almost infantile (4.6.202–3). He must be captured by love. The final two-act cycle turns on his reunion with Cordelia (4.7), the most moving epiphany and the focal point of Lear's deepest shame; and the cycle concludes with the traumatic stripping away of her life, for which Lear is partly responsible, and the horror of his powerlessness to revive her. As Cavell notes, Lear in these acts operates at a peak of defensive denial,[39] despite the transparency of Cordelia's affection: she is the only epiphanal figure without any duplicity. In act 4 he evades guilt by proclaiming universal absolution from moral law, but then flees Cordelia. In act 5 he refuses to confront the wicked daughters, then denies Cordelia's death. That she must invade England stresses Cordelia's aggressive charity and Lear's active evasion. Lear's love-test, his ardent avoiding of love, and his shameful-joyous reunion all imply the main theme, the valuation of love (what Augustine calls "love of love," *amor amoris*).[40] Lear's best self is shaped by Cordelia's presence; healthy love, including self-love, must be learned.

The revelation of Cordelia again uses supernatural terms ("Thou art a soul in bliss") and a provocative image of Fortune's wheeling that moves deeper than the cycles of courtly power in acts 1–2, deeper than the whirling of the mind in stormy madness in act 3:

> . . . I am bound
> Upon a wheel of fire.
> (4.7.47–48)

Assisted by Elton's glossary of analogues for the fire-wheel,[41] one perceives three levels of meaning—each deriving from varied mythic sources. As a Wheel of Hell (Ixion's wheel or Dante's complex vision in the *Inferno* of circles within circles, all turning around Satan's paralyzing fury) it springs from Lear's proud, willful rage at his failure to command Cordelia's love. As a Wheel of Purgatory it is Lear's penitent shame ("mine own tears do scald like molten lead"), causing him to avoid her presence. As a Wheel of Heaven (a fiery "wheel of the sun") it is Lear's illumination through love. All three levels of passion's cyclic burning focus on Cordelia, the "revealed heart."[42] With her tearful joy, the rage and shame dissolve, leaving love dominion.

Cordelia's forgiving love is the axis of acts 4–5; her death, the only means of complete communion, is the cycle's fitting end.[43] This paradox is the most complex element of Shakespeare's retelling of the *Everyman* morality, where Good Deeds' accompanying Everyman into the grave comforts the audience in the hope of activating their own goodness. Cordelia is a suggestive realization of Charity or Good Deeds, her generosity inspiring but also reflecting her father's sovereign instinct for charity (his prayer for the poor, his empathy for the Fool and Tom): she is indeed his "child" (though, like Marina in *Pericles,* she has also become her father's mother). At first Cordelia's preceding Lear into the grave gives no comfort; and the moral lesson (that Everyman can keep only what he gives away) seems insufficiently realized in Lear's experience. But as he stands immersed in affection for a child whose virtue surpasses the Cynics, sustaining him with faithful bonding and kind deeds, Lear at her death extends and consummates the epiphanic attentiveness of the earlier reunion scene. Not only is he distracted from mortal fears, but his mysterious final words (in the folio version) suggest that Lear sees—internalizes, becomes one with—her parting spirit.[44]

Like Lear, we perceive Cordelia's immortal spirit only through epiphanic awareness, for this theatrical production subjects the audience to psychological stripping similar to his. Kiefer observes that *King Lear*—unlike *Julius Caesar, Hamlet, Macbeth,* and *Antony and Cleopatra*—has no outward manifestation of the supernatural: "no evidence of magic, no witchcraft, no portents . . . , no ghosts or other spirits, and no miracles."[45] Kiefer, however, does not acknowledge the many *immanent* manifestations of the supernatural in *King Lear:* the genuinely "fiendish" behavior of Goneril, Regan, Edmund, Cornwall; the "spirit" of naked Tom and the "magic" of Edgar's artful performance and language; the "miracle" of Gloucester's revivification in faith; the absoluteness of Cordelia's "bond" and the persistence of her spiritual presence even after death. *King Lear* is charged with the supernaturalism of human figures who reflect or deflect God's image, engaged in paradoxical cycles of action which suggest providential order.[46]

Each manifestation of spirit—Goneril's fiendish power-hunger, Tom's resistance of fiends and quest for charity, above all, Cordelia's appearance as a "soul in bliss" (4.7.47), a gracious, forgiving "spirit" (4.7.50)—serves as axis in a cycle of humiliating divestiture and self-exposure for Lear. Each shameful vision of an Other promotes deepening levels of self-awareness. The encounter with Goneril, focusing the initial cycle, dismantles the superego's contrived image of parental-kingly-Godlike authority. The meeting with Poor Tom focuses the middle cycle, an interplay of ego with its doubles in a quest for philosophical insight. The reunion with Cordelia focuses the final cycle, exposing yearnings of the childlike id for absolute love, the nexus for Lear's "wheel of fire."

In Ezekiel's spectacular vision of God's providential working, "like a wheel inside a wheel" (or "wheels within wheels")[47] each multidimensional "wheel" revolves around the spiritual power and radiance of an animal-human-angelic "beast," which in its composite and dynamic form reflects the Creator's nature. This complex revelation supersedes those fatalistic emblems which show Fortune, or Death, at the wheel's center.[48] So too, mature Shakespearean dramaturgy consists of reiterated cycles of action, each revolving around an epiphanic encounter with a natural-supernatural figure whose "spirit . . . was in the wheel."

As in the prophet's vision, King Lear also portrays "wheels within wheels": subsumed in the three great turnings of Lear's fortune are other characters' revolutions of selfhood, each shaping his/her own cycle by choosing an authority-figure as the axis defining the wheel's process. Oswald, Edmund, and the soldier who kills Cordelia adopt the rising arc of the new power clique; Kent, the Fool, Edgar, and Cordelia submit to Lear's and Gloucester's falling arc and, in so doing, attain the freedom of moral solidarity and purpose:

> [O]f a number of spheres turning about the same centre, the innermost one approaches the simplicity of middleness and is a sort of pivot for the rest . . . ; that which is furthest separated from the principal mind is entangled in the tighter meshes of fate.[49]

Lear, rather than Macbeth, pushes toward the inmost simplicity of the "principal mind," that is, conscience, the voice and vision of God-likeness.

In the last two-act cycle of King Lear, the inward pilgrimage of act 4, culminating in reunion with Cordelia, is countered by the arc of warfare in act 5, culminating in the vision of her dead body. At the end of this final cycle Edmund's choric reflection on Fortune is quite different in tone from the remarks of Kent and Edgar when each touched bottom to conclude the play's first two cycles of action: "The wheel is come full circle; I am here" (5.3.174). Giving no credence to spiritual reality, Edmund lacks the optimism that Kent finds because of his shaming in the stocks ("A good man's fortune may grow out at heels. . . . Nothing almost sees miracles / But misery," 2.2.164, 172–73) and that Edgar finds in nakedness and contemnation: "The worst returns to laughter" (4.1.1–9). In striking contrast, Edmund's remark is resoundingly final, not only because he is dying but because he views the wheel of human being reductively, as a cycle of materialistic self-assertion. His "I am" is swallowed by "here," the lowly dust at the wheel's bottom, where he began. Equally ironic and reductive is Edmund's boast of conquering the hearts of Goneril and Regan ("all three / Now marry in an instant"), for none of them has enjoyed truly companionate marriage, the consummation of oneself as another. The Fool, who at first seemed to affirm Edmund's materialistic ego-tism when he advised hitching one's cycle only to the "great wheels" that move upward (2.4.70–73), ignores his own opportunistic maxim by following Lear into the storm. His foolish loyalty epitomizes *King Lear*'s paradoxical cycles. As in Boethius's *Consolation* and Dante's *Commedia,* the way up may be achieved by enduring the way down.

Lear, Gloucester, Edgar, Kent, and Cordelia engage in cycles of abasement that ultimately exalt: "the last shall be first." Edgar, in assuming the humblest human form, the Bethlehem beggar, learns the agony of spinning privilege into poverty, and vice versa; and, like Boethius, he learns self-reflection, that he must "on himself turn back the light of his inward vision, / Bending and forcing his far-reaching movements / Into a circle."[50] This self identity is achieved by social awareness and bonding, the cycle of "good pity" (4.6.220) which restores the gratitude of children to parents and of parents to the Creator, "the love common to all things":

> . . . they seek to be bound by their end, the good,
> Since in no other way could they endure,
> If the causes that gave them being did not flow back
> Under the power of returning love.[51]

Vincenzo Cioffari notes that Aquinas, Dante, Boccaccio, and Petrarch conceived God as the "*causa per se* of our Fortune" ("the love that moves the spheres"), and viewed human will as a subordinate cause.[52] The ending of *King Lear* (both quarto and folio) suggests that the wheel of Lear's destiny, not just the resolutional cycle of acts 4–5 but the drama as a whole, is moved by love. It is a force much larger than Lear himself, as shown by the many who extend it so assiduously on his behalf (Cordelia, Kent, Albany, Gloucester, Edgar, the King of France, gentlemen, servants) and by Lear's persistent failure to receive and reciprocate it with grace. The authenticity of the play's final psychological triumph stresses Lear's residual inadequacies when he finally engages wholeheartedly in this mysterious force.

For Shakespeare the fundamental cause of "fortune" is not philosophical attraction to the idea of the Good but creaturely fellow-feeling, which draws the comedies and romances to a final communal celebration, and which the tragedies affirm as the best resource for confronting death. Such bonding redefines the cycles of historical change and the wheels of our inner being. Edgar, the heir apparent, is the best final *sprecher,* and the best candidate for sovereignty, not only by his former exposure to aloneness, nakedness, and death-terror but also by his modest admission of partial detachment from the "wheel of fire"—the burning of shame and love which so consumed his father, then still more terribly his godfather Lear. Humbled by their vision and passion, he does not presume to "see so much" or "live so long."

Notes

INTRODUCTION

All Shakespearean quotations are taken from David Bevington's updated 4th edition of *The Complete Works of Shakespeare* (New York: Longman, 1997).

1. Kenneth Muir, *The Singularity of Shakespeare* (Oxford: Clarendon Press, 1983); cf. Anthony Brennan, *Shakespeare's Dramatic Structures* (London: Routledge and Kegan Paul, 1968).

2. Harold Bloom, *The Western Canon* (New York: Harcourt Brace, 1994), 59.

3. Shakespeare's creative complementarity, often noted in the contrary handling of Pyramus and Thisbe's love-death in *Romeo and Juliet* and in *A Midsummer Night's Dream,* is also apparent in the two history tetrads and in various neighboring plays: the garden world of *As You Like It* vs. the courtly world of *Twelfth Night,* Cressida's fickleness vs. Desdemona's constancy, Lear's divestiture vs. Macbeth's usurpation, Timon's overgenerosity vs. Coriolanus's overcontempt, female authority in *The Winter's Tale* vs. male authority in *The Tempest.* Cf. Richard P. Wheeler's psychoanalytic reading of complementarity in *Shakespeare's Development and the Problem Comedies: Turn and Counter-turn* (Berkeley and Los Angeles: Univerisity of California Press, 1981).

4. See Barbara A. Mowat, *The Dramaturgy of Shakespeare's Romances* (Athens: University of Georgia Press, 1976), chap. 4.

5. For discussion of the *sprecher*-figure, see John Greenwood, *Shifting Perspectives and the Stylish Style: Mannerism in Shakespeare and His Jacobean Contemporaries* (Toronto: University of Toronto Press, 1988), 22, 53–96, 176–77, 186–87.

6. See Anne Righter, *Shakespeare and the Idea of the Play* (London: Chatto and Windus, 1962); David Young, *Something of Great Constancy* (New Haven: Yale University Press, 1966); Robert Egan, *Drama Within Drama: Shakespeare's Sense of His Art* (New York: Columbia University Press, 1975); Anthony Brennan, *Shakespeare's Dramatic Structures.*

7. See Richard Levin, ("Direct Contrast Plots" in *The Multiple Plot in English Renaissance Drama* (Chicago: University of Chicago Press, 1971), 21–54.

8. Levin discusses "Three-Level Hierarchies" of plot in *Much Ado about Nothing, As You Like It, 1 Henry IV,* and other English Renaissance dramas (ibid., 55–108).

9. Shakespeare's *tragedies of mutuality* include *Romeo and Juliet, King Lear,* and *Antony and Cleopatra. Tragedies of insularity* include *Macbeth, Timon of Athens,* and *Coriolanus.* Some tragic protagonists—Brutus, Hamlet, Othello, Timon—though inclined to bonding, are estranged mainly through deception. These plays show features of mutuality: a partial secondary plot and the protagonist's affirmative engagement with servants or commoners, who assist in the attainment of epiphanal awareness. *Titus Andronicus* shows no clear commitment to mutuality or insularity.

Chapter 1: Shakespearean Dramaturgy

1. For selected commentaries on Shakespearean dramaturgy, to most of which I am indebted, see Bibliography, Section 1.

2. If one envisions Shakespearean drama as *completed form* (static, holistic, "atomic"), its three sets of linked scenes form concentric cycles; as in Dante's *Commedia*, each cycle subsumes prior cycles, narrowing or widening around an epiphanic disclosure. Viewed as *process*, Shakespearean drama consists of undular, constantly reversing fluctuations, rises and falls ("waves"), as noted by John Velz, "Undular Structure in *Julius Caesar*," *MLR* 66 (1971): 21–30.

3. "Poetics" in *The Complete Works of Aristotle*, ed. Jonathan Barnes (Oxford: Clarendon Press, 1984).

4. *Collected Works of Erasmus: Adages Ii1 to Iv100*, trans. Margaret Mann Phillips (Toronto: University of Toronto Press, 1987), 177. There is little relation between Greek drama's "prologos, episodes, exodos" and Roman drama's "protasis, epitasis, catastrophe"—the latter terms designating not just placement but function. "Episodes" are a variable number of complicating events; the "epitasis" is a turbulent central development, usually involving discovery and reversal.

5. Horace, *Epistles* 2:3, 189–90. Cf. William Beare, "The Roman Origin of the Law of Five Acts," in *The Roman Stage* (London: Methuen, 1950), 196–218; R. T. Weissinger, *A Study of Act Divisions in Classical Drama* (Iowa Studies in Classical Philology, No. IX, 1940); J. Dover Wilson, "Act- and Scene-Divisions in the Plays of Shakespeare," *RES* 3 (1927): 385–97; W. W. Greg, "Act-Divisions in Shakespeare," *RES* 4 (1928): 152–58; T. W. Baldwin, *Shakspere's Five-Act Structure* (Urbana: University of Illinois Press, 1947), 1–52, 97–119, 228–51, 312–32, 691–718. For discussion of Plautus's five-act structuring, see Wolfgang Riehle, *Shakespeare, Plautus, and the Humanist Tradition* (Cambridge: D. S. Brewer and Rochester: Boydell and Brewer, 1990).

6. A. C. Bradley, *Shakespeare's Tragedies* (New York: Macmillan, 1904), 41–70. Ruth Nevo, in *Tragic Form in Shakespeare* (Princeton: Princeton University Press, 1972), affirms Baldwin's five-act thesis but does not resolve the debate between three-part or five-part structure. Agreeing with Bradley on the functioning of acts 1, 3, and 5, she synthesizes Bradley and the humanists on the varied function of act 2 (initiate conflicts, or complete those begun in the exposition) and act 4 (intensify the epitasis, introduce the resolution, or withdraw into pathos and false-climax before the conclusive resolution of act 5).

7. For discussion of the protagonist's absence in act 4, see Bradley, *Shakespeare's Tragedies*, 54–55; and Maynard Mack, "The Jacobean Shakespeare: Some Observations on the Construction of the Tragedies," in *Jacobean Theatre*, ed. John Russell Brown and Bernard Harris (Stratford-upon-Avon Studies. London: Edward Arnold, 1960), 11–41.

8. *Shakspere's Five-Act Structure*, 228–51. Baldwin's valuable study rightly stresses the influence of Donatus and the fifteenth–sixteenth century commentators. But his massive work, which is often distracted by etymologies, superficially summarizes the plays (neglecting dramaturgic and moral-psychological development) and observes no exceptions as he forces all plots into one pattern, which is partly incorrect.

9. The Battle of Agincourt in acts 3–4 serves as *epitasis* for *Henry V* and, with the triumphant courtship in act 5, also serves as *catastrophe* for the entire *Henriad*.

King Lear's epitasis may also seem to extend into act 4 (the continuing madness);

yet act 3 is a coherent whole, ending with Lear's sleep, the Fool's parting, and Gloucester's blinding. In act 4 Lear vanishes for six scenes, displaced by Gloucester's suicidal pilgrimage, and reappears with a more defensive lunacy; act 4 thus begins the resolution, depicting not the stormy madness of wounded authority but a deepening shame, anticipating the father-child reunions.

10. Emrys Jones argues for two-part structure, a *3–2 pattern of acts* with a definitive break after act 3, also noting in some plays a strong pause after act 2 (*Scenic Form in Shakespeare* [Oxford: Clarendon Press, 1971], chap. 3). Jones is correct, except in downplaying the break after act 2. Cf. Bradley, *Shakespeare's Tragedies*, 56. On Shakespeare's structural echoes of "the two phased moral play," see Alan C. Dessen, *Shakespeare and the Late Moral Plays* (Lincoln: University of Nebraska Press, 1986), chaps. 2–5.

11. Baldwin, *Shakspere's Five-Act Structure*, 232–35, 294–96, 304–11. S.v. "*parasceve*" in the *O.E.D.* According to Lancelot Andrewes, "It is called by the Fathers, *Parasceue Spiritus*, 'the preparation,' as there was one for the Passover, so here for Pentecost." See *The Works of Lancelot Andrewes*, 11 vols. (1854; reprint, New York: AMS Press, 1967), 2:254, 3:112.

12. Robert Wilcher, "Double Endings and Autonomous Acts: A Feature of Shakespearean Design," *CahiersE* 51 (1997): 47–61.

13. Clifford Leech, "Shakespeare's Use of a Five-Act Structure," in *Die Neueren Sprachen* 6 (1957): 249–63. Cf. Baldwin, *Shakspere's Five-Act Structure*, 112. Leech further describes the five-act/three-phase pattern in his Arden edition of *Two Gentlemen of Verona* and in "The Structure of the Last Plays," *ShS* 11 (1958): 19–30.

14. According to Willichius, act 1 "unfolds the argument and embraces for the most part the *protasis*," and act 2 "completes the same." Act 3, as *epitasis*, "has the increment of turbations and contentions." Acts 4–5 effect the *catastrophe:* the fourth "seeks a medicine for the turbations" and is "preparatory to the catastrophe, which the fifth demands by right for itself." See Leech, "Shakespeare's Use of a Five-Act Structure," 251; Baldwin, *Shakspere's Five-Act Structure*, 231–32.

15. Wilfred Thomas Jewkes, *Act Division in Elizabethan and Jacobean Plays 1583–1616* (Hamden: Shoestring Press, 1958). Cf. Greg, "Act-Divisions in Shakespeare"; Henry Snuggs, *Shakespeare and Five Acts: Studies in a Dramatic Convention* (New York: Vantage Press, 1960).

16. Baldwin, *Shakspere's Five-Act Structure*, 325–29.

17. James E. Hirsh, *The Structure of Shakespearean Scenes* (New Haven: Yale University Press, 1981).

18. G. K. Hunter, "Were There Act-Pauses on Shakespeare's Stage?" in *English Renaissance Drama: Essays in Honor of Madeleine Doran and Mark Eccles*, ed. Standish Henning, Robert Kimbrough, and Richard Knox (Carbondale and Edwardsville: Southern Illinois University Press, 1976), 15–35.

19. Gary Taylor, "The Structure of Performance: Act-Intervals in the London Theatres, 1576–1642," in Gary Taylor and John Jowett, *Shakespeare Reshaped: 1606–1623* (Oxford: Clarendon Press, 1993), 4–25. In this early period Taylor finds "only one (dubious) piece of manuscript evidence, one (dubious) plot, no external references to act-intervals, no directions to 'long' intervals, no dialogue references to a break in the playing, no directions identifying 'the act' as an interval between two stretches of continuous dramatic action, and only one play [Jonson's] which calls for music between the acts."

20. Ibid., 23.

21. For Lyly's symmetry and its influence on Shakespearean dramaturgy, see Albert Feuillerat, *John Lyly* (Cambridge: Cambridge University Press, 1910), 385–89; T. W. Baldwin, "John Lyly and Five-act Structure," in *Shakspere's Five-act Structure*, 493–543; Muriel Bradbrook, *The Growth and Structure of Elizabethan Comedy* (London: Chatto and Windus, 1955), 72–76; G. K. Hunter, *John Lyly: The Humanist as Courtier* (London: Routledge and Kegan Paul, 1962), 159–62, 298–349; Lester Beaurline, *Jonson and Elizabethan Comedy* (San Marino, CA: Huntington Library, 1978), 86–102. Cf. Michael R. Best, "Lyly's Static Drama," *RenD* 1 (1968): 75–86; Barry Thorne, "*Love's Labors Lost:* The Lyly Gilded," *Humanities Association Bulletin* 21 (1970): 32–37.

22. G. Taylor, "The Structure of Performance," 20–21.

23. Ibid., 36. To Beare also, "The essential characteristic of act-division is the pause in performance"; "'acts' have no reality unless there is some external mark of division [or a choral interlude] between them"; "Continuous performance . . . is the negation of act-division" (*Roman Stage*, 202, 205, 217). In stressing "external" signals, Beare utterly neglects dramaturgy.

24. See Jean Howard, *Shakespeare's Art of Orchestration: Stage Technique and Audience Response* (Urbana: University of Illinois Press, 1984).

25. On coherence of time and place in each act, see Clifford Leech's introduction to the Arden *Two Gentlemen of Verona*.

26. Joan Hartwig, in *Shakespeare's Analogical Scene: Parody as Structural Syntax* (Lincoln: University of Nebraska Press, 1983), explains the parodic principle linking disparate scenes (heroic and comic).

27. G. Taylor, "The Structure of Performance," 48–50.

28. The folio retains the bridge-dialogue of Lear and the Fool between acts 1 and 2, for it develops Lear's own character, anticipating madness and lamenting his treatment of Cordelia.

29. Mack, "The Jacobean Shakespeare," 11–41.

30. In act 3 of *The Comedy of Errors* each Antipholus inverts his relational experience; other topsy-turvydoms, which take on increasing complexity and symbolic suggestiveness, include Titania's vow to Bottom, Lysander's to Helena, Touchstone's to Audrey, Phebe's to "Ganymede," Olivia's to "Cesario," Malvolio's to Olivia. The chaotic distortions at the center are sometimes intentional and have positive aims: Petruchio at the wedding shows Katherine how to enact one's own antithesis; and other discerning lovers (Portia, Rosalind, Viola, Helena) advance their desires through disguise and gender-reversal in act 3.

31. Mark Rose, *Shakespearean Design* (Cambridge: Harvard University Press, 1972), 13–15, 35, 43–44, 126, 151, 179 n. 21.

32. Ibid., 50–59.

33. The first cycle, acts 1–2, though activating all three plot strands (the king's counsel, Falstaff's riot, Hotspur's rebellion), focuses mainly on the tavern and builds to Hal's long verbal duel with Falstaff (2.4). The final cycle, acts 4–5, though engaging all four principals at Shrewsbury, focuses on Hal's comparison with Hotspur and builds to their combat.

34. Rose briefly sketches *The Tempest*'s perfect symmetry (173–74) but does not structurally relate the three character-groups' development.

35. Howard, *Shakespeare's Art of Orchestration.*

36. *Ibid.*, 160–64.

37. Jones, "The Growth of Scenes," in *Scenic Form in Shakespeare*, 89–113.

38. Brennan, *Shakespeare's Dramatic Structures*, 13–103.

39. Robert L. Reid, "Macbeth's Three Murders: Shakespearean Psychology and Tragic Form," *RenP 1991* (Durham: Duke University Press, 1992), 75–92; "Lear's Three Shamings: Shakespearean Psychology and Tragic Form," *RenP 1996* (Columbia, SC: Camden House, 1997), 93–112.

40. In Jonson's *The Magnetic Lady* the Boy says of Classical drama's protasis-epitasis-catastrophe format, "I understand that, sin' I learn'd *Terence*, i' the third forme at *Westminster*." See Baldwin, *Shakspere's Five-act Structure*, 327. Cf. chaps. 15–16.

41. For discussion of Plautus's symmetrical dramaturgy, see Riehle, *Shakespeare, Plautus, and the Humanist Tradition;* for Lyly's symmetries, see the commentaries listed in note 21 above.

42. For the view that Gower's seven choruses divide the action of *Pericles* into a simulacrum of Augustine's Seven Ages of History, see Cynthia Marshall, *Last Things and Last Plays: Shakespearean Eschatology* (Carbondale: Southern Illinois University Press, 1991), 61–85.

43. Shakespeare makes a two-act cycle of acts 1–2 (and of acts 4–5) either by *intensified repetition* or by *reversal*, often both. Intensified repetition informs acts 1–2 of *The Comedy of Errors, Romeo and Juliet, 1 Henry IV, Measure for Measure, King Lear*, and *Winter's Tale*. Reversal in acts 1–2 informs all the above and also *Titus Andronicus, Two Gentlemen of Verona, As You Like It, Julius Caesar, Hamlet, All's Well That Ends Well, Othello, Macbeth, Timon of Athens, Antony and Cleopatra, Coriolanus, Pericles, Cymbeline*, and *Tempest*.

44. For discussion of Shakespearean epiphany, see chapter 3.

45. As "epiphanal encounter," this turning-point for the cycle of acts 1–2 in *Antony and Cleopatra* does not seem comparable to the spectacular confrontation that occurs at this point in the other mature tragedies.

46. In Nevo's emendation of the act-division of *Love's Labors Lost* (Nevo, *Tragic Form in Shakespeare*), Boyet remains on stage between acts 4 and 5. While the break between acts 1 and 2 and between 4 and 5 is minimized, or is made into a fulcrum between complementary arcs of action, act 3 is usually set apart by distinctive closure on either side—most ingeniously in *A Midsummer Night's Dream*, where sleepers remain on stage just before and after act 3: instead of clearing the stage Shakespeare renders all personae inactive, emphasizing that act 3 is a dream.

47. Howard, in *Shakespeare's Art of Orchestration*, 160–63, explains how mood, setting, and flow of action connect the adjoining scenes of acts 1–2 of *Julius Caesar*. I would add: the fire-storm of 1.3 provides climactic closure for act 1, yet it also serves as axis for a longer cycle of action. Though scenes 1–2 of act 2 continue the storm as background noise, they turn deeply reflective as Brutus broods over the conspiracy and as he and Caesar resist their wives' sense of coming crisis—thus intensifying the anticipated assassination. Act 3, fulfilling those preparations, is presented as a separate cycle of action, signaled by a trumpet flourish and by the shift from secretive private scenes to the central ceremonious public events.

48. Two partial qualifications to the linkage of acts 1 and 2 are *Hamlet* and *Othello:* Though Hamlet vows hasty revenge, the final couplet in act 1 signals his imminent paralysis, which pervades the tense mutual surveillances of act 2. Hamlet's caution toward the court, doubt of the ghost, and disgust with sexual/emotional relationship after his mother's easy change all enforce tense repression. Moreover, his extravagant response to the ghost drains him and the audience, inducing the break in

action that contradicts his vow. In *Othello* a similar but contrary climax ends act 1, bringing respite from the trial's tension and a sense of having established true love's eternal durance. The residual presence and soliloquy of Iago (as, in other plays, of Aaron, Romeo, and Hamlet) thus enforces the connection of acts 1 and 2.

49. Of the tragic protagonists only Macbeth does not engage in a (usually humiliating) public encounter at the end of act 2.

50. In act 3 we note the Fury-arousing spectacle in Titus Andronicus; invocations to the vengeful spirits of Tybalt, Mercutio, Julius Caesar; literal ghosts of old Hamlet and Banquo; Edgar-as-Tom's evocation of "fiends" twisting his mind; Othello's "monstrous" transformation into "black vengeance" (3.3.462). Only the mature Roman plays *(Antony and Cleopatra, Coriolanus)* do not evoke supernatural causation for the central turbulence, though Hercules's spirit is said to abandon Antony in 4.3.

51. Laurence Michel, "The Possibility of a Christian Tragedy," in *Tragedy: Modern Essays in Criticism,* ed. Michel and Arthur Sewall (Englewood Cliffs, NJ: Prentice-Hall, 1963), and *The Thing Contained: Theory of the Tragic* (Bloomington: Indiana University Press, 1970), 12, 133–35. Cf. Erich Frank on Sartre: "The higher developed the moral consciousness of the individual . . . , the more clearly he will understand the inevitability of guilt in the very process of perfecting himself" (cited in Michel, 24–25).

52. Act 3 of *The Tempest* presents a comprehensive disclosure of consciences, matching the servants' unworthy desire for Miranda against the young lovers' betrothal, and the guilty power-hunger of the indicted courtiers against Prospero's true power as he glories from on high over each group—though he has not yet fully mastered the corresponding parts of his own nature.

53. "The finest form of discovery is one attended by reversal," "Poetics," trans. R. Kassel, in *The Complete Works of Aristotle,* The Revised Oxford Translation, ed. Jonathan Barnes (Princeton: Princeton University Press, 1984), 2:2324.

54. Gerald F. Else, *Aristotle's Poetics: The Argument* (Cambridge: Harvard University Press, 1957), 353. Cf. 252–57, 338–58.

55. William Arrowsmith, "A Greek Theatre of Ideas," in *Euripides: A Collection of Critical Essays,* ed. Erich Segal (Englewood Cliffs, NJ: Prentice-Hall, 1968), 13–33; "The Criticism of Greek Tragedy," in *Tragedy: Vision and Form,* ed. R. W. Corrigan (San Francisco: Chandler, 1965), 317–42: "moral action is obscured and prevented by a deep discord in the nature of things" (328). As in *Oedipus Rex* the *anagnorisis* of evil brings not clarity but confusion, paralysis, and self-abuse to Hamlet, Lear, Othello, Timon, Macbeth, Antony and Cleopatra, and Coriolanus.

56. On the dread of defilement, see Paul Ricoeur, *The Symbolism of Evil,* trans. Emerson Buchanan (1967; reprint, Boston: Beacon Press, 1969), 25–46.

57. On the sacrifice of women from dread of maternal power and from narcissistic rage, see William Beers, *Women and Sacrifice: Male Narcissism and the Psychology of Religion* (Detroit: Wayne State University Press, 1992).

58. See Wilcher, "Double Endings and Autonomous Acts"; cf. Anne Barton, "'Nature's Piece 'Gainst Fancy': The Divided Catastrophe in *Antony and Cleopatra,*" in *Modern Critical Interpretations: William Shakespeare's Antony and Cleopatra,* ed. Harold Bloom (New York: Chelsea House, 1988), 35–55.

59. M. A. Screech, *Ecstasy and the Praise of Folly* (London: Duckworth, 1980), esp. 63–67 and chaps. 5–6.

60. See Michel, "The Possibility of a Christian Tragedy," 212.

61. For the debate over five-act structure in Roman comedy, see n. 5 above; W. M. Lindsay, *The Ancient Editions of Plautus* (Oxford: James Parker, 1904), 88–104.

62. Riehle, *Shakespeare, Plautus, and the Humanist Tradition,* 89–97: "the view that the 'theory of the five-act structure is largely a red herring' should at last be discarded." Cf. Robert S. Miola, *Shakespeare and Classical Comedy: The Influence of Plautus and Terence* (Oxford: Clarendon Press, 1994), 19–38.

63. The line-count is taken from *The Menaechmi: The Original of Shakespeare's "Comedy of Errors": The Latin Text Together with the Elizabethan Translation,* ed. W. H. D. Rouse (New York: Duffield and London: Chatto and Windus, 1912). See Erma M. Gill, "The Plot-Structure of 'The Comedy of Errors' in Relation to Its Sources," *Texas University Studies in English* 8 (1928): 13–65.

64. Act-divisions are those of Joannes Baptista Pius, who first inserted them in Plautus's texts   (1500, 1514). Shakespeare apparently used Lambinus's 1576 edition, which does not indicate act division. (Lambinus's notation repeatedly uses "errors"— the first edition to do so.) See Baldwin, *Shakespere's Five-Act Structure,* 666–70, 691–94, 700–702; *The Comedy of Errors,* ed. T. W. Baldwin (London: Heath, 1928), 127–29.

65. The 2–1–2 structure of *Amphitryon* is different: the lock-out of the husband, rather than occupying the play's center, initiates the cycle of acts 1–2 and then that of acts 4–5: Jupiter must sustain repeatedly his trick of human impersonation, most climactically when he confronts Alcmena in act 3.

66. Despite the Christian-romance values implicit in the anagnorisis at the priory (the strangely detached reunion of Egeon and Emilia, the presumed reconciliation of Adriana and Antipholus E, the implicit betrothal of Luciana and Antipholus S), neither romantic nor Christian values are emphasized as much as the attainment of fraternal communion by the twins.

67. William Shakespeare, *Measure for Measure,* ed. J. W. Lever (London: Methuen, 1965), xli—xliii.

68. Ibid., xli.

69. For discussion of Shakespeare's optimistic portrayal of Vincentio, perhaps in part to flatter or to educate James I, see Josephine Waters Bennett, *Measure for Measure as Royal Entertainment* (New York: Columbia University Press, 1966); Darryl Gless, *"Measure for Measure," the Law, and the Convent* (Princeton: Princeton University Press, 1979).

70. Skalliger for Oswald, Perillus and Mumford for Kent, motifs of kneeling and sending letters, the dwindling of Lear's rage, the daughters' moral polarity, as summarized by R. A. Foakes in the Arden edition of *King Lear* (Walton-on-Thames: Thomas Nelson and Sons, 1997), 92–110.

71. Ibid., 94.

72. Ibid., 100–102.

73. See William Elton, *King Lear and the Gods* (1966; reprint, Lexington: University Press of Kentucky, 1988); Leo Salingar, "*King Lear,* Montaigne and Harsnett," *Dramatic Form in Shakespeare and the Jacobeans* (Cambridge: Cambridge University Press, 1986), 107–39; Reid, "Lear's Three Shamings," 98–99, 104–6.

74. In *Shakespeare's Mouldy Tales: Recurrent Plot Motifs in Shakespearian Drama* (New York: Longman, 1992), Leah Scragg surveys six recurrent motifs in the comedies and romances: *sibling confusion* (two plays), *gender exchange* (five plays), *scolding* (four plays), *substitute coupling* (five plays), *exile* (nine plays), *putative death* (nine plays). Motifs involving darker passion and moral errancy are even more pervasive in the canon

as a whole: *revenge* (twenty-three plays), *slander of love* (ten plays), *abdication* (seven plays), *usurpation by assassination* (six plays), *actual love-death* (seven plays).

75. For discussion of Shakespeare's uses of contrariety, see Marion Bodwell Smith, *Dualities in Shakespeare* (Toronto: University of Toronto Press, 1966), citing opposites in nature, human nature, and being. On these dualisms' intellectual history, see Robert Grudin, *Mighty Opposites: Shakespeare and Renaissance Contrariety* (Berkeley and Los Angeles: University of California Press, 1979); Colin N. Manlove, *The Gap in Shakespeare: The Motif of Division from Richard II to The Tempest* (London: Vision Press and Totowa: Barnes and Noble, 1981); Thomas McAlindon, *Shakespeare's Tragic Cosmos* (Cambridge: Cambridge University Press, 1991), chaps. 1–2.

76. See Robert B. Heilman, *This Great Stage: Image and Structure in "King Lear"* (Baton Rouge: Louisiana State University Press, 1948).

77. Cf. the ironic reversals in the recurrent discovery-scenes of *The Comedy of Errors, The Taming of the Shrew,* and *Richard III.*

78. See Mowat, *The Dramaturgy of Shakespeare's Romances.*

79. One might except *Seinfeld:* its flexible formula of interlaced plot-strands, geared to each character's metadramatic self-promotion and meddling stage-management of others, building to ironic discovery-scenes where characters hoist themselves with their own petards while evading epiphany and self-change, offers intriguing comparison with Shakespeare's mature comedies.

CHAPTER 2: A PROBLEM OF DRAMATIC FORM

1. Madeleine Doran, *Endeavors of Art: A Study of Form in Elizabethan Drama* (Madison: University of Wisconsin Press, 1964), 259. Cf. 17–18, 259–94, 370–76.

2. See Susan Snyder, *The Comic Matrix of Shakespeare's Tragedies* (Princeton: Princeton University Press, 1979), 137–79.

3. Mack, "The Jacobean Shakespeare"; cf. Richard Levin, "Comic Subplots: Foil, Parody, Magic," in *The Multiple Plot in English Renaissance Drama* (Chicago: University of Chicago Press, 1971).

4. See Enid Welsford, *The Fool: His Social and Literary History* (1935; reprint, New York: Doubleday, 1961); Robert Goldsmith, *Wise Fools in Shakespeare* (East Lansing: Michigan State University Press, 1955); Robert Weimann, *Shakespeare and the Popular Tradition in the Theater: Studies in the Social Dimension of Dramatic Form and Function,* ed. Robert Schwartz (1967; reprint, Baltimore: Johns Hopkins University Press, 1978), 11–14, 30–48, 190–92.

5. For discussion of the *sprecher*-figure, see Greenwood, *Shifting Perspectives and the Stylish Style,* 22, 53–96, 176–77, 186–87. For the view of *Hamlet* as Western culture's watershed drama, endowing virtually every character with metatheatrical self-consciousness so that each conceives the action as springing from his/her own devising and direction, see Lionel Abel, "*Hamlet* Q.E.D.," in *Metatheatre: A New View of Dramatic Form* (New York: Hill and Wang, 1963), 41–58.

6. For discussion of symbolic stage divisions (central action at *locus,* marginal commentators at *platea*), see Weimann, *Shakespeare and the Popular Tradition in the Theater,"* 224–37.

7. Douglas Bruster, "Comedy and Control: Shakespeare and the Plautine *Poeta,"*

in *Drama and the Classical Heritage,* ed. Clifford Davidson, Rand Johnson, and John H. Stroupe (New York: AMS Press, 1993), 117–31.

8. On the complex nesting of plots in *A Midsummer Night's Dream,* see Young, *Something of Great Constancy,* 86–106.

9. See Levin, *The Multiple Plot in English Renaissance Drama,* 21–54, 148–91.

10. Ibid., chap. 3 ("Three-Level Hierarchies"), 55–108. Here I differ from Levin's astute analysis of multiple plots: Shakespeare's ultimate model is a four-level hierarchy of plots, the fourth level, that of the *sprecher-magus,* being most potent and definitive.

11. In drawing upon the imaginative gifts of Falstaff, Hal (even as Henry V) does not merit full comparison with Oberon's governance of Puck's energies, nor with Prospero's mastery of Ariel's more refined spirit. Yet the analogy is evident.

12. Shakespeare's darker *sprecher-magi* have been traced to the medieval Vice, the Renaissance Machiavel, and a demonic artificer by Bernard Spivack, *Shakespeare and the Allegory of Evil* (New York: Columbia University Press, 1958), 28–59; Sidney R. Homan, "Iago's Aesthetics: *Othello* and Shakespeare's Portrait of an Artist," *ShS* 5 (1969): 141; Richard Abrams, "*The Tempest* and the Concept of the Machiavellian Playwright," *ELR* 8 (1978): 44. For the view of Prospero as a positive revision of Dr. Faustus, see Alvin B. Kernan, *The Playwright as Magician: Shakespeare's Image of the Poet in the English Public Theater* (New Haven: Yale University Press, 1979), 146–59.

13. Northrop Frye, *Fools of Time: Studies in Shakespearean Tragedy* (Toronto: University of Toronto Press, 1967).

14. Janette Dillon, *Shakespeare and the Solitary Man* (Totowa, NJ: Rowman and Littlefield, 1981), chaps. 2–3.

15. See Sigmund Freud, "Mourning and Melancholia" [1917], *SE;* Hans W. Loewald, "Internalization, Separation, Mourning, and the Superego," *PsyQ* 31 (1962): 483–504.

16. For discussion of the lack of a source for expanding the roles of Polonius's family, see Ann Pasternak Slater, *Shakespeare the Director* (Brighton: Harvester Press and Totowa, NJ: Barnes and Noble, 1982), 191–93. Equally radical is Shakespeare's revision of the Lear history by adding the plot from *Arcadia.*

17. See Riehle, *Shakespeare, Plautus and the Humanist Tradition;* Miola, *Shakespeare and Classical Comedy,* 174–201.

18. Likewise, despite the powerful bedroom encounter, Gertrude's psyche is largely unvocalized, except in reaction to others. See Janet Adelman, *Suffocating Mothers: Fantasies of Maternal Origin in Shakespeare's Plays, Hamlet to the Tempest* (New York and London: Routledge, 1992), 11–37; and cf. 79, 104, 166, 246–49, 254–55.

19. A. C. Bradley, "Construction in Shakespeare's Tragedies," in *Shakespearean Tragedy* (London: Macmillan, 1904); Jones, *Scenic Form in Shakespeare,* 152–94.

20. Augustus W. von Schlegel, *A Course of Lectures on Dramatic Art and Literature* trans. J. Black 1815; reprint, New York: AMS Press n.d.), 412. Ernest Dowden, *Shakspere: A Critical Study of His Mind and Art* (New York: Capricorn Books, 1962), 265–72. Cf. Jay Halio, "The Double Plot of *King Lear,*" in *Readings on the Tragedies of William Shakespeare* (San Diego: Greenhaven Press, 1996), 188–93; Elton, "Double Plot," in *King Lear and the Gods,* 267–83.

21. For the view that Lear's erotic fixation reverses the Oedipus complex, see Arpad Pauncz, "Psychopathology of Shakespeare's *King Lear,*" *AI* 9 (1952): 57–77, esp. 58.

22. See William C. Carroll, *Fat King, Lean Beggar: Representations of Poverty in the Age of Shakespeare* (Ithaca: Cornell University Press, 1996).

23. See F. T. Flahiff, "Edgar: Once and Future King," in *Some Facets of "King Lear": Essays in Prismatic Criticism*, ed. Rosalie L. Colie and F. T. Flahiff (Toronto: University of Toronto Press, 1974), 221–37.

24. See Stanley Cavell, "The Avoidance of Love: A Reading of *King Lear*," in his *Disowning Knowledge in Six Plays of Shakespeare* (1969; reprint, Cambridge: Cambridge University Press, 1987), 39–123.

25. To some extent Duke Vincentio also changes through sexual-social engagement, with its suffering and compromise. See Mark Taylor, "Farther Privileges: Conflict and Change in *Measure for Measure*," *PQ* 73 (1994): 169–93.

26. Stephen Booth, *King Lear, Macbeth, Indefinition and Tragedy* (New Haven: Yale University Press, 1983), chap. 1.

Chapter 3: Epiphanal Encounters

1. See Revelation 21–22. The New Jerusalem, a city covered with jewels, reveals an Edenic core: "[The Angel] shewed me a pure riuer of water of life, cleare as crystal, proceding out of the throne of God, and of the Lambe. In the middes of the strete of it, and of ether side of the riuer, was the tre of life" (22.1–2).

This apocalyptic unveiling is the supreme epiphany: the city's tenants, who see God's face and know God's name, are filled with light, needing "no candle, nether light of the sunne," "for the glorie of God did light it: & the Lambe is the light of it" (Rev. 22.5, 21.23).

2. Epiphany, the "showing forth" of Christ's divine nature and glory, is a solemnity established in the third century in Eastern Orthodox Christianity to celebrate Jesus' baptism (when the Trinity was fully disclosed), as well as the Magi's visit to the nativity and Jesus' first miracle at Cana. The Western church focuses on the Magi's visit (6 January, the twelfth day after Jesus' birth, climax of the Christmas festival) to stress that Christ's glory was now shared with the Gentiles. See K. Pruman, "Epiphany," in *The New Catholic Encyclopedia*, 18 vols. (New York: McGraw-Hill, 1967); and note 15. For discussion of epiphany in Jewish and Christian scriptures and in the "pagan anticipations" of Plato, the Eleusinian mysteries, and Neoplatonism, see K. E. Kirk, *The Vision of God: The Christian Doctrine of the Summum Bonum* (1931; reprint, New York: Harper, 1966).

3. For Lancelot Andrewes's distinction between "the thing to be seen" (the physical pain, soul-sorrow, and shame of Jesus' Passion) and "the act of seeing" (love transforming tragedy to joy, "His cross into ease, "His shame into glory"), see *The Works of Lancelot Andrewes*, 11 vols. (1854; reprint, New York: AMS Press, 1967), 2:121, 160, 183.

4. Richard Hooker, *Of the Laws of Ecclesiastical Polity*, Book V, ed. W. Speed Hill, Folger Library Edition of the Works of Richard Hooker, 2 (Cambridge: Harvard University Press, 1977), 334.

5. Andrewes, *Works*, 2:130.

6. Emrys Jones, *The Origins of Shakespeare* (New York: Oxford University Press, 1977), 51–55.

7. Ibid., 51.

8. See Robert G. Hunter, *Shakespeare and the Comedy of Forgiveness* (New York: Columbia University Press, 1965); G. Wilson Knight, *The Crown of Life: Essays in Interpretation of Shakespeare's Final Plays* (1947; reprint, New York: Barnes and Noble, 1966), 76–128; S. L. Bethell, *The Winter's Tale: A Study* (London: Athlone Press, 1947); Raymond E. Brown, *The Semitic Background of the Term "Mystery" in the New Testament* (Philadelphia: Fortress, 1968).

9. Despite the value-inversions provoked by mortality crises in the problem comedies, tragedies, and romances, Shakespeare remains firmly committed to embodiment and natural creation, not to ascetic other-worldliness and contempt for bodily pleasures.

10. See V. A. Kolve, *The Play Called Corpus Christi* (Stanford: Stanford University Press, 1966), 124–74.

11. *The Sermons of John Donne*, 10 vols., ed. George R. Potter and Evelyn M. Simpson (Berkeley and Los Angeles: University of California Press, 1953–62), 9:131.

12. Ibid., 7:279, 286.

13. See Scott Colley, "Richard III and Herod," *SQ* 37 (1986): 451–58; Glynne Wickham, *Shakespeare's Dramatic Heritage* (London: Routledge and Kegan Paul, 1969), 225–31. For the argument that Shakespeare in *Macbeth, Richard III,* and other plays subverts the primal power of motherhood, see Adelman, *Suffocating Mothers.*

14. For other metaphoric male pregnancies, see Sonnets 1–18, 22, 59, 86, 97, 98, 102, 114; *Tempest* 1.2.92–97, 155–57.

15. Anselm Strittmatter, "Christmas and the Epiphany, Origins and Antecedents," *Thought* 17 (1942): 600–626; Theodor E. Mommsen, "Aponius and Orosius on the Significance of the Epiphany," in *Medieval and Renaissance Studies,* ed. Eugene F. Rice, Jr. (Ithaca: Cornell University Press, 1959), 299–324; Augustine, *Sermons for Christmas and Epiphany,* trans. Thomas Comerford Lawler (New York: Newman Press, 1952).

16. Andrewes, *Works,* 3:241–60.

17. See also Pilate's hand-washing in, for example, the York Tilemakers' play (*The York Plays,* ed. Richard Beadle [London: Edward Arnold, 1982]), 304–5.

18. For baptismal storms, see E. J. Devereux, "Sacramental Imagery in *The Tempest,*" *Bulletin de l'Association Canadienne des Humanités* 19 (1968): 50–62; John Cunningham, "*King Lear,* the Storm, and the Liturgy," *Christianity and Literature* 34 (1984): 9–30.

19. Cunningham, "*King Lear,* The Storm, and the Liturgy."

20. See Arthur Kirsch, *Shakespeare and the Experience of Love* (New York: Cambridge University Press, 1981), 160–63.

21. As with the brutal effort to convert Malvolio, Shylock's forced baptism is, of course, not likely to induce change of heart or genuine epiphany: both men's self-deifying, self-deceiving contempt for others is answered not with Christlike loving forgiveness but with correspondingly bitter, vengeful force, setting apart rather than integrating. See Joseph A. Bryant, Jr., *Hippolyta's View: Some Christian Aspects of Shakespeare's Plays* (Lexington: University Press of Kentucky, 1961), 33–51; Allan Holaday, "Antonio and the Allegory of Salvation," *ShakS* 4 (1968): 109–18; Ruth Levitsky, "Shylock as Unregenerate Man," *SQ* 28 (1977): 58–64; Lawrence Danson, *The Harmonies of "The Merchant of Venice"* (New Haven: Yale University Press, 1978), 164–69.

22. Andrewes, *Works,* 3:243, citing 1 Tim. 6.9, 2 Pet. 2.22.

23. John Anthony McGuckin, *The Transfiguration of Christ in Scripture and Tradition* (Lewiston/Queenston: Edwin Mellen, 1986); Kirk, *The Vision of God,* 97–101.

24. Bryant, *Hippolyta's View,* 1–18.

25. McGuckin, *The Transfiguration of Christ,* 15.

26. Shakespeare qualifies Hal's messianic activity by mixing pagan theology and Ovidian myth. See Bryant, *Hippolyta's View,* "Prince Hal and the Ephesians," 52–67; *Shakespeare's Christian Dimension: An Anthology of Criticism,* ed. Roy Battenhouse (Bloomington: Indiana University Press, 1994), 315–26. Paul Siegel surveys various resurrection motifs in "Shakespeare's Kneeling-Resurrection Pattern and the Meaning of *King Lear,*" *Shakespeare in His Time and Ours* (South Bend: University of Notre Dame Press, 1968), 108–21.

27. For discussion of Shakespeare's enlisting pagan deities for the anagnorises of the romances, see Kenneth Muir, "Theophanies in the Last Plays," in *Shakespeare: Contrasts and Controversies* (Norman: University of Oklahoma Press, 1985).

28. For examples of the Passion as the main object of contemplation and epiphanal vision in Reformation England, see Louis Martz, *The Poetry of Meditation* (New Haven: Yale University Press, 1954), 19, 26–30, 71–117, 132–35, 193–97, 250–53, 282–87, 295–309.

29. *Spiritual Exercises and Devotions of Blessed Robert Southwell, S. J.,* trans. P. E. Hallett (London: Sheed and Ward, 1931), 47–48, as quoted in Martz, ibid., 29.

30. Andrewes, *Works,* 2:122–23, 132–33. I cite Andrewes's Good-Friday sermon on Zechariah 12.10 ("And they shall look upon Me, Whom they have pierced").

31. See Thomas H. Bestul, *Texts of the Passion: Latin Devotional Literature and Medieval Society* (Philadelphia: University of Pennsylvania Press, 1996), chap. 2 ("Medieval Narratives of the Passion of Christ") and chap. 5 ("The Passion of Christ and the Institution of Torture"), 26–68, 145–64.

32. Cordelia's death also recalls the virgin mother's, as in Robert Southwell's "The Death of Our Ladie":

> Weepe, living thinges, of life the mother dyes;
> The world doth loose the summ of all her blisse,
> The Quene of Earth, the Empresse of the skyes,
> By Maryes death mankind an orphan is,
> Lett nature weepe, yea lett all graces mone,
> Their glory, grace, and giftes dye all in one.

(Robert Southwell, *The Complete Poems,* ed. James H. McDonald and Nancy Pollard Brown [Oxford: Clarenden Press, 1967], 11). See also the "Meditation by Bernard on the Lamentation of the Blessed Virgin," in Bestul, *Texts of the Passion,* 165–85.

33. See, for example, Elton, *King Lear and the Gods;* Howard Felperin, *Shakespearean Romances* (Princeton: Princeton University Press, 1972). Cf. Roy Battenhouse, *Shakespearean Tragedy: Its Art and Its Christian Premises* (Bloomington: Indiana University Press, 1969), 269–302, and *Shakespeare's Christian Dimension,* 444–72; Cherrell Guilfoyle, *Shakespeare's Play Within Play* (Kalamazoo, MI: Medieval Institute, 1990), 111–27; Peter Milward, "Notes on the Religious Dimension in *King Lear,*" *English Literature and Language* (Tokyo) 23 (1986): 5–27; Russell A. Peck, "Edgar's Pilgrimage: High Comedy in *King Lear,*" *SEL* 7 (1967): 219–37; Joseph H. Summers, "The Ending of *King Lear,*" in *Dreams of Love and Power* (Oxford: Clarendon Press, 1984), 111–13.

34. See John Freccero, "Medusa: The Letter and the Spirit," in *Dante: The Poetics of Conversion* (Cambridge: Harvard University Press, 1986), 119–35; and the seminal ideas in Sigmund Freud, "Medusa's Head," *SE* 18:273–74.

35. On the coordination of plays with religious festivals, see C. L. Barber, *Shakespeare's Festive Comedy: A Study of Dramatic Form and Its Relation to Social Custom* (Princeton: Princeton University Press, 1959); R. Chris Hassel, Jr., *Renaissance Drama and the English Church Year* (Lincoln: University of Nebraska Press, 1979); Glynne Wickham, *Early English Stages, 1300 to 1660, Volume Three: Plays and Their Makers to 1576* (London and Henley: Routledge and Kegan Paul, 1981), 23–50.

36. See Nevill Coghill, "*All's Well* Revalued," in *Studies in Language and Literature in Honor of Margaret Schlauch,* ed. Mieczyslaw Brahmer et al. (Warsaw: Polish Scientific Publishers, 1966), 71–83; Andrew Turnbull, "Motifs of Bedmate Substitution and Their Reconciliatory Functions in Shakespearean and Jacobean Drama," Ph.D. diss., Indiana University, 1977, 281–326; Gless, *Measure for Measure, the Law, and the Convent,* 56–59, 179–80; Kirsch, *Shakespeare and the Experience of Love,* 80–83, 116–18; Kathleen Ashley, "The Guiler Beguiled: Christ and Satan as Theological Tricksters," *Criticism* 24 (1982): 126–37; Marliss C. Desens, *The Bed-Trick in English Renaissance Drama* (Newark: University of Delaware Press, 1994), 20–24, 139–42.

37. For Kirsch, *Measure for Measure* has "no sense . . . of the epiphanies of the last plays, and perhaps not even of the wonder that characterizes *All's Well That Ends Well*"; yet "the play is nevertheless not without marvellousness, and its own miracles are not less great because we are aware of how they have been contrived" (*Shakespeare and the Experience of Love,* 105–6).

38. For the ghost's nature, provenance, and psychic impact, see, for example, Eleanor Prosser, *Hamlet and Revenge* (Stanford: Stanford University Press, 1967, 1971), chap. 5; John Russell, *Hamlet and Narcissus* (Newark: University of Delaware Press, 1995), chap. 3. Battenhouse calls the vengeful spirit "a reverse analogy to a baptism or a Pentecost" (*Shakespearean Tragedy,* 260–61); Guilfoyle sees it elaborately parodying Christ's nativity in the mystery cycles (*Shakespeare's Play within Play,* 21–39).

39. In *Shakespearean Representation* (Princeton: Princeton University Press, 1977), 64–65, 104–5, Howard Felperin notes Hamlet's obscuring of genuine salvation; Lear's speeches also evoke "Christian mystery" yet vacillate "between demystification and mystification of the self," leaving characters and audiences in a "state of aporia, of being completely at a loss."

40. For fuller discussion of Shakespeare's systematic assault on the three main object relations—authority figures, rival siblings, and infant-nurturers—see chapters 5–6.

41. For Augustine's account of the trinitarian image in human nature, see *The Works of Saint Augustine,* ed. John E. Rotelle, trans. Edmund Hill, pt. 1, 24 vols. (Brooklyn, NY: New City Press, 1990–), 9:1–5; 10:11–12; 14; 15:6–7, 21–23; *The City of God,* 11:24–28, in *Basic Writings of Saint Augustine,* ed. Whitney J. Oates, 2 vols. (New York: Random House, 1948), 2:166–71.

42. David Bakan, *Disease, Pain, and Sacrifice: Toward a Psychology of Suffering* (Boston: Beacon Press, 1968), 79, 99. Cf. Beers, *Women and Sacrifice.*

43. Jean-Paul Sartre, *Being and Nothingness: An Essay on Phenomenological Ontology,* trans. Hazel E. Barnes (1943; reprint, New York: Philosophical Library, 1956), lvii; cf. xlv–lxvii ("The Pursuit of Being"), 221–351 ("Being for Others"), 361–430 ("Concrete Relations with Others").

44. See S. B. Hemingway, "The Relation of *A Midsummer Night's Dream* to *Romeo and Juliet,*" *MLN* (1911); Henry Alonzo Myers, "*Romeo and Juliet* and *A Midsummer Night's Dream:* Tragedy and Comedy," in *Tragedy: A View of Life* (Ithaca: Cornell University Press, 1956).

45. R. S. White, *"Let Wonder Seem Familiar": Endings in Shakespeare's Romance Vision* (London: Athlone Press, 1985), 172; cf. Northrop Frye, *Fables of Identity: Studies in Poetic Mythology* (New York, 1963), 107–18, and *A Natural Perspective: The Development of Shakespearean Comedy and Romance* (New York, 1965); Frank Kermode, *William Shakespeare; The Final Plays* (London: Longman, Green, 1963). See Bibliography, 2A, "Shakespearean Epiphany."

46. Henri Bergson, *Essai sur les données immédiates de la conscience,* 11th ed. (1889; reprint, Paris: F. Alcan, 1912), as translated by Robert Langbaum in *The Word from Below: Essays on Modern Literature and Culture* (Madison: University of Wisconsin Press, 1987), 51.

47. Hunter, *Shakespeare and the Comedy of Forgiveness.*

48. See René Girard, *Violence and the Sacred,* trans. Patrick Gregory (Baltimore: Johns Hopkins University Press, 1977), 250–308; Naomi Liebler, *Shakespeare's Festive Tragedy: The Ritual Foundations of Genre* (London and New York: Routledge, 1995), 85–111, 155–72.

49. For the argument that the mystery cycles, miracle plays, and martyred saint plays (especially Thomas Becket) exercised greater influence on Elizabethan tragedy than morality plays, see John Wasson, "The Morality Play: Ancestor of Elizabethan Drama?" in *The Drama in the Middle Ages: Comparative and Critical Essays,* ed. Clifford Davidson, C. J. Gianakaris, and John H. Stroupe (New York: AMS Press, 1982), 316–27.

50. See Rowland Wymer, *Suicide and Despair in the Jacobean Drama* (New York: St. Martin's Press, 1986), esp. Chap. 6, "Deaths for Love." Cf. Paul N. Siegel, "Christianity and the Religion of Love in *Romeo and Juliet,*" *SQ* 12 (1961): 371–92; Battenhouse, *Shakespearean Tragedy,* 102–30; *Shakespeare's Christian Dimension,* ed. Battenhouse, 363–81; Roland M. Frye, *Shakespeare and Christian Doctrine* (Princeton: Princeton University Press, 1963), 24–31; Walter C. Foreman, *The Music of the Close: The Final Scenes of Shakespeare's Tragedies* (Lexington: University Press of Kentucky, 1978), 29–30, 50–56.

51. See D. Douglas Waters, *Christian Settings in Shakespeare's Tragedies* (London: Associated University Presses, 1994).

52. Foreman, *The Music of the Close,* 1–71.

53. See Frye, *Shakespeare and Christian Doctrine,* 43–45, 57–60.

54. James Joyce, *Stephen Hero,* ed. Theodore Spencer (New York: New Directions, 1963), 211. See Richard Ellmann, *James Joyce* (New York: Oxford University Press, 1959), 87–89, 98, 108, 113, 125, 132, 137, 149; Irene Hendry, "Joyce's Epiphanies," *SR* 54 (1946): 449–67.

55. Morris Beja, *Epiphany in the Modern Novel* (Seattle: University of Washington Press, 1972), 15. Beja cites Gerard Manley Hopkins and T. S. Eliot as exceptions.

56. Ellmann, *James Joyce,* 87.

57. Joyce, *Stephen Hero,* 30.

58. Many of these offers are compromised: Hal, "to save the blood on either side," offers to "try fortune with [Hotspur] in a single fight" (*1 Henry IV* 5.1.99–100); but Battenhouse notes the Augustinian and Erasmian warnings against such privileging of worldly glory, especially through militarism ("*Henry V* in the Light of Erasmus," *ShakS* 17 [1985]: 77–88); see also Harold C. Goddard, *The Meaning of Shakespeare,* 2 vols. (1951; reprint, Chicago: University of Chicago Press, 1960), 217–60.

59. Beja, *Epiphany in the Modern Novel,* 16–17.

60. See Bibliography, 2B, "Epiphany in Modern Literature."

61. *Much Ado* 5.4.69. See also Felperin, *Shakespearean Romances,* for discussion of the use of colloquial language in these plays.

62. See Muir, "Theophanies in the Last Plays."

63. Exceptions include Flannery O'Connor and Walker Percy.

64. William Faulkner, "The Bear," in *Go Down, Moses* (New York: Random House, 1940), 209, 254–315, 330–31. See Francis Lee Utley, "Pride and Humility: The Cultural Roots of Ike McCaslin," in *Bear, Man, and God: Seven Approaches to William Faulkner's "The Bear,"* ed. F. L. Utley et al. (New York: Random House, 1964), 233–60; Irving Malin, *William Faulkner: An Interpretation* (Stanford: Stanford University Press, 1957), 70–73; R. W. B. Lewis, "The Hero in the New World: William Faulkner's *The Bear,*" *Kenyon Review* 13 (1951): 641–60; Olga W. Vickery, *The Novels of William Faulkner* (Baton Rouge: Louisiana State University, 1959), 130–34.

65. See Paul Weiss, *Modes of Being* (Carbondale: Southern Illinois University Press, 1958).

66. Andrewes, *Works,* 3:371–72.

CHAPTER 4: IMMANENT EPIPHANIES

1. See Odon Lottin, *Psychologie et morale aux xii et xiii siècles,* 2 vols. (1942; reprint, Gembloux, Belgium: J. Duculot, 1960); G. Verbeke, *L'Évolution de la doctrine du pneuma du Stoicisme à S. Augustin* (Paris: Desclée de Brouwer and Louvain: Éditions de l'Institut Superieur de Philosophie, 1945).

2. An Aristotelian bias properly governs studies of Shakespearean psychology, as in the classic study by Ruth L. Anderson, *Elizabethan Psychology and Shakespeare's Plays* (Iowa City: University of Iowa Press, 1927). Many scholars, however, assume this Aristotelean-Galenic model as virtually the exclusive Renaissance psychology, ignoring the continued vitality of Pythagorean, Platonic, and Augustinian idealism, as noted in studies by S. K. Heninger. Of the major general studies of Renaissance psychology, only Herschel Baker has acknowledged the varied provenances of body-soul models (*The Dignity of Man* [Cambridge: Harvard University Press, 1947]). See the studies listed in Bibliography, 3A.

3. For discussion of English Renaissance access to Platonic and Christian-Platonic psychology, see Robert L. Reid, "Psychology, Platonic," in *SpEncy.*

4. A. G. van Kranendonk, "Spenserian Echoes in *A Midsummer Night's Dream,*" *ES* 14 (1932): 209–13; "Shakespeare's Platonische Wende," in *Anglo-Americana,* ed. Karl Brunner (Stuttgart: Wilhelm Braumuller, 1955), 62–71; James P. Bednarz, "Imitations of Spenser in *A Midsummer Night's Dream,*" *RenD* 14 (1983): 79–102; the Arden *A Midsummer Night's Dream,* ed. Harold Brooks (London: Methuen, 1979), xxxiv–xxxix, lviii–lxii; Robert L. Reid, "The Fairy Queen: Gloriana or Titania?" *UCrow* 13 (1993): 16–32.

5. Augustine, *Soliloquia* 1.2.7. Cf. *De quantitate animae* 14.24; *De ordinantia* 2.18.47: "The study of philosophy . . . treats of two problems: one regarding the soul, the other regarding God. The goal of the first is to know ourselves; the goal of the second is to know our origin. . . . The former makes us fit for a happy life; the latter gives us happiness."

6. Northrop Frye, *Words with Power, Being a Second Study of "The Bible and Literature"* (New York: Harcourt, Brace, Jovanovitch, 1990), 97–135, esp. 121–29.

7. Verbeke, *L'Évolution de la doctrine du pneuma du Stoicisme à S. Augustin*, 11–174, 175–220. For links between Stoicism and the Renaissance, especially Avicenna's *Canon*, see E. Ruth Harvey, "Psychology," in *SpEncy*.

8. John Donne, "The Exstasie," in *The Complete Poetry and Selected Prose of John Donne*, ed. John Hayward (New York: Modern Library, 1946), 35.

9. Hankins, *Backgrounds of Shakespeare's Thought*, 87. See Levinus Lemnius, *The Touchstone of Complexions*, trans. Thomas Newton (London, 1576), 1.2.12–15.

10. Harvey, "Psychology," *SpEncy*, 565–68. Cf. Anderson, *Elizabethan Psychology and Shakespeare's Plays.*

11. Pierre de la Primaudaye, *The French Academie*, trans. Thomas Bowes (London, 1586; reprint, 1618), 2.63.522, 2.78.564.

12. La Primaudaye's highlighting the tripartism of body and of soul (as in his conclusion) corresponds to the main structural principle of Spenser's allegory. Both syncretize pagan and Christian tripartite structures (Platonic, Aristotelian, Galenic, Neoplatonic, Augustinian) throughout their work, especially in Spenser's mythic structures—three chambers in every house, temple, garden, cave or underworld, as well as three graces, nine muses, six stages of lechery and of jealousy, six virtues in Venus's Temple.

13. La Primaudaye's *French Academie*, Pt. 2 (1580; Eng. trans. 1586), established the pattern for many English and French treatises on the theme of "know thyself," including Sir John Davies, *Nosce Teipsum* (1592–94, 1599); Thomas Barckley, *Felicitie of Man* (1598); Pierre Charron, *Of Wisdome* (1601); John Davies of Hereford, *Microcosmus* (1603), *Mirum in Modum* (1604), *Summa Totalis* (1607).

14. Timothy Bright, *A Treatise of Melancholie* (London, 1586). Cf. Mary Isabelle O'-Sullivan, "Hamlet and Dr. Timothy Bright," *PMLA* 41 (1926): 667–79; Babb, *The Elizabethan Malady;* Lyons, *Voices of Melancholy.*

15. Robert Burton, *The Anatomy of Melancholy*, ed. Holbrook Jackson (New York: Vintage Books, 1977).

16. See Graham Bradshaw, *Shakespeare's Skepticism* (Brighton, England: Harvester Press and New York: St. Martin's Press, 1987); Elton, *King Lear and the Gods;* Cavell, *Disowning Knowledge in Six Plays of Shakespeare;* and cf. the studies of Renaissance skepticism in Bibliography, 4.

17. For Shakespeare's use of clouds to express skepticism, see *Hamlet* 3.1.65, 3.2.393; *Timon of Athens* 4.2.34; *Antony and Cleopatra* 4.14.2; 5.2.74, 302; *Coriolanus* 4.5.109; *Tempest* 4.1.150–56.

18. The medieval hierarchy of dream-types ranges from the nightmarish *insomnium* and hallucinative *visium* to the ordinary but enigmatic *somnium*, to the prophetic *oraculum* and exalted *visio*. See Constance B. Hieatt, *The Realism of Dream Visions* (The Hague and Paris: Mouton, 1967), 14–33. Cf. Manfred Weidhorn, *Dreams in Seventeenth-Century English Literature* (The Hague and Paris: Mouton, 1970); Carol Schneider Rupprecht, "Dreams," in *SpEncy.*

19. See Plato, *Phaedrus;* Sidney, *Astrophil and Stella* 1, 15; Spenser, *Faerie Queene* 2.12.47; Shakespeare, Sonnets 1–18, 22, 59, 86, 97, 98, 102, 114, interweaving metaphors of generation, self-generation, and imaginative generation by the pregnant poet whose love-labors and art-labors seek to bring forth a more refined and constant beauty in the beloved. Cf. the motif's greater complexity in *Tempest* 1.2.155–57, 92–97.

20. Shakespeare's dreams include wishful self-delusions and fear-generated nightmares, oracular prophecies and holy visions, and comic parodies (*Taming of the Shrew* Induc.2.71, 114; *A Midsummer Night's Dream* 4.1.203; *2 Henry IV* 5.5.53; *Measure for Measure* 3.1.34; *Antony and Cleopatra* 5.2.76–97; *Pericles* 4.5.5, 5.1.163, 250; *Cymbeline* 4.2.309, 349–54, 5.4.128–46, 5.5.180; *Tempest* 3.2.149, 4.1.157–58. See Frankie Rubinstein, "Shakespeare's Dream-Stuff: A Forerunner of Freud's 'Dream-Material,'" *AI* 43 (1986): 335–55.

21. Bullough, *Mirror of Minds*, 2–4. I have synthesized Bullough's list of ten common assumptions about human nature.

22. Joseph B. Collins, *Christian Mysticism in the Elizabethan Age* (Baltimore: Johns Hopkins University Press, 1940).

23. For discussion of number symbolism in Pythagorean-Platonic psychology, epitomized by Plato's *Timaeus* and fully exploited in the allegories of Dante and Spenser, see the commentaries in the Bibliography, 3B.

24. For Shakespeare's many allusions to Paul's letters and for Pauline Christianity's predominance in Reformation England, see Roger Cox, "*King Lear* and the Corinthian Letters," in *Between Earth and Heaven* (New York: Holt, Rinehart, 1969), 82–90; Peter Milward, *Shakespeare's Religious Background* (Bloomington: Indiana University Press, 1973) and *Biblical Influences in Shakespeare's Great Tragedies* (Bloomington: Indiana University Press, 1987).

25. Cf. Petruchio's abuse of Kate; Richard III's seduction-disposal of Lady Anne; Oberon's subjecting Titania to bestiality; the monstrous power-hunger in Goneril, Regan, Lady Macbeth, Volumnia; the public shaming of Hero, Ophelia, Desdemona, Cordelia, Hermione.

26. For Spenser's and Shakespeare's uses of androgyny and hermaphroditism, see Lauren Silberman, "The Hermaphrodite and the Metamorphosis of Spenserian Allegory," *ELR* 17 (1987): 207–23, and "Hermaphrodite," in *SpEncy;* Albert R. Cirillo, "The Fair Hermaphrodite: Love-Union in the Poetry of Donne and Spenser," *SEL* 9 (1969): 81–95; Donald Cheney, "Spenser's Hermaphrodite and the 1590 *Faerie Queene*," *PMLA* 87 (1972): 192–200; Camille Paglia, "The Apollonian Androgyne and the *Faerie Queene*," *ELR* 9 (1979): 42–63; Margaret Boerner Beckman, "The Figure of Rosalind in *As You Like It*," *SQ* 29 (1978): 44–51; Robert Kimbrough, *Shakespeare and the Art of Humankindness: the essay toward androgyny* (Atlantic Highlands: Humanities Press International, 1990).

27. For commentary on epiphanal recognition in Shakespeare's romances, see the Bibliography, 2A.

28. A. C. Bradley, "On Coriolanus," noted in the Arden edition of *As You Like It*, ed. Harold Jenkins (5.1.6–7 n).

29. For discussion of Plato's and Spenser's tripartite hierarchic model of self, family, and commonwealth, see Robert L. Reid, "Spenserian Psychology and the Structure of Allegory in Books I and II of *The Faerie Queene*," *MP* 79 (1981–82): 359–75.

30. Andrewes, *Works*, 1:33.

31. Ibid., 1:34.

32. See Kolve, *The Play Called Corpus Christi*, 124–74.

33. Paul Ricoeur, *Oneself as Another*, trans. Kathleen Blamey (Chicago: University of Chicago Press, 1992), 355. Cf. C. S. Lewis, *Till We Have Faces* (1958; Old Tappan: Macmillan, 1998).

34. The exception is *Henry VIII*, with twenty-one uses.

35. Lear's possible vision of Cordelia's spirit at the words "Look there! Look there!" is noted by Elton, *King Lear and the Gods,* 258 n; Thomas Clayton, "'Is this the promis'd end?' Revision in the Role of the King," *The Division of the Kingdom: Shakespeare's Two Versions of King Lear,* ed. Gary Taylor and Michael Warren (Oxford: Clarendon Press, 1983), 121–41; Bettie Anne Doebler, *"Rooted Sorrow": Dying in Early Modern England* (Rutherford: Fairleigh Dickinson University, 1994), 168–69.

36. See Harold Skulsky, "Despair," in *SpEncy.*

37. Schwartz, *The Mortal Worm: Shakespeare's Master Theme* (Port Washington: Kennikat Press, 1977).

38. Where Shakespeare activates empirical and spiritual meanings in the same usage, I have counted it both ways.

39. For discussion of the questionable reality of the Weird sisters and of evil, see Curry, *Shakespeare's Philosophical Patterns* (1937; reprint, Magnolia: Peter Smith, 1990); Robert H. West, *Shakespeare and the Outer Mystery* (Lexington: University Press of Kentucky, 1968).

40. See Janet Clare, *"Art made tongue-tied by authority": Elizabethan and Jacobean Dramatic Censorship* (Manchester: Manchester University Press, 1990), 103–4.

41. On Spenser's complex symbolism of human psychology by means of pagan deities, notably Venus and Cupid, see the works listed in Bibliography, 3C, esp. those of Roche, Nestrick, Nohrnberg, and Hyde.

42. On the subordination of pagan deities to Christian doctrine in Medieval (and Spenserian) mythography and psychological symbolism, see the commentaries in the Bibliography, 3C, especially Conti, Panofsky, and Seznec. On the reversal of this practice by Marlowe, Shakespeare, and other Renaissance poets, see Daniel Javitch, "Rescuing Ovid from the Allegorizers," *CL* 30 (1978): 97–107; Leonard Barkan, *The Gods Made Flesh: Metamorphosis & the Pursuit of Paganism* (New Haven: Yale University Press, 1986), chaps. 3–5.

43. For discussion of pluralistic attitudes toward supernatural beings in the English Renaissance, see Robert H. West, *The Invisible World: A Study of Pneumatology in Elizabethan Drama* (1939; reprint, New York: Octagon Books, 1969), 1–53.

44. See Augustine, *The City of God,* trans. Henry Bettenson (Baltimore: Penguin Books, 1972), 13:17–18; 20:6; 22:4–5, 11–21.

CHAPTER 5: MACBETH'S THREE MURDERS

1. Freud's argument for the second instinctual drive, the aggressive death-wish, grew out of his reflections on the "repetition compulsion"—obsessive reenacting of a pleasurable sensation, or of a painful and self-destructive behavior. The motive, he felt, was not simply to sustain pleasure or pain, but subconsciously to use it as a means of recovering primal experience, especially in the case of the aggressive and destructive obsession, which he attributed to a desire to return to peaceful nothingness. See Bibliography, 5H, "Repetition Compulsion."

2. See Bibliography, 5E, "Oedipal Conflict (*Macbeth*)." For revisionary studies of gender-psychology, shifting attention from embattled father to devouring mother, or reformulating gender roles, see Bibliography, 5F, "Preoedipal Conflict (*Macbeth*)," and 5B, "Gender Stereotyping, Reversal, and Transference."

3. Foakes, "Images of Death: Ambition in *Macbeth*," *Focus on Macbeth*, ed. John Russell Brown (London: Routledge and Kegan Paul, 1982), 18.

4. Julian Markels, "The Spectacle of Deterioration: Macbeth and the 'Manner' of Tragic Deterioration," *SQ* 12 (1961): 293–303.

5. Heilman, Muir, and Sanders insist on Macbeth's greatness of spirit but also on the sordid depths of his degradation (Robert B. Heilman, "The Criminal as Tragic Hero: Dramatic Methods," *ShS* 19 [1966]: 12–24; Kenneth Muir, introduction, *Macbeth*, New Arden Ed. [London: Methuen, 1987], xliii–liii, lxv; Wilbur Sanders, *The Dramatist and the Received Idea* [Cambridge: Cambridge University Press, 1968], 253–316). Cf. A. C. Bradley, *Shakespearean Tragedies,* 2nd ed. (1905; reprint, New York: Macmillan, 1949), 349–65; A. P. Rossiter, *Angel with Horns,* ed. Graham Storey (New York: Theatre Arts, 1961), 209–34; Paul A. Jorgensen, *Our Naked Frailties: Sensational Art and Meaning in Macbeth* (Berkeley: University of California Press, 1971), 185–216; Maynard Mack, Jr., *Killing the King* (New Haven: Yale University Press, 1973), 138–85; Arthur Kirsch, "Macbeth's Suicide," *ELH* 51 (1984): 269–96.

6. This "object relations" pattern was (in slightly different form) first noted by L. Veszy-Wagner, "*Macbeth:* 'Fair is Foul and Foul is Fair,'" *AI* 25 (1968): 242–57. Though she subordinates each victim to a patriarchal version of the Oedipal struggle, she acutely observes that Macbeth's "main problem is . . . uncertain identity" with regard to gender.

7. See Jones, *Scenic Form in Shakespeare,* 195–224.

8. For detailed treatment of this three-part structure of *Macbeth*, see *ibid.* For discussion of three stages of self-discovery in Shakespeare's tragic form, see Maynard Mack, "The Jacobean Shakespeare," 11–42.

9. See Muir's Introduction to *Macbeth,*" xxxvi–xliii; Muriel C. Bradbrook, "The Sources of *Macbeth*," *ShS* 4 (1951): 35–48; David Norbrook, "*Macbeth* and the Politics of Historiography," in *Politics of Discourse: The Literature and History of 17th-Century England,* ed. Kevin Sharpe and Steven N. Zwicker (Berkeley and Los Angeles: University of California Press, 1987), 78–116.

10. Sanders, *The Dramatist and the Received Idea,* 253–316. Cf. Harry Berger, Jr., "The Early Scenes of *Macbeth:* Preface to a New Interpretation," *ELH* 47 (1980): 1–31; James L. Calderwood, *If It Were Done: Macbeth and Tragic Action* (Amherst: University of Massachusetts Press, 1986), 119–21; Graham Bradshaw, *Shakespeare's Skepticism* (New York: St. Martin's Press, 1987), 244–50; Adelman, "'Born of Woman,'" 93–94.

11. Berger, "The Early Scenes of *Macbeth*" Calderwood, *If It Were Done.* Other sharp questioners of Banquo include Bradley, *Shakespearean Tragedies,* 379–87; Roy Walker, *The Time Is Free* (London: Andrew Dakers, 1949), 89–92; Richard J. Jaarsma, "The Tragedy of Banquo," *L&P* 17 (1967): 87–94.

12. Adelman, "'Born of Woman'"; Hunter, "Doubling, Mythic Difference."

13. See Bibliography, 5J, "Superego-formation."

14. See D. W. Harding, Robert Kimbrough, Marilyn French, Coppélia Kahn, Janet Adelman, and Dianne Hunter in Bibliography, 5B, "Gender Stereotyping, Reversal, and Transference," and 5F, "Preoedipal Conflict."

15. See Stephen Orgel and Louis A. Montrose in *Rewriting the Renaissance: The Discourses of Sexual Difference in Early Modern Europe,* ed. Margaret W. Ferguson, Maureen Quilligan, and Nancy J. Vickers (Chicago: University of Chicago Press, 1986), 58–59, 65–87.

For the Renaissance view of conscience or synteresis as a means of consolidating mental powers and gender-components of human nature, see Pierre de la Primaudaye, *The French Academie*, 2:364–511, esp. on restoring the Edenic communion between heart (437–511) and head (364–436).

16. See Bibliography, 5I, "Sublimation." In *The Ego and the Mechanisms of Defense* Anna Freud described ego-functions as not only defensive but constructive. Hartmann and other ego psychologists, by replacing "sublimation" with "neutralization" and "desexualization," tended to villify the libido and to ignore the constructive activity of sublimation. It plays a vital role in the struggle for what Kohut calls "grandiose selfhood," the process so travestied by the Macbeths. For discussion of the closely-related processes of sublimation, superego formation, and therapeutic transference, see Loewald, *Sublimation*, chaps. 1–2; and Kohut, *The Analysis of the Self*, 309–24.

17. Aquinas, *Summa Theologica*, 2 vols. (Chicago: Encyclopedia Britannica, 1952), 1.63.2.

18. For a different view of the analogy between Cain and Macbeth, see Jorgensen, *Our Naked Frailties*, 47–51, 190–95, 200, 213.

19. Ibid., 194. Robert Weimann similarly explains Lear's shifts from dialogue to monologue during his madness (*Shakespeare and the Popular Tradition in the Theater*, 217–21). Cf. Barry Weller, "Identity and Representation in Shakespeare," *ELH* 49 (1982): 356–58.

20. On the key role of projection in psychological development, see Bibliography, 5G, "Projection and Projective Identification." Melanie Klein, in "Notes on Some Schizoid Mechanisms" and in *The Psychoanalysis of Children* (142–48, 178), established a pattern in childhood development of *introjection-projection-reintrojection*. But the reintrojection-phase occurs on a higher level, as in sublimation, and this higher level is made possible by the stimulating effect of projection. Thus reintrojection, like Wordsworth's "recollection in tranquillity", is a culminating mode of psychic internalization and identity-construction occurring on a more comprehensive, controlled, and "sublime" level. Cf. Knight, "Introjection, Projection, and Identification"; and Anna Freud, *The Ego and the Mechanisms of Defense*, 50–53.

21. This theory, first advanced by Allan Park Paton, *N&Q* (1869), was lucidly reformulated by Harold Goddard in Vol. 2 of *The Meaning of Shakespeare*, 122–26.

22. George W. Williams, "The Third Murderer in *Macbeth*," *SQ* 23 (1972): 261.

23. George W. Williams, "*Macbeth:* King James's Play," *SoAR* 47 (1982): 12–21.

24. See Bibliography, 5A, "Dissociation, Doubling, Multiple Personality, and Splitting." No critic has fully considered Banquo as Macbeth's "double." Robert N. Watson briefly mentions Banquo as "doppelgänger" ("'Thriftless Ambition,' Foolish Wishes, and the Tragedy of *Macbeth*," in *William Shakespeare's Macbeth*, ed. Harold Bloom [New York: Chelsea House, 1987], 142–47); James Kirsch describes the "participation mystique" of the two men, Macbeth being more attuned to the unconscious, but the weaker ego (*Shakespeare's Royal Self* [New York: G. P. Putnam, 1965], 331–39); Matthew N. Proser describes Banquo's ghost "as a kind of analogy for Macbeth's mutilated soul" (*The Heroic Image in Five Shakespearean Tragedies* [Princeton: Princeton University Press, 1965], 76–78). In *A Psychoanalytic Study of the Double in Literature*, Robert Rogers builds on Freud's reading of *Macbeth* when he identifies Macbeth and Lady Macbeth as doubles; Rogers does not distinguish between the customary homoerotic phenomenon of mirror-transference (between close friends,

sibling rivals, or hero and alter-ego) and the more complex psychic transference between heterosexual partners in marriage.

25. Hogan, "*Macbeth:* Authority and Progenitorship," sees the slaughter as repeating the Oedipal struggle, an indirect blow at Macduff as threatening authority and as fertile progenitor.

26. See Bibliography, 5D, "Narcissism and Self-love." One must distinguish Macbeth's tyrannous infantilism (culminating in narcissistic rage) from the healthy oral-narcissistic bond, involving mutual respect between parent and child during the sucking stage. For negative aspects of narcissism, see S. Freud, "On Narcissism: An Introduction"; Kernberg, *Borderline Conditions and Pathological Narcissism;* and the important Shakespearean studies by Kirsch, "Macbeth's Suicide"; and Adelman, "'Born of Woman,'" and "'Anger's My Meat.'" For positive modes of narcissism, see Kohut, "Forms and Transformations of Narcissism"; and Benjamin, *The Bonds of Love.* Shakespeare seems particularly attuned to this primitive cathexis which forms the core of human identity, emphasizing not just negative but positive aspects of mother-child bonding in the cathartic sequence of each mature tragedy, most strikingly in Cleopatra's death-scene ("Dost thou not see the baby at my breast / That sucks the nurse asleep?").

27. See Bibliography, 5C, "Introjection, Internalization, Identification."

28. Though the cathartic valuation of womanly/matronly nurture in acts 4–5 holds true for all of Shakespeare's major tragedies, *Hamlet* requires qualification. Never fully reunited with Ophelia or Gertrude, Hamlet only incipiently comprehends the meaning of a grave holding his "fool" and his beloved (a synthesis so richly explored in *King Lear*). *Hamlet's* final focus on the killing of a false parent-king, of an inadequate sibling-double (Laertes), and of a disloyal nurturing mother suggests unresolved Oedipal (and pre-Oedipal) anxieties and an incomplete quest for identity.

29. See Bibliography, 5K, "Vagina Dentata and Penis Dentata," especially Roy Schafer, *Language and Insight,* who provides a broad gender analysis (153–60). The demoniac symbolism in *Macbeth* combines male and female perversions. In tempting Macbeth to annihilate children, the demon masters' "armed head" (*penis dentata*) joins the witches' devouring cauldron (*vagina dentata*) (4.1.69–86). This satanic collusion of perverted gender components, a marital travesty which promotes mutual deception and annihilation rather than mutual support and procreation, evolves throughout the play.

CHAPTER 6: LEAR'S THREE SHAMINGS

1. In "The Uniqueness of *King Lear*," *ShJE* (1984): 44–61, E. A. J. Honigmann calls *Lear* an "Oedipus-Everyman play," in which "a sinner who becomes a thinker . . . suffers rather than initiates action" (47). To this universal sufferance-myth one might add the stories of Job and Prometheus, who also figure as prominent analogues for Lear. Yet all of these, except Job, actively initiate and sustain their own suffering—and none more than Lear.

2. Bradley, "Construction in Shakespeare's Tragedies," in *Shakespearean Tragedy;* Jones, *Scenic Form in Shakespeare,* 152–94.

3. Snyder, *The Comic Matrix of Shakespeare's Tragedies,* 137–79; Stephen Booth, *King*

Lear, Macbeth, Indefinition and Tragedy (New Haven: Yale University Press, 1983), chap. 1.

4. Ernest Becker, *The Denial of Death* (New York: Free Press, 1973), 36–46, 115–23.

5. Elton, *King Lear and the Gods,* 63–71; Harry Berger, Jr., "*King Lear:* The Lear Family Romance," *Centennial Review* 23 (1979): 348–76.

6. For discussion of act divisions in the folio *Lear,* see Jones, *Scenic Form in Shakespeare,* 160; G. Taylor, "The Structure of Performance," 48–50; Jewkes, *Act Division in Elizabethan and Jacobean Plays, 35–40.*

7. George W. Williams, by examining "twenty-one specific petitions . . . to the gods, to the heaven(s), and to Nature or Fortune," discovers a more optimistic dialogue with divinity than that described by William R. Elton, Susan Snyder, and others ("Petitionary Prayer in *King Lear,*" *SAQ* 85 (1986): 360–73.

8. Gary Taylor, *To Analyze Delight: A Hedonist Criticism of Shakespeare* (Newark: University of Delaware Press, 1985), 162–236.

9. Heilman, *This Great Stage;* Mack, *Everybody's Shakespeare: Reflections Chiefly on the Tragedies* (Lincoln: University of Nebraska Press, 1993), 172–75.

10. See, for example, Soellner, *Shakespeare's Patterns of Self-Knowledge;* Paul Jorgensen, *Lear's Self-Discovery* (Berkeley and Los Angeles: University of California Press, 1981).

11. Lawrence Josephs, *Character Structure and the Organization of the Self* (New York: Columbia University Press, 1992), chap. 5 ("The Archaic Relational Matrix").

12. See Frederick Kiefer, *Fortune and Elizabethan Tragedy* (San Marino, CA: Huntington Library, 1983), 296. See the comments on Fortune by Kent (2.2.176, 5.3.282–83), the Fool (2.4.70–73; 3.2.76), Edgar (3.6.101–114; 4.1–12; 5.2.9–11), Cordelia (5.3.3–6), Lear (5.3.16–19), and Edmund (5.3.29–34). Cf. Vincenzo Cioffari, "Fortune, Fate, and Chance," in *Dictionary of the History of Ideas,* 2:225–36, and *Fortune and Fate from Democritus to St. Thomas Aquinas* (New York. Privately Printed, 1935); Rolf Soellner, "*King Lear* and the Magic of the Wheel," *SQ* 35 (1984): 274–89; Howard R. Patch, *The Goddess Fortuna in Medieval Literature* (Cambridge: Harvard University Press, 1927); Raymond Chapman, "The Wheel of Fortune in Shakespeare's Historical Plays," *RES* 1 (1950): 1–7; Russell A. Fraser, *Shakespeare's Poetics in Relation to King Lear* (London: Routledge and Kegan Paul, 1962), 46–60; Samuel C. Chew, *The Pilgrimage of Life* (New Haven: Yale University Press, 1962), 22–69; Elton, *King Lear and the Gods;* Northrop Frye, *Fools of Time,* 13–14, 88–95, 116; Leo Salingar, *Shakespeare and the Traditions of Comedy* (Cambridge: Cambridge University Press, 1974), 129–74.

13. Elton, *King Lear and the Gods,* 63–71.

14. See Bibliography, 5H, "Repetition Compulsion."

15. Mark Rose, *Shakespearean Design,* 13–15, 35–39, 43–44, 126, 151, 179 n. 21.

16. For discussion of Lady Macbeth's demonism, see W. Moelwyn Merchant, "'His Fiend-like Queen,'" *ShS* 19 (1966): 75–94.

17. Inga-Stina Ewbank traces the sterility wish in *Lear* and *Macbeth* to *Medea,* "The Fiend-like Queen: A Note on 'Macbeth' and Seneca's 'Medea,'" *ShS* 19 (1966): 82–94.

18. Cf. 1.4.170, 268, 274–88, 2.4.129–31, 172–73, 278–85, 3.2.7–9.

19. See Bibliography, 5I, "Sublimation."

20. On the universal psychological content of Lear's love-test, see Alan Dundes, "'To Love My Father All': A Psychoanalytic Study of the Folktale Source of *King Lear,*" *Southern Folklore Quarterly* 40 (1976): 353–66.

21. See Ricoeur, *Oneself as Another,* 336–39.

22. Boethius, "The Consolation of Philosphy," trans. S. J. Tester, in *The Theological Tractates and The Consolation of Philosophy* ed. E. H. Warmington (Cambridge: Harvard University Press and London: William Heinemann 1978), 325–31.

23. That Lear in his central cycle induces his own madness in self-exile on a stormy heath, while Macbeth deceitfully hosts an inaugural banquet, epitomizes their contrary developments.

24. For the iconographic linking of fortune with tempest, apparently as synonyms (both driven by time, temporality), see Edgar Wind, *Giorgione's "Tempesta" with Comments on Giorgione's Poetic Allegories* (Oxford: Clarendon Press, 1969); Kiefer, *Fortune and Elizabethan Tragedy,* 287.

25. See Stephen Greenblatt, "Shakespeare and the Exorcists," in *Shakespearean Negotiations* (Berkeley: University of California Press, 1988), 94–128; John L. Murphy, *Darkness and Devils: Exorcism in King Lear* (Athens: Ohio State University Press, 1984), chap. 7.

26. Nicholas Grene, *Shakespeare's Tragic Imagination* (New York: St. Martin's Press, 1992), 178.

27. William Gulstad, "Mock-Trial or Witch-Trial in *King Lear?*" *N&Q* 239 (4) (1994): 494–97.

28. See Bibliography, 5G, "Projection and Projective Identification."

29. Berger, "The Lear Family Romance," 356–64; Alexander Leggatt, *King Lear* (New York: Harvester Press, 1988), 33, 79-81; Jonathan Dollimore, *Radical Tragedy: Religion, Ideology and Power in the Drama of Shakespeare and His Contemporaries* (Chicago: Chicago University Press, 1984), 189–203; and Sears Jayne, "Charity in *King Lear,*" *SQ* 15 (1964): 277–88, who finds "no compensating love anywhere in the world of this play" (285). A more balanced view is Kent Cartwright's tracing of the audience's alternating engagement with and detachment from Lear, in *Shakespearean Tragedy and Its Double: The Rhythms of Audience Response* (University Park: Pennsylvania State University, 1991), 181–226, esp. 202–16.

30. For St. Augustine, sane self-love reflects Creator love (*De moribus ecclesiae* 25.46–29.61; *De trinitate* 8–15). See Bibliography, 5D, "Narcissism and Self-love."

31. Berger, "The Lear Family Romance," 367–76.

32. On the Cynic philosophers' wise madness in connection with Poor Tom, see E. M. M. Taylor, "Lear's Philosopher," *SQ* 6 (1955): 364–65; Soellner, *Shakespeare's Patterns of Self-Knowledge,* 300–302; Jane Donawerth, "Diogenes the Cynic and Lear's Definition of Man, *King Lear* III iv 101–109," *ELN* (Sept. 1977): 10–14; F. G. Butler, "Who Are King Lear's Philosophers? An Answer, with Some Help from Erasmus," *ES* 67 (1986): 511–24; Steven Doloff, "'Let me talk with this philosopher': The Alexander/Diogenes Paradigm in *King Lear,*" *HLQ* 54 (1991): 253–55. Cf. John Leon Lievsay, "Some Renaissance Views of Diogenes the Cynic," *Joseph Quincy Adams Memorial Studies,* ed. J. G. McManaway, G. E. Dawson, and E. E. Willoughby (Washington, D. C.: Folger Library, 1948), 447–55. In Elton's more pessimistic reading, Lear's "philosopher" visually parodies Stoic denial of passion, and asking him the cause of thunder undermines belief in providence (97–98, 197–213).

33. For Erasmus's and Montaigne's satire of presumption and praise of folly (exemplified on the heath and in Lear's "sermon" to Gloucester in act 4), see Peter McNamara, "*King Lear* and Comic Acceptance," *Erasmus Review* 1 (1971): 95–105; Elton, *King Lear and the Gods,* 192–94, 231–33, 259; Soellner, *Shakespeare's Patterns of Self-*

Knowledge, 296–97, 314; and Leo Salingar, "*King Lear,* Montaigne and Harsnett," in *Dramatic Form in Shakespeare and the Jacobeans* (Cambridge: Cambridge University Press, 1986), 107–39.

34. Dieter Mehl's critique of Lear's largely unrealized prayer for the poor ("Lear and the 'Poor Naked Wretches,'" *Deutsche Shakespeare Gesellschaft West* [1975]: 154–62) is made a crux in Dollimore's Marxist reading (*Radical Tragedy*). Cf. Dollimore, "Shakespeare, Cultural Materialism and the New Historicism," in *Political Shakespeare,* ed. Jonathan Dollimore and Alan Sinfield (Manchester: Manchester University Press, 1985), 2–17.

35. Interpretations of Macbeth's "great bond" include his complicity with witches, his friendship with Banquo, the general bond of universal siblinghood, and, for Garry Wills, the baptismal bond with God (*Witches and Jesuits: Shakespeare's Macbeth* [New York: Oxford University Press, 1995], 59–61).

36. Elton, *King Lear and the Gods,* 197–212.

37. See Josephine W. Bennett, "The Storm Within: The Madness of Lear," *SQ* 13 (1962): 137–55.

38. On the establishing of self-identity in reaction to the death of a beloved nurturer, see Bibliography, 5C, "Introjection, Internalization, Identification."

39. Stanley Cavell, "The Avoidance of Love: A Reading of *King Lear,*" in *Must We Mean What We Say? A Book of Essays* (New York: Scribner's, 1969), 267–353.

40. See Augustine, *De trinitate.* On Cordelia's aggressive charity, see Berger, "The Lear Family Romance," 374.

41. Elton, *King Lear and the Gods,* 135–36, 175 and n, 234–38, 258, 326.

42. Murray J. Levith, *What's in Shakespeare's Names* (New Haven, CT: Archon Books, 1978), 57.

43. Compare the *liebestod* of Pyramus and Thisbe, Romeo and Juliet, and especially Antony and Cleopatra, whose communion in the final scene of act 4 is axis for the final two-act cycle.

44. The optimistic potential of Lear's final words (in the folio) is noted by Elton in *King Lear and the Gods,* 258 n.; Thomas Clayton, in *The Division of the Kingdoms,* 121–41; Doebler, in *"Rooted Sorrow,"* 168–69. Cf. Williams, "Petitionary Prayer," 371.

45. Kiefer, *Fortune and Elizabethan Tragedy,* 295.

46. In its cycles of action that revolve around immanent epiphanies, and in the development of these axial visions from lovelessness to love, Shakespeare's *King Lear* forms an intriguing analogue with Dante's spiritual pilgrimage: from frustration in the *Vita Nuova* (12.26–34), where Dante is excluded from the circle of Love, to the joyous end of the *Paradiso,* where, in the presence of God, Dante's desire is made perfect, "like a wheel in even revolution":

Ma gia volgeva il mio disiro e 'l *velle,*
Si come rota ch' igualmente e mossa,
L'Amor che move il sole e l' altre stelle.
(33.143–45).

Dante Alighieri, *La Divina Commedia,* ed. C. H. Grandgent (Boston: D. C. Heath, 1933), 972 n. 144: "The circle, being the perfect figure, is an emblem of perfection; and circular motion symbolizes full and faultless activity" (St. Thomas, *In Librum B. Dionysii Di Divinis Nominibus,* caput iv, Lectio 7).

47. "They foure had one forme, . . . and their worke *was* as one whele in *another* whele. . . . Whether their spirit led them, they went . . . & when they were lifted vp from the earth, the wheles were lifted vp besides them: for the spirit of the beastes [*the cherubim*] *was* in the wheles" (Ezekiel 1:16, 20–21; see 10:9–13, 16–17).

48. Soellner, "*King Lear* and the Magic of the Wheel," *SQ* 35 (1984): 283–84.

49. Boethius, *The Theological Tractates and The Consolation of Philosophy*, 361–63.

50. Ibid., 297; and see 273.

51. Ibid., 375.

52. Cioffari, "Fortune, Fate, and Chance."

Bibliography

1. SHAKESPEAREAN DRAMATURGY

A. General

Barber, C. L. *The Whole Journey: Shakespeare's Power of Development.* Berkeley and Los Angeles: University of California Press, 1986.

Berry, Ralph. *Shakespearean Structures.* Totowa, NJ: Barnes and Noble, 1981.

Bradbrook, Muriel C. *Shakespeare the Craftsman.* London: Chatto and Windus, 1969.

Brennan, Anthony. *Shakespeare's Dramatic Structures.* London: Routledge and Kegan Paul, 1986.

Brown, John Russell. *Shakespeare's Dramatic Style.* New York: Barnes and Noble, 1971.

Calderwood, James L. *Shakespearean Metadrama.* Minneapolis: University of Minnesota Press, 1971.

Cox, John D. *Shakespeare and the Dramaturgy of Power.* Princeton: Princeton University Press, 1989.

Egan, Robert. *Drama Within Drama: Shakespeare's Sense of His Art.* New York: Columbia University Press, 1975.

Granville-Barker, Harley. *Prefaces to Shakespeare* 2 vols. Princeton: Princeton University Press, 1946–47.

Hartwig, Joan. *Shakespeare's Analogical Scene: Parody as Structural Syntax.* Lincoln: University of Nebraska Press, 1983.

Hirsh, James E. *The Structure of Shakespearean Scenes.* New Haven: Yale University Press, 1981.

Howard, Jean E. *Shakespeare's Art of Orchestration: Stage Technique and Audience Response.* Urbana: University of Illinois Press, 1984.

Jones, Emrys. *Scenic Form in Shakespeare.* Oxford: Clarendon Press, 1971; and *The Origins of Shakespeare.* New York: Oxford University Press, 1977.

Kastan, David. *Shakespeare and the Shapes of Time.* Hanover, NH: University Press of New England, 1982.

Righter, Anne. *Shakespeare and the Idea of the Play.* London: Chatto and Windus, 1962.

Salingar, Leo. *Dramatic Form in Shakespeare and the Jacobeans.* Cambridge: Cambridge University Press, 1986.

171

B. Dramaturgy of the Comedies

Barber, C. L. *Shakespeare's Festive Comedy.* Princeton: Princeton University Press, 1959.

Berry, Edward. *Shakespeare's Comic Rites.* Cambridge: Cambridge University Press, 1984.

Berry, Ralph. *Shakespeare's Comedies: Explorations in Form.* Princeton: Princeton University Press, 1972.

Carroll, William C. *The Metamorphoses of Shakespearean Comedy.* Princeton: Princeton University Press, 1985.

Charlton, H. B. *Shakespearian Comedy.* London: Macmillan, 1938.

Frye, Northrop. "The Argument of Comedy." In *English Institute Essays 1948.* New York: Columbia University Press, 1949; *A Natural Perspective.* New York: Columbia University Press, 1965.

Kermode, Frank. "The Mature Comedies." In *Early Shakespeare,* ed. John Russell Brown and Bernard Harris. Stratford-upon-Avon Studies. London: Edward Arnold, 1961.

Levin, Richard A. *Love and Society in Shakespearean Comedy: A Study of Dramatic Form and Content.* Newark: University of Delaware Press, 1986.

Nevo, Ruth. *Comic Transformations in Shakespeare.* London: Methuen, 1980.

Salingar, Leo. *Shakespeare and the Traditions of Comedy.* Cambridge: Cambridge University Press, 1974.

C. Dramaturgy of the Problem Plays

Frye, Northrop. *The Myth of Deliverance.* Toronto: University of Toronto Press, 1983.

Schanzer, Ernest. *The Problem Plays of Shakespeare.* New York: Schocken Books, 1963.

Westlund, Joseph. *Shakespeare's Reparative Comedies.* Chicago: University Of Chicago Press, 1984.

Wheeler, Richard P. *Shakespeare's Development and the Problem Comedies: Turn and Counter-Turn.* Berkeley and Los Angeles: University of California Press, 1981.

D. Dramaturgy of the Histories

Berry, Edward I. *Patterns of Decay: Shakespeare's Early Histories.* Charlottesville: University of Virginia Press, 1975.

Blanpied, John W. *Time and the Artist in Shakespeare's English Histories.* Newark: University Of Delaware Press, 1983.

Calderwood, James L. *Metadrama in Shakespeare's Henriad.* Berkeley and Los Angeles: University of California Press, 1979.

Dean, Paul. "Shakespeare's *Henry VI* Trilogy and Elizabethan 'Romance' Histories: The Origin of a Genre." *SQ* 33 (1982): 34–48.

Hunter, G. K. "*Henry IV* and the Elizabethan Two-Part Play." *RES,* n.s. 5 (1954): 236–48.

Jenkins, Harold. *The Structural Problem in Shakespeare's "Henry IV."* London: Folcroft Library, 1973; c. 1956.

Knowles, Richard. "Unquiet and the Double Plot of *2 Henry IV*," *ShakS* 2 (1966): 133–40.

Leech, Clifford. "The Two-Part Play: Marlowe and the Early Shakespeare." *ShJE* 94 (1958): 90–106.

Price, Hereward T. *Construction in Shakespeare*. Ann Arbor: University of Michigan Press, 1951.

E. Dramaturgy of the Tragedies

Barroll, J. Leeds. *Shakespearean Tragedy: Genre, Tradition, and Change in "Antony and Cleopatra."* Washington, D. C.: Folger Library Press, 1984.

Bonjour, Adrien. *The Structure of "Julius Caesar."* Liverpool: University of Liverpool Press, 1958.

Bradley, A. C. *Shakespearean Tragedy*. London: Macmillan, 1904.

Calderwood, James L. *If It Were Done: "Macbeth" and Tragic Action*. Amherst: University of Massachusetts Press, 1986.

Fergusson, Francis. "*Macbeth* as the Imitation of an Action," *English Institute Essays, 1951*. New York: Columbia University Press, 1952. 31–43.

Hamilton, A. C. "*Titus Andronicus*: The Form of Shakespearean Tragedy." *SQ* 14 (1963): 201–13.

Heilman, Robert B. *This Great Stage: Image and Structure in "King Lear."* Baton Rouge: Louisiana State University Press, 1948

Kirsch, Arthur. *The Passions of Shakespeare's Tragic Heroes*. Charlottesville: University of Virginia Press, 1990.

Levin, Harry. "Form and Formality in *Romeo and Juliet*," *SQ* 11 (1960): 1–11.

Mack, Maynard. "The Jacobean Shakespeare: Some Observations on the Construction of the Tragedies," *Jacobean Theatre*, ed. John Russell Brown and Bernard Harris. Stratford-upon-Avon Studies. London: Edward Arnold, 1960. 11–41.

Mack, Maynard, Jr. *Killing the King: Three Studies in Shakespeare's Tragic Structure*. New Haven: Yale University Press, 1973.

Nevo, Ruth. *Tragic Form in Shakespeare*. Princeton: Princeton University Press, 1972.

Ribner, Irving. *Patterns in Shakespearian Tragedy*. New York: Barnes and Noble, 1960.

Snyder, Susan. *The Comic Matrix of Shakespeare's Tragedies*. Princeton: Princeton University Press, 1979.

Velz, John W. "Undular Structure in *Julius Caesar*," *MLR* 66 (1971): 21–30.

Wilson, Harold S. *On the Design of Shakespearean Tragedy*. Toronto: University of Toronto Press, 1957.

Young, David. *The Action to the Word: Structure and Style in Shakespearean Tragedy*. New Haven: Yale University Press, 1990.

F. Dramaturgy of the Romances

Frye, Northrop. *The Secular Scripture: A Study of the Structure of Romance*. Cambridge: Harvard University Press, 1976.

Gesner, Carol. *Shakespeare and the Greek Romance: A Study of Origins*. Lexington: University Press of Kentucky, 1970.

Hartwig, Joan. *Shakespeare's Tragicomic Vision*. Baton Rouge: Louisiana State University Press, 1972.

Kermode, Frank. *William Shakespeare: The Final Plays*. London: Longmans, Green, 1963.

Kirsch, Arthur C. "*Cymbeline* and Coterie Dramaturgy," *ELH* 34 (1967): 285–306.

Leech, Clifford. "The Structure of the Last Plays," *ShS* 11 (1958): 19–30.

McDonald, Russ. "Poetry and Plot in *The Winter's Tale*," *SQ* 36 (1985): 315–29.

Mowat, Barbara. *The Dramaturgy of Shakespeare's Romances*. Athens: University of Georgia Press, 1976.

Peterson, Douglas L. *Time, Tide, and Tempest: A Study of Shakespeare's Romances*. San Marino, CA: Huntington Library Press, 1973.

Proudfoot, G. Richard. "Verbal Reminiscence and the Two-Part Structure of *The Winter's Tale*." *ShS* 29 (1976): 67–78.

Pyle, Fitzroy. *"The Winter's Tale": A Commentary on the Structure*. New York: Barnes and Noble, 1969.

Schanzer, Ernest. "The Structural Pattern of *The Winter's Tale*." *REL* 5 (1964): 72–82.

White, R. S. *Let Wonder Seem Familiar: Endings in Shakespeare's Romance Vision*. London: Athlone Press and Atlantic Highlands: NJ Humanities Press International, 1985.

2. Epiphany: Shakespearean and Modern

A. *Shakespearean Epiphany*

Aronson, Alex. *Psyche and Symbol in Shakespeare*. Bloomington: Indiana University Press, 1972.

Barber, C. L. "'Thou that beget'st him that did thee beget': Transformation in 'Pericles' and 'The Winter's Tale.'" *ShS* 22 (1969): 59–67.

Battenhouse, Roy, *Shakespearean Tragedy: Its Art and Its Christian Premises*. Bloomington: Indiana University Press, 1969; and *Shakespeare's Christian Dimension: An Anthology of Criticism*. Ed. Roy Battenhouse. Bloomington: Indiana University Press, 1994.

Bethell, S. L. *The Winter's Tale: A Study*. London: Athlone Press, 1947.

Bonjour, Adrien. "The Final Scene of *The Winter's Tale*," *ES* 33 (1952): 193–208.

Bryant, Joseph A., Jr. *Hippolyta's View*. Lexington: University Press of Kentucky, 1967.

Elton, William. *King Lear and the Gods*. 1966; reprint, Lexington: University Press of Kentucky, 1988.

Felperin, Howard. *Shakespearean Romances*. Princeton: Princeton University Press, 1972.

Frye, Northrop. "Recognition in *The Winter's Tale*." In *Fables of Identity: Studies in Poetic Mythology*. New York, 1963, 107–18; *A Natural Perspective: The Development of Shakespearean Comedy and Romance*. New York, 1965.

Gourlay, Patricia Southard. "'O my most sacred lady': Female Metaphor in *The Winter's Tale*," *ELR* 5 (1975): 375–95.

Grant, Patrick. "*The Tempest* and the Magic of Charity," *Images and Ideas in Literature of the English Renaissance*. Amherst: University of Massachusetts Press, 1979. 82–85.

Grantley, Darryl. "*The Winter's Tale* and Early Religious Drama," *CompD* 20 (1986): 17–34.

Grudin, Robert. "Prospero's Masque and the Structure of *The Tempest*," *SAQ* 71 (1972): 401–9.

Guilfoyle, Cherrell. *Shakespeare's Play Within Play*. Kalamazoo, MI: Medieval Institute, 1990. 111–27.

Hanna, Sara. "Christian Vision and Iconography in *Pericles*," *UCrow* 11 (1991): 92–116.

Hunt, Maurice. *Shakespeare's Romance of the Word*. Lewisburg, PA: Bucknell University Press, 1990.

Hunter, Robert G. *Shakespeare and the Comedy of Forgiveness*. New York: Columbia University Press, 1965.

Kermode, Frank. *William Shakespeare: The Final Plays*. London: Longmans, Green, 1963.

Knight, G. Wilson. *The Crown of Life: Essays in Interpretation of Shakespeare's Final Plays*. 1947; reprint, New York: Barnes and Noble, 1966.

Milward, Peter. "Notes on the Religious Dimension in *King Lear*." *English Literature and Language* (Tokyo) 23 (1986): 5–27; and "A Theology of Grace in *The Winter's Tale*." In *Shakespeare's Other Dimension*. Tokyo: Renaissance Institute, Sophia University, 1989. 102–24.

Muir, Kenneth. "The Conclusion of *The Winter's Tale*," *The Singularity of Shakespeare and Other Essays*. Liverpool: University of Liverpool Press, 1977. 76–91; and "Theophanies in the Last Plays." In *Shakespeare: Contrasts and Controversies*. Norman: University of Oklahoma Press, 1985.

Peck, Russell A. "Edgar's Pilgrimage: High Comedy in *King Lear*." *SEL* 7 (1967): 219–37.

Schwartz, Murray M. "*The Winter's Tale*: Loss and Transformation." *AI* 32 (1975): 145–99.

Siegel, Paul. "Shakespeare's Kneeling-Resurrection Pattern and the Meaning of *King Lear*." In *Shakespeare in His Time and Ours*. South Bend, IN: University of Notre Dame Press, 1968. 108–21.

Summers, Joseph H. "The Ending of *King Lear*." In *Dreams of Love and Power*. Oxford: Clarendon Press, 1984. 111–13.

White, R. S. *"Let Wonder Seem Familiar": Endings in Shakespeare's Romance Vision*. London: Athlone Press, 1985.

B. Epiphany in Modern Literature

Beja, Morris. *Epiphany in the Modern Novel*. Seattle: University of Washington Press, 1972.

Bergson, Henri. *Essai sur les données immédiates de la conscience,* 11th ed. (1889; reprint, Paris, 1912).

Bidney, Martin. *Patterns of Epiphany: From Wordsworth to Tolstoy, Pater, and Barrett Browning.* Carbondale: Southern Illinois University Press, 1997.

Ellmann, Richard. *James Joyce.* New York: Oxford University Press, 1965. See esp. 87–89, 98, 108, 113, 125, 132, 137, 149.

Gilkey, Langdon. *Naming the Whirlwind: The Renewal of God Language.* New York: Bobbs-Merrill, 1969.

Hendry, Irene. "Joyce's Epiphanies." *SR* 54 (1946): 449–67.

Langbaum, Robert. "Wordsworth and the Epiphanic Mode in Modern Poetry." *NLH* 14 (1983): 335–58; and *Word from Below.* Madison: University of Wisconsin Press, 1987.

Nichols, Ashton. *The Poetics of Epiphany: Nineteenth-Century Origins of the Modern Literary Moment.* Tuscaloosa: University of Alabama Press, 1987.

Weiskel, Thomas. *The Romantic Sublime: Studies in the Structure and Psychology of Transcendence.* Baltimore: Johns Hopkins University Press, 1976.

3. RIVAL PSYCHOLOGIES IN THE ENGLISH RENAISSANCE

A. Renaissance Psychology

Anderson, Ruth L. *Elizabethan Psychology and Shakespeare's Plays.* Iowa City: University of Iowa Press, 1927.

Babb, Lawrence. *The Elizabethan Malady.* East Lansing: Michigan State University Press, 1951.

Baker, Herschel. *The Dignity of Man.* Cambridge: Harvard University Press, 1947. Reprinted as *The Image of Man.* New York, 1952.

Bamborough, John B. *The Little World of Man.* London, 1952.

Barkan, Leonard. *Nature's Work of Art.* New Haven: Yale University Press, 1975.

Barroll, J. Leeds. *Artificial Persons: The Formation of Character in the Tragedies of Shakespeare.* Columbia: University of South Carolina Press, 1974.

Bullough, Geoffrey. *Mirror of Minds.* London: Athlone Press, 1962.

Craig, Hardin. *The Enchanted Glass.* 1936; reprint, Oxford: Blackwell, 1952.

Curry, Walter Clyde. *Shakespeare's Philosophical Patterns.* Baton Rouge: Louisiana State University Press, 1937.

Draper, John W. *The Humors and Shakespeare's Characters.* Durham, NC: Duke University Press, 1945.

Hankins, John Erskine. *Backgrounds of Shakespeare's Thought.* Hamden, CT: Archon Books, 1978.

Harvey, E. Ruth. "Psychology." *SpEncy.* Toronto: University of Toronto Press, 1990.

Heninger, S. K., Jr. *Touches of Sweet Harmony: Pythagorean Cosmology and Renaissance Poetics.* San Marino, CA: Huntington Library, 1974; *The Cosmographical Glass.* San Marino: Huntington Library, 1977. Chap. 4, "The Pythagorean-Platonic Tradition."

Kocher, Paul H. *Science and Religion in Elizabethan England*. San Marino: Huntington Library Press, 1953.

Lewis, C. S. *The Discarded Image*. Cambridge: Cambridge University Press, 1964.

Lottin, Odon. *Psychologie et morale aux xii et xiii siècles*, 2 vols. 1942; rev. ed. Gembloux, Belgium: J. Duculot, 1960.

Lyons, Bridget Gellert. *Voices of Melancholy*. New York: Barnes and Noble, 1971.

Reid, Robert L. "Psychology, Platonic." *SpEncy*.

Soellner, Rolf. *Shakespeare's Patterns of Self-Knowledge*. Athens: Ohio State University Press, 1972.

Spencer, Theodore. *Shakespeare and the Nature of Man*. New York: Macmillan, 1942.

Tillyard, E. M. W. *The Elizabethan World Picture*. London: Chatto and Windus, 1943.

B. Number Symbolism in Christian-Platonic Psychology

Butler, Christopher. *Number Symbolism*. London: Routledge, 1970.

Fowler, Alastair. *Spenser and the Numbers of Time*. London: Routledge and Kegan Paul, 1964; and *Silent Poetry: Essays in Numerological Analysis*. London: Routledge, 1970.

Heninger, S. K., Jr. *Touches of Sweet Harmony: Pythagorean Cosmology and Renaissance Poetics*. San Marino, CA: Huntington Library, 1974; *The Cosmographical Glass*. San Marino, CA: Huntington Library, 1977.

Hieatt, A. Kent. *Short Time's Endless Monument*. New York: Columbia University Press, 1960.

Hopper, Vincent Foster. *Medieval Number Symbolism*. New York: Columbia University Press, 1938.

Rostvig, Maren-Sofie. *Fair Forms*. Cambridge: D. S. Brewer, 1975; "Number symbolism, tradition of," *SpEncy*.

C. Christian-Platonic Psychology: Allegorizing Pagan Deities

Conti, Natali. *Mythologiae sive explicationum fabularum libri decem*. Venice, 1567; reprint, New York and London: Garland, 1976.

Donno, Elizabeth S. "The Triumph of Cupid: Spenser's Legend of Chastity." *Yearbook of English Studies* 4 (1974): 37–48.

Hyde, Thomas. *The Poetic Theology of Love: Cupid in Renaissance Literature*. Newark: University of Delaware Press, 1986.

Javitch, Daniel. "Rescuing Ovid from the Allegorizers," *CL* 30 (1978): 97–107.

Lotspeich, Henry G. *Classical Mythology in the Poetry of Edmund Spenser*. Princeton: Princeton University Press, 1932.

Nestrick, William V. "Spenser and the Renaissance Mythology of Love." *Literary Monographs* 6 (1975): 3570, 161–66.

Nohrnberg, James. *The Analogy of The Faerie Queene*. Princeton: Princeton University Press, 1976.

Ovide moralisé. Ed. Cornelius de Boer et al. Wiesbaden: M. Sändig, 1915–36.

Panofsky, Erwin. *Studies in Iconology*. 1939; reprint, New York: Harper and Row, 1967.

Thomas P. Roche, *The Kindly Flame: A Study of the Third and Fourth Books of Spenser's "Faerie Queene."* Princeton: Princeton University Press, 1964.

Seznec, Jean. *The Survival of the Pagan Gods*, trans. Barbara F. Sessions. 1940; reprint, New York: Harper, 1953.

Spenser Encyclopedia, The. Toronto: University of Toronto Press, 1990.

4. RENAISSANCE SKEPTICISM

Allen, D. C. "The Degeneration of Man and Renaissance Pessimism." *SP* 35 (1938): 210–30; *Doubt's Boundless Sea: Skepticism and Faith in the Renaissance.* Baltimore: Johns Hopkins University Press, 1964.

Bradbrook, Muriel C. *The School of Night.* Cambridge: Cambridge University Press, 1936.

Bradshaw, Graham. *Shakespeare's Skepticism.* Brighton, England: Harvester Press and New York: St. Martin's Press, 1987.

Cavell, Stanley. *Disowning Knowledge in Six Plays of Shakespeare.* Cambridge: Cambridge University Press, 1987.

Elton, William. *King Lear and the Gods.* 1966; reprint, Lexington: University Press of Kentucky, 1988.

Febvre, Lucien. *The Problem of Unbelief in the Sixteenth Century: The Religion of Rabelais,* trans. Beatrice Gottlieb. 1942; reprint, Cambridge: Harvard University Press, 1982. 174–239.

Felperin, Howard. *Shakespearean Romances.* Princeton: Princeton University Press, 1972.

Harris, Victor. *All Coherence Gone.* Chicago: Chicago University Press, 1949.

Kaiser, Walter. *Praisers of Folly: Erasmus, Rabelais, and Shakespeare.* Cambridge: Harvard University Press, 1963.

Kocher, Paul H. *Science and Religion in Renaissance England.* San Marino: Huntington Library Press, 1953.

Popkin, Richard H. *The History of Scepticism from Erasmus to Descartes.* Assen, Netherlands: Van Gorcum, 1960.

5. PSYCHOANALYTIC FUNCTIONS IN SHAKESPEAREAN TRAGEDY

A. Dissociation, Doubling, Multiple Personality, Splitting

Braude, Stephen E. *First Person Plural: Multiple Personality and the Philosophy of Mind.* London: Routledge, 1991.

Brook, J. A. "Freud and Splitting." *International Review of Psychoanalysis* 19 (1992): 335–50.

Bryant, Doris, Judy Kessler, and Lunda Shirar. *The Family Inside: Working with the Multiple.* New York: Norton, 1992.

Coates, Paul. *The Double and the Other: Identity as Ideology in Post-Romantic Fiction.* 1990; New York: St. Martins, 1991.

Confer, William N. & Billie S. Ables. *Multiple Personality.* New York: Human Sciences Press, 1983.

Crabtree, Adam. *Multiple Man: Explorations in Possession and Multiple Personality.* Toronto: Collins, 1985.

Crook, Eugene J., ed. *Fearful Symmetry: Doubles and Doubling in Literature and Film.* Tallahassee: University Presses of Florida, 1981.

Eder, Doris, L. "The Idea of the Double," *PsyR* 65 (1978): 579–614.

Fineman, Joel. "Fratricide and Cuckoldry: Shakespeare's Doubles." *PsyR* 64 (1977): 409–53.

Freud, Sigmund. "Splitting of the Ego in the Process of Defence." 1938. *SE* 23: 271–78.

Goettman, Carole, George B. Greaves, and Philip M. Coons. *Multiple Personality and Dissociation, 1791–1992: A Complete Bibliography.* 2nd ed. Lutherville, Md.: Sidran Press, 1994.

Greaves, George B. "A History of Multiple Personality Disorder." In *Clinical Perspectives on Multiple Personality Disorder.* Ed. R. P. Kluft and C. G. Fine. Washington, D. C.: American Psychiatric Press, 1993. 355–80.

Grotstein, James S. *Splitting and Projective Identification.* New York: Jason Aronson, 1981.

Guntrip, Harry. *Schizoid Phenomena, Object Relations, and the Self.* London: Hogarth, 1968.

Hacking, Ian. *Rewriting the Soul: Multiple Personality and the Sciences of Memory.* Princeton: Princeton University Press, 1995; "Two Souls in One Body." *Critical Inquiry* 17 (1991): 838–67.

Harrington, Anne. *Medicine, Mind, and the Double Brain: A Study in Nineteenth-Century Thought.* Princeton: Princeton University Press, 1987.

Hawthorn, Jeremy. *Multiple Personality and the Disintegration of the Literary Character.* London: Edward Arnold and New York: St. Martins, 1983.

Herdman, John. *The Double in Nineteenth-century Fiction: The Shadow Life.* London: Macmillan, 1990, and New York: St. Martins, 1991.

Hilgard, Ernest. *Divided Consciousness: Multiple Controls in Human Thought and Action.* New York: John Wiley, 1977.

Janet, Pierre. *The Major Symptoms of Hysteria.* London: Macmillan, 1907.

Josephs, Lawrence. *Character Structure and the Organization of the Self.* New York: Columbia University Press, 1992.

Jung, C. G. *The Structure and Dynamics of the Psyche.* New York: Pantheon, 1960.

Keppler, C. F. *The Literature of the Second Self.* Tucson: University of Arizona Press, 1972.

Kluft, Richard P., ed. *Childhood Antecedents of Multiple Personality.* Washington, D. C.: American Psychiatric Press, 1985.

Laing, R. D. *The Divided Self: A Study of Sanity and Madness.* London: Tavistock, 1959.

Lichtenberg, Joseph D. and Joseph W. Slap. "Notes on the Concept of Splitting and Defense Mechanism of Splitting Representations." *JAPA* 21 (1973): 722–87.

Lustman, J. "On Splitting." *PSOC* 32 (1977): 119–54.

Miller, Karl. *Doubles: Studies in Literary History.* 2nd ed, corrected. Oxford: Oxford University Press, 1987.

Myoshi, Masao. *The Divided Self: A Perspective on the Literature of the Victorians.* New York: New York University Press, and London: University of London Press, 1969.

North, Carol S. et al. *Multiple Personalities, Multiple Disorders: Psychiatric Classification and Media Influence.* New York: Oxford University Press, 1993.

Prince, Morton. *The Dissociation of a Personality.* New York: Longmans, Green and Co., 1905; *Psychotherapy and Multiple Personality: Selected Essays.* Ed. Nathan G. Hale, Jr. Cambridge: Harvard University Press, 1975.

Rank, Otto. *The Double: A Psychoanalytic Study,* 1914. Trans. Harry Tucker, Jr. New York: New American Library, 1979.

Rivera, Margo. "Am I a Boy or a Girl? Multiple Personality as a Window on Gender Differences." *Resources for Feminist Research/ Documentation sur la Recherche Feministe* 17 (1987):41–43.

Rogers, Robert. *A Psychoanalytic Study of the Double in Literature.* Detroit: Wayne State University Press, 1970.

Rosenfield, Claire. "The Shadow Within: The Conscious and Unconscious Use of the Double." *Daedalus* 92 (1963): 326–44.

Ross, Colin A. *The Osiris Complex: Case Studies in Multiple Personality Disorder.* Toronto: University of Toronto Press, 1994.

Stoller, Robert. *Splitting: A Case of Female Masculinity.* London: Hogarth Press, 1974.

Tymms, Ralph. *Doubles in Literary Psychology.* Cambridge: Bowes and Bowes, 1949.

Walker, Mitchell. "The Double: An Archetypal Configuration." *Spring* (1976): 165–75.

Wangh, M. "*Othello:* The Tragedy of Iago." *PQ* 19 (1950): 202–12.

B. Gender Stereotyping, Reversal, and Transference (Macbeth).

Asp, Carolyn. "'Be bloody, bold, and resolute': Tragic Action and Sexual Stereotyping in *Macbeth,*" *SP* 78 (1981): 153–69. French, Marilyn. *Shakespeare's Division of Experience* (New York: Ballantine, 1981), 242–53.

Galenson, Eleanor and Roiphe, Herman. "The Preoedipal Development of the Boy." *JAPA* 24 (1980): 805–27.

Harding, D. W. "Women's Fantasy of Manhood: A Shakespearean Theme," *SQ* 20 (1969): 245–53.

Kahn, Coppélia. *Man's Estate: Masculine Identity in Shakespeare.* Berkeley: University of California Press, 1981. 151–55, 172–92.

Kimbrough, Robert. "Macbeth: Prisoner of Gender," *ShS* 6 (1972): 175–90.

Meyer, J. "The Theory of Gender Identity Disorders." *JAPA* 30 (1982): 381–418.

Micale, Mark S. "Charcot and the Idea of Hysteria in the Male: Gender, Mental Science, and Medical Diagnosis in Late Nineteenth-Century France." *Medical History* 34 (1990): 363–411.

Showalter, Elaine. "Hysteria, Feminism, and Gender." In *Hysteria beyond Freud*. Ed. S. L. Gilman et al. Berkeley: University of California Press, 1993. 286–344.

Stoller, Robert. *Sex and Gender,* vol. 2. New York: Jason Aronson, 1975.

C. Introjection (Internalization, Identification).

Behrends, Rebecca Smith and Blatt, Sidney J. "Internalization and Psychological Development throughout the Life Cycle," *PSOC* 40 (1985): 11–39.

Ferenczi, Sandor. "Introjection and Transference." In *Sex in Psychoanalysis*. New York: Basic Books, 1909. 35–93.

Freud, Anna. *The Ego and the Mechanisms of Defense*. New York: International Universities Press, 1966.

Freud, Sigmund. "Mourning and Melancholia" (1917), *SE* 14: 237–58.

Greenberg, Jay R. and Stephen A. Mitchell. *Object Relations in Psychoanalytic Theory*. Cambridge: Harvard University Press, 1983.

Heimann, Paula. "Certain Functions of Introjection and Projection in Early Infancy." In *Developments in Psycho-Analysis*. Klein, Melanie, Paula Heimann, S. Isaacs, and Joan Riviere, eds. London: Hogarth Press, 1952. 122–68.

Klein, Melanie. *Contributions to Psycho-Analysis, 1921–1945*. London: Hogarth Press, 1948.

Jacobson, Edith. *The Self and the Object World*. New York: International Universities Press, 1964.

Loewald, Hans W. "Internalization, Separation, Mourning, and the Superego," *PsyQ* 31 (1962): 483–504, and "On Internalization," *IJP* 54 (1973): 9–17.

Meissner, William W. "Internalization and Object Relations," *JAPA* 27 (1979): 345–60, and *Internalization in Psychoanalysis*. New York: International Universities Press, 1981.

Schafer, Roy. *Aspects of Internalization*. New York: International Universities Press, 1968.

D. Narcissism and Self-love

Adelman, Janet. "'Born of Woman,'" and "'Anger's My Meat': Feeding, Dependency, and Aggression in *Coriolanus*," *Representing Shakespeare*, 129–49.

Augustine, *De moribus ecclesiae* 25.46–29.61; *De trinitate* 8–15.

Bach, Sheldon. *Narcissistic States and the Therapeutic Process*. New York: Aronson, 1985.

Benjamin, Jessica. *The Bonds of Love*. New York: Pantheon Books, 1988. 11–50.

Ferrari, T. M. De. *The Problem of Charity for Self, A Study of Thomistic and Modern Theological Discussion*. Washington, D. C., 1962.

Freud, Sigmund. "On Narcissism: An Introduction," *SE* 14:69–102.

Furnish, Paul. *The Love-Command in the New Testament*. London, 1973.

Kernberg, Otto F. *Borderline Conditions and Pathological Narcissism*. New York: Aronson, 1975.

Kirsch, Arthur. "Macbeth's Suicide." *ELH* 51 (1984): 269–96.

Kohut, Heinz. "Forms and Transformations of Narcissism," *JAPA* (1966): 243–72.

Moore, B. E. "Toward a Clarification of the Concept of Narcissism." *PSOC* 30 (1975): 243–76.

O'Donovan, Oliver. *The Problem of Self-Love in St. Augustine.* New Haven: Yale University Press, 1980. 37–45, 112–21.

Outka, Gene. *Agape.* New Haven: Yale University Press, 1972.

Pulver, S. "Narcissism." *JAPA* 18 (1970): 319–40.

E. Oedipal Conflict (Macbeth)

Atkins, N. "The Oedipus Myth, Adolescence, and the Succession of Generations." *JAPA* 18 (1970): 18:860–75.

Blos, Peter. *Son and Father.* New York: Free Press, 1985.

Freud, Sigmund. "The Dissolution of the Oedipus Complex." 1924. *SE* 19:173–79; "Those Who Are Wrecked by Success." 1916. *SE* 14:318–24.

Frye, Northrop. *Fools of Time. Studies in Shakespearean Tragedy.* Toronto: University of Toronto Press, 1967. 3–39.

Greene, James J. "Macbeth: Masculinity as Murder," *AI* 41 (1984): 155–80.

Hogan, Patrick Colm. "*Macbeth:* Authority and Progenitorship," *AI* 40 (1983): 385–95.

Holland, Norman H. *Psychoanalysis and Shakespeare.* New York: McGraw-Hill, 1964. 219–30.

Janton, Pierre. "Sonship and Fatherhood in *Macbeth.*" *CahiersE* 35 (1989): 47–58.

Jekels, Ludwig. "The Riddle of Shakespeare's *Macbeth.*" 1917; reprint, in *The Design Within: Psychoanalytic Approaches to Shakespeare.* Ed. M. D. Faber. New York: Science House, 1970. 235–49.

Krohn, Janis. "Addressing the Oedipal Dilemma in *Macbeth.*" *PsyR* 73 (1986): 333–47.

Loewald, Hans W. "The Waning of the Oedipus Complex." *JAPA* 27 (1959): 751–56.

F. Preoedipal Conflict (Macbeth)

Adelman, Janet. "'Born of Woman': Fantasies of Maternal Power in *Macbeth,*" in *Cannibals, Witches, and Divorce: Estranging the Renaissance.* Ed. Marjorie Garber. Baltimore: Johns Hopkins Press, 1987. 90–121.

Barber, C. L. and Wheeler, Richard P. *The Whole Journey: Shakespeare's Power of Development.* Berkeley: University of California Press, 1986.

Barron, David. "The Babe That Milks: An Organic Study of *Macbeth.*" 1960; reprint, in *The Design Within.* 251–79.

Galenson, Eleanor and Roiphe, Herman. "The Preoedipal Development of the Boy." *JAPA* 24 (1980): 805–27.

Hunter, Dianne. "Doubling, Mythic Difference, and the Scapegoating of Female Power in *Macbeth,*" *PsyR* 75 (1988): 129–52.

Kahn, Coppélia. *Man's Estate: Masculine Identity in Shakespeare.* Berkeley: University of California Press, 1981.

Kirsch, Arthur. "Macbeth's Suicide." *ELH* 51 (1984): 269–96.

Luborsky, L. "Measuring a Pervasive Psychic Structure in Psychotherapy: The Core Conflictual Relations Theme." In N. Freedman and S. Grand, eds. *Communicative Structures and Psychic Structures*. New York: Plenum Press, 1977.

Mitchell, S. A. *Relational Concepts in Psychoanalysis: An Integration*. Cambridge: Harvard University Press, 1988.

G. Projection and Projective Identification

Balint, Michael. *The Basic Fault: Therapeutic Aspects of Regression*. London: Tavistock, 1968.

Freud, Anna. *The Ego and the Mechanisms of Defense*. New York: International Universities Press, 1966, 50–53. *The Writings of Anna Freud* 4:509–85.

Freud, Sigmund. "Psychoanalytic Notes on an Autobiographical Account of a Case of Paranoia." 1911. *SE* 12:3–82.

Klein, Melanie. "Notes on Some Schizoid Mechanisms," *IJP* 27 (1946): 99–110; *The Psychoanalysis of Children*, trans. Alix Strachey. 1932; rev. ed., New York: Delacorte Press, 1975, 142–48, 178; *Envy and Gratitude and Other Works (1946–1963)*. New York: Free Press, 1975.

Knight, Robert P. "Introjection, Projection, and Identification," *PsyQ* 9 (1940): 334–41.

Ornston, Darius. "On Projection," *PSOC* 33 (1978): 117–66.

H. Repetition Compulsion

Bibring, Edward. "The Conception of the Repetition Compulsion," *PsyQ* 12 (1941): 486–519.

Freud, Sigmund. "Remembering, Repeating, and Working-through" (1914), *SE* 12:147–56; "Beyond the Pleasure Principle" (1920), *SE* 18:7–64.

Loewald, Hans W. "Some Considerations on Repetition and Repetition Compulsion," *IJP* 52 (1971): 59–65.

I. Sublimation

Boesky, Dale. "Questions about Sublimation." In *Psychoanalysis the Science of Mental Conflict*. Ed. A. D. Richards and M. S. Willick. Hillsdale, N.J.: Analytic Press, 1986. 153–76.

Freud, Anna. "Some Remarks on Infant Observation" (1952) in *The Writings of Anna Freud*, 8 vols. New York: International Universities Press, 1968, 4:509–85; and *The Ego and the Mechanisms of Defense*, 1936.

Freud, Sigmund. *The Ego and the Id*. 1923. *SE* 19:30; "The Dissolution of the Oedipal Complex." 1924. *SE* 19:173–79.

Glover, Edward. "Sublimation, Substitution, and Societal Anxiety." *IJP* 12 (1931): 263–97.

Hartmann, Heinz. "Notes on the Theory of Sublimation." *PSOC* 10 (1955): 9–29; "The Development of the Ego Concept in Freud's Work." *IJP* 37 (1956): 425–38.

Hoffer, Willi. "Defensive Process and Defensive Organization: Their Place in Psychoanalytic Technique," *IJP* 35 (1954): 194–98.

Kohut, Heinz. *The Analysis of the Self.* New York: International Universities Press, 1971. 309–24.

Kubie, Lawrence S. "The Fallacious Misuse of the Concept of Sublimation." *PsyQ* 31 (1962): 73–79.

Loewald, Hans W. *Sublimation* (New Haven: Yale University Press, 1988), chaps. 1–2.

J. Superego–formation

Freud, Sigmund. "The Ego and the Id" (1923), *SE* 19:3–66; "Civilization and Its Discontents." (1930). *SE* 21: 59–145.

Furer, Manuel. "The History of the Superego Concept in Psychoanalysis." In *Moral Value and the Superego Concept in Psychoanalysis,* ed. Seymour C. Post. New York: International Universities Press, 1972. 11–62.

Holder, Alex. "Preoedipal Contributions to the Formation of the Superego," *PSOC* 37 (1982): 245–72.

Kohut, Heinz. *The Analysis of the Self: A Systematic Approach to the Psychoanalytic Treatment of Narcissistic Personality Disorders.* New York: International Universities Press, 1971; *The Restoration of the Self.* New York: International Universities Press, 1977.

Sandler, Joseph. "On the Concept of the Superego." *PSOC* 15 (1960): 128–62.

Tyson, Phyllis & Tyson, Robert L. "Narcissism and Superego Development." *JAPA* 34 (1984): 75–98.

K. Vagina Dentata and Penis Dentata

Ferenczi, Sandor F. *The Theory and Technique of Psychoanalysis.* New York, Basic Books, 1925. 278–81.

Rank, Otto. *The Trauma of Birth.* 1924; reprint, New York: Robert Brunner, 1952. 48–49.

Schafer, Roy. *Language and Insight.* New Haven: Yale University Press, 1978. 153–60.

Schuster, Daniel B. "Bisexuality and Body as Phallus," *PsyQ* 38 (1969): 72–80.

Shengold, Leonard. "The Effects of Overstimulation," *IJP* 48 (1967): 403–15.

Wilson, C. Philip. "Stone as a Symbol of Teeth," *PsyQ* 36 (1967): 418–27.

Index

Numbers in boldface refer to pages in which the topic is discussed in depth.

Abel, Lionel, 152n.5
Abrams, Richard, 153n.12
Act of Abuses (1606), 87, 106
Adelman, Janet, 13, 114, 153n.18, 155n.13, 165n.26
Aeschylus, 82
alternating (mirroring) plots. *See* dramaturgy
anagnorisis. *See* dramaturgy
Andrewes, Lancelot, 70–72, 74, 87, 99–100, 146n.11, 154n.3, 155n.22, 156n.30
Aquinas, Thomas, 87, 90, 96, 116, 143
Aristotle, 23, 36, 90–92, 96, 150nn.53 and 54, 159n.2, 160n.12
Arrowsmith, William, 36, 150n.55
Ashley, Kathleen, 157n.36
Augustine, St., 77, 90–92, 96, 107, 132, 140, 155n.15, 157n.41, 159n.5, 162n.44, 167n.30, 168n.40

Bakan, David, 78
Baldwin, Thomas, 24, 26–27, 146nn.5 and 8, 148n.21, 149n.40, 151n.64
Barber, C. L., 13, 157n.35
Barton, Anne, 150n.58
Battenhouse, Roy, 156nn.26 and 33, 157n.38, 158n.58
Beare, William, 146n. 5, 148n.23
Beaurline, Lester, 27
Becker, Ernest, 123
Beckman, Margaret Boerner, 161n.26
Beers, William, 150n.57, 157n.42
Beja, Morris, 83, 156n.55

Bennett, Josephine Waters, 151n.69, 168n.37
Berger, Harry, Jr., 113, 124, 132, 163n.10
Bergson, Henri, 81
Best, Michael, 148n.21
Bestul, Thomas H., 156nn.31 and 32
Bevington, David, 12
Bible: Ezekiel, 141–42; 1 Corinthians, 73, 80, 98, 100; Isaiah, 109; James, 87; Job, 64, 123–25, 137, 165n.1; Matthew, 86, 121; Psalms, 86; Revelation, 69, 154n.1; 1 Timothy, 100
Bidney, Martin, 84
Bloom, Harold, 14
Boethius, 43, 129, 134, 142–43
Booth, Stephen, 64, 123, 154n.26
Bradbrook, Muriel, 148n.21, 163n.9
Bradley, A. C., 24–27, 60–61, 99, 112, 123, 146n.6, 163nn.5 and 11
Bradshaw, Graham, 163n.10
Brennan, Anthony, 27, 31, 145nn.1 and 6
Bright, Timothy, 92–93
Bruster, Douglas, 53
Bryant, Joseph A., Jr., 155n.21, 156n.26
Bullough, Geoffrey, 13, 96, 161n.21
Burton, Robert, 93

Calderwood, James L., 113, 163n.10
Carroll, William C., 154n.22
Cartwright, Kent, 27, 167n.29
catastrophe. *See* dramaturgy
Cavell, Stanley, 139, 154n.24
center. *See* dramaturgy

185

Chapman, Raymond, 166n.12
Cheney, Donald, 161n.26
Chew, Samuel C., 166n.12
Cinthio, Giraldi: *Epitia,* 23, 38, 41
Cioffari, Vincenzo, 143, 166n.12
Cirillo, Albert R., 161n.26
Clayton, Thomas, 162n.35
Coghill, Nevill, 157n.36
Colley, Scott, 155n.13
Collins, Joseph B., 96–97
commoners (or clowns), 15, 48–55, 57, 60–62, 99–100
contrariety (or complementarity), 15, 29, 33–36, 45, 50–51, 54–55, 59–63, 95, 99, 125–26, 130
Cox, Roger, 161n.24
Curry, Walter Clyde, 162n.39

Danson, Lawrence, 155n.21
Dante, Alighieri, 80, 83, 87, 140, 143, 168n.46
Desens, Marliss C., 157n.36
Dessen, Alan, 147n.10
Dillon, Janette, 56
Diogenes, 134
Doebler, Bettie Anne, 162n.35
Dollimore, Jonathan, 132, 168n.34
Doloff, Stephen, 167n.32
Donatus, 24, 31, 146n.8
Donawerth, Jane, 167n.32
Donne, John, 71, 91
Doran, Madeleine, 48
Dowden, Edward, 61
doubling. *See* psychological functions
dramaturgy, **21–47, 48–65;** alternating (or mirroring) plots, 15, 48–49, 54, 58–63, 124, 136; anagnorisis (*see* reversal); catastasis (or paraskeue), 26, 147n.11; catastrophe, 24–26, 36–37, 46, 49, 146n.4, 147n.14; center, 24–26, 29–37, 40–45, 58–59, 61, 76–80, 89, 111, 118–19, 125–28, 130–32, 137, 139–42; chorus, 25, 27–28, 31; continuous performance, 24, 27–29; discovery (*see* reversal); double ending, 26, 36–38, 41, 44, 112, 125, 138–42; embedded plot (or embedded scenes), 15, 53–54, 63–65;

epitasis, 24, 26, 35–37, 43–44, 49, 63, 146n.4, 147n.14; five-act structure, 14, 23, 26–29, 31–38, 39–44, 146n.5; foil, 15, 50–52, 54, 59–65, 278–81; framing plot (or framing scenes), 15, 53, 63–64; multilevel (four-level) hierarchy of plots, 15, 49, 52, 54–55, 63–65, 153n.10; open form, 14, 47; protasis, 24, 26, 37, 49, 146n.4, 147n.14; reversal (or anagnorisis, discovery), 14, 23–24, 29, 32–38, 41–45, 58–61, 76–81, 89, 111, 118–19, 125–28, 130–32, 140–43; three-cycle plot (or 2–1–2 act structure), 14, 16, 23, 26, 28–29, **31–47,** 49, 58, 62, 65, 111–12, 125–26, 129–30, 139
Dundes, Alan, 166n.20

Ellmann, Richard, 83
Else, Gerald, 36
Elton, William R., 124, 127, 137, 140, 151n.73, 153n.20, 156n.33, 162n.35, 166n.7, 167nn.32 and 33
embedded plot. *See* dramaturgy
epiphany, 14, 16, 32–38, 46, 50–51, 67, **69–88,** 89–90, 93–94, 97–100, 103–8, 111, 125–27, 136, 138–43, 149n.45, 168n.46
epitasis. *See* dramaturgy
Erasmus, Desiderius, 24, 37, 43, 72, 90, 92, 134, 137, 146n.4, 158n.58, 167n.33
Euripides, 36, 82, 150n.55
Evanthius, 24, 31
Everyman, 123–25, 140
Ewbank, Inga-Stina, 166n.17

Famous Victories of Henry V, The, 23
Faulkner, William, 83, 86–87, 159n.64
Felperin, Howard, 156n.3, 157n.39, 159n.61
Feuillerat, Albert, 27, 148n.21
five-act structure. *See* dramaturgy
Flahiff, F. T., 154n.23
Foakes, R. A., 111, 151n.70
Foreman, Walter, 82
fortune, 29, 34–35, 42, 46, 107, 127,

138, 140–44, 166n.12, 167n.24.
  See also wheel
framing plot (or framing scenes).
  See dramaturgy
Frank, Erich, 150n.51
Fraser, Russell A., 166n.12
Freccero, John, 156n.34
Freud, Anna, 116, 164n.16
Freud, Sigmund, 16, 87, 111, 114–16,
  120, 153n.15, 156n.34, 162n.1
Frye, Northrop, 13, 55, 80, 91

Galen, 90–93, 96, 160n.12
gender stereotyping, reversal, or trans-
  ference. *See* psychological functions
Geoffrey of Monmouth, 43
Gill, Erma M., 151n.63
Girard, Rene, 158n.48
Gless, Darryl, 151n.69, 157n.36
Gl'Ingannati, 23
Goddard, Harold C., 111, 158n.58,
  164n.21
Goldsmith, Robert, 152n.4
Greenblatt, Stephen, 167n.25
Greenwood, John, 145n.5, 152n.5
Greg, W. W., 26, 146n.5
Grene, Nicholas, 167n.26
Grudin, Robert, 152n.75
Guilfoyle, Cherrell, 156n.33, 157n.38
Gulstad, William, 131

Halio, Jay, 153n.20
Hankins, John Erskine, 92, 160n.9
Harding, D. W., 162n.2, 163n.14
Hartmann, Heinz, 164n.16
Hartwig, Joan, 28, 148n.26
Harvey, E. Ruth, 160n.7
Heilman, Robert B., 112, 126, 152n.76,
  163n.5
Hemingway, S. B., 157n.44
Hirsh, James, 27
Holaday, Allan, 155n.21
Holinshed's *Chronicles,* 23, 112–14
Holland, Norman, 13
Homan, Sidney R., 153n.12
Honigmann, E. A. J., 165n.1
Hooker, Richard, 70

Horace's "law of five acts," 24–26,
  146n.5
Howard, Jean, 27, 30–31, 148n.24,
  149n.47
Hunter, Dianne, 114
Hunter, G. K., 27–28, 148n.21
Hunter, Robert G., 81, 155n.8

introjection (or internalization, identification). *See* psychological functions

Jaarsma, Richard J., 163n.11
Jayne, Sears, 167n.29
Jekels, George, 114
Jewkes, Wilfred T., 26–27
Jones, Emrys, 26, 31, 60, 70, 81, 123,
  147n.10, 163n.8, 166n.6
Jonson, Ben, 26–28, 31, 147n.19,
  149n.40
Jorgensen, Paul, 112, 117, 163n.5,
  164n.19, 166n.10
Josephs, Lawrence, 166n.11
Joyce, James, 82–88, 158n.54

Kermode, Frank, 80
Kernan, Alvin B., 153n.12
Kernberg, Otto F., 165n.26
Kiefer, Frederick, 127, 141
Kimbrough, Robert, 161n.26
King Leir, 23, 38, 42–43
Kirk, K. E., 154n.2, 155n.23
Kirsch, Arthur, 112, 157nn.36 and 37,
  163n.5, 165n.26
Kirsch, James, 164n.24
Klein, Melanie, 164n.20
Knight, Robert P., 164n.20
Kohut, Heinz, 116, 128, 132, 164n.16,
  165n.26
Kolve, V. A., 155n.10

Landino, Christopher: *Horace,* 26
Langbaum, Robert, 84, 158n.46
Leech, Clifford, 26, 147n.13, 148n.25
Leggatt, Alexander, 132
Lemnius, Levinus, 160n.9
Lever, J. W., 41
Levin, Richard, 145n.8, 152n.3,
  153n.10

Levith, Murray J., 168n.42
Levitsky, Ruth, 155n.21
Lewis, C. S., 161n.33
Liebler, Naomi, 158n.48
Lievsay, John Leon, 167n.32
Loewald, Hans, 116, 128, 153n.15, 164n.16
Lyly, John, 13, 27, 31, 148n.21

McAlindon, Thomas, 152n.75
Mack, Maynard, 29, 50, 112, 126, 146n.7, 152n.3, 163n.8
Mack, Maynard, Jr., 163n.5
McNamara, Peter, 167n.33
Manlove, Colin N., 152n.75
Markels, Julian, 163n.4
Martz, Louis, 74, 156n.28
Mehl, Dieter, 168n.34
Merchant, W. Moelwyn, 166n.16
Michel, Laurence, 35, 37, 150n.51
Milward, Peter, 156n.33, 161n.24
Miola, Robert S., 151n.62, 153n.17
Mommsen, Theodore E., 155n.15
Montaigne, Michel de, 43, 90, 137, 167n.33
Montrose, Louis A., 115
Moulton, Richard G., 23
Mowat, Barbara, 14, 145n.4
Muir, Kenneth, 13, 112, 156n.27, 163nn.5 and 9
multilevel hierarchy of plots. See dramaturgy
multiplicity, 13–16, **48–65,** 92, 96–97
Murphy, John L., 167n.25
Myers, Henry Alonzo, 157n.44
mystery plays, 13, 16, 36, 70, 74, 82, 99–100, 155n.17, 157n.38, 158n.49

narcissism (or self-love). See psychological functions
Nevo, Ruth, 31, 146n.6, 149n.46
Nichols, Ashton, 84
Norbrook, David, 163n.9
nothing, 17, 44, 53, 61–62, 64–65, 73, 79, 103, 123–24, 134–36, 142
number symbolism, 92, 96–97

object relations. See psychological functions
O'Connor, Flannery, 85, 159n.63
Oedipal conflict. See psychological functions
Oedipus Rex, 23–24, 48, 124–25, 150n.55
Orgel, Stephen, 115
O'Sullivan, Mary Isabelle, 160n.14
otherness, 24, 29–30, 33–37, 41–42, **48–65,** 75, 77–79, 83–88, 102, 120–24, 126, 130–38, 141–42
Ovid, 13, 73, 108
Ovide moralise, 82, 162n.42

Paglia, Camille, 161n.26
Patch, Howard R., 166n.12
Paton, Alan Park, 164n.21
Paul, St., 73, 91, 161n.24
Pauncz, Arpad, 153n.21
Pius, Joannes Baptista, 40, 151n.64
Plato, 17, 90–93, 96–97, 99, 159nn.2, 3, and 4, 160nn.12 and 19
Plautus, 13, 31, 38–41, 53, 149n.41, 151nn.61, 62, 64, and 65, 153n.17; Amphytrion, 38, 151n.65; Menaechmi, 23, 38–41, 151n.63
Plutarch, 23, 82
projection and projective identification. See psychological functions
Proser, Matthew N., 164n.24
Prosser, Eleanor, 157n.38
protasis. See dramaturgy
Proust, Marcel, 83–85
psychological functions: doubling (or dissociation, multiple personality, splitting), 16, 33–38, 41–42, 50–51, 60–62, 116–20, 123–24, 129–38, 164n.24; ego, 16, 77, 115, 120, 126, 129, 131, 136, 141, 163n.16; gender stereotyping, reversal, or transference, 34, 60–61, 98–99, 113, 115, 128, 148n.30, 164n.24; id, 16, 77, 120–22, 138–44, 163n.13, 164n.16; introjection (or internalization, identification), 120–22, 138–44, 165n.27, 168n.38; narcissism or self-love (normative or pathological), 74, 120–22,

132, 138–42, 165n.26; object relations, 33–38, 79, 81, 112–16, 126, 157n.40; Oedipal conflict, 61, 111, 114–16, 120, 123, 125, 153n.21, 165nn.25 and 28; projection and projective identification, 116–20, 129–38, 164n.20; repetition compulsion, 111, 127, 162n.1; sublimation, 116–17, 126, 128–29, 131; superego formation (or collapse), 16, 77, 114–16, 123–24, 126–29, 131, 141, 163n.13; *vagina dentata* (and *penis dentata*), 121, 165n.29

Rabelais, François, 90
Reid, Robert L., 149n.39, 159n.3, 159n.4, 161n.29
repetition compulsion. *See* psychological functions
reversal (or anagnorisis, discovery). *See* dramaturgy
Ricoeur, Paul, 102, 123, 129, 150n.56, 161n.62
Riehle, Wolfgang, 39, 146n.5, 149n.41, 151n.62
Righter, Anne, 145n.6
Rogers, Robert, 164n.24
Rose, Mark, 27, 30, 148n.34
Rossiter, A. P., 112, 163n.5
Rubinstein, Frankie, 161n.20
Russell, John, 157n.38

Salingar, Leo, 151n.73, 166n.12, 168n.33
Sanders, Wilbur, 112–13, 163n.5
Sartre, Jean-Paul, 79, 150n.51, 157n.43
Schlegel, Wilhelm, 61
Scragg, Leah, 151n.74
Schwartz, Elias, 104
Schwartz, Murray, 13
Screech, M. A., 150n.59
Seinfeld, 152n.79
Seneca, 13, 166n.17; *Medea*, 128
Shakespeare, William: *All's Well That Ends Well*, 16, 25, 35, 52, 54–55, 69, 71–73, 76, 83, 85–86, 88, 97, 99, 107, 148n.30, 149n.43, 157nn.36 and 37;

Antony and Cleopatra, 14–15, 26, 29, 33–38, 47–58, 72, 77–78, 81–82, 85–86, 88, 95, 97–100, 103, 107, 119, 121, 145n.9, 149nn.43 and 45, 150nn.50 and 55, 160n.17, 161n.20, 165n.26, 168n.43; *As You Like It*, 25, 35, 52–54, 72, 75, 83, 85, 97, 99, 119, 145nn.3 and 8, 148n.30, 149n.43; *Comedy of Errors, The*, 25, 35, 38–42, 53, 75, 94, 97, 107, 148n.30, 149n.43, 151nn.63, 64, and 66, 152n.77; *Coriolanus*, 16, 25–26, 29, 32–36, 50, 56, 70, 81–83, 99, 114–15, 121, 145nn.3 and 9, 149n.43, 150nn.50 and 55, 160n.17, 161nn.25 and 28; *Cymbeline*, 13–14, 31–32, 6–47, 51, 53–55, 69, 72–73, 80, 84–87, 96, 103, 107, 113–14, 149n.43, 161n.20; *Hamlet*, 15–16, 25, 29, 32–36, 46, 48, 50–53, 55–60, 62, 69, 76–79, 81–82, 85, 92, 94, 96–98, 101–4, 106–7, 113–14, 121, 125, 127, 131, 136–37, 145n.9, 149nn.43 and 48, 150nn.50 and 55, 152n.5, 153nn.16 and 18, 157n.38, 160n.17, 161n.25, 165n.28; *Henriad*, 15, 55, 61, 101, 107; *1 Henry IV*, 30, 35, 42, 52, 54, 61, 72–73, 75, 81, 85–86, 99, 101, 119, 133, 137, 145n.8, 148n.33, 149n.43, 153n.11, 156n.26, 158n.58; *2 Henry IV*, 85, 101, 104, 161n.20; *Henry V*, 25–26, 28, 31, 52, 54, 61, 73, 75, 83, 101, 104, 146n.9, 158n.58; *Henry VI, Parts 1–3*, 46–47, 70, 83, 94, 98, 100, 125, 127; *Henry VIII*, 71, 81, 161n.34; *Julius Caesar*, 25, 30, 32–36, 50, 81, 97, 145n.9, 146n.2, 149nn.43 and 47, 150n.50; *King John*, 25, 107; *King Lear*, 14–17, 24–25, 28–38, 42–46, 48–65, 69–70, 72–75, 77, 81–83, 85–86, 88, 90, 93–94, 97–99, 102–7, 111, 113–14, 119–21, **123–44,** 145nn.5 and 9, 146n.9, 148n.28, 149n.43, 150nn.50 and 55, 151n.70, 152n.76, 153nn.16 and 21, 156n.26, 161n.25, 162n.35, 164n.19, 165n.28; *Love's Labours Lost*, 25, 31, 35, 52–53, 55, 75, 149n.46; *Macbeth*,

Shakespeare, William (continued)
14, 16–17, 25–26, 32–36, 45–46,
49–53, 55–56, 71–72, 75, 81–83, 86,
94, 97, 99, 102, 106–7, **111–22,**
125–32, 137–39, 141–42, 145nn.3
and 9, 149n.43, 150nn.49, 50, and
55, 161n.25; *Measure for Measure,* 16,
35, 38, 41–43, 52–55, 64, 69, 73, 76,
80, 85–86, 95, 100, 104, 107, 127,
149n.43, 151n.69, 154n.25, 157nn.36
and 37, 161n.20; *Merchant of Venice,
The,* 35, 46, 52–55, 72, 75–76, 80–81,
86, 99, 107, 148n.30, 155n.21; *Merry
Wives of Windsor, The,* 25, 35, 72; *Midsummer Night's Dream, A,* 13, 15, 25,
30, 33, 35, 46, 49, 52–55, 60–61, 64,
73, 80–81, 85– 86, 91, 95, 97, 99–100,
107–8, 145nn.3 and 9, 148n.30,
149n.46, 153nn.8 and 11, 159n.4,
161nn.20 and 25; *Much Ado about
Nothing,* 13, 32, 35, 46, 52–54, 72, 75,
85, 97, 99, 145n.8, 161n.25; *Othello,*
13, 16, 25, 32–36, 38, 48–50, 52, 55,
57–58, 69–70, 72, 76–79, 82–83, 86,
88, 97, 101–3, 106, 115, 119, 121,
131, 145nn.3 and 9, 149nn.43 and
48, 150nn.50 and 55, 153n.12,
161n.25; *Pericles,* 14, 26, 28, 31, 47,
51–52, 69, 71–73, 80, 84–88, 95, 100,
103, 107, 140, 149nn.42 and 43,
161n.20; *Richard II,* 25, 35, 70, 82, 97,
101, 125, 127; *Richard III,* 25, 35, 45,
52, 54, 70–71, 82–83, 100–1, 107, 112,
125, 152n.77, 161n.25; *Romeo and
Juliet,* 13, 15, 25, 28, 32–34, 37–38,
48–49, 52–53, 55, 72–73, 79–80, 82,
94, 96, 98, 145nn.3 and 9, 150nn.43,
48, and 50, 168n.43; *Sonnets,* 102,
104–6, 160n.19; *Taming of the Shrew,
The,* 25, 35, 46, 52–55, 72, 75, 81, 85,
95, 107, 148n.30, 152n.77, 161nn.20
and 25; *Tempest, The,* 15, 26, 35, 46,
49, 51–55, 69, 71–73, 79–81, 84–89,
91, 94–97, 100, 103, 105–7, 125, 127,
136, 145n.3, 149n.43, 150n.52,
153nn.11 and 12, 160nn.17 and 19,
161n.20; *Timon of Athens,* 26, 29,
32–34, 36, 48–50, 52–54, 56–58, 70,
95, 145nn.3 and 9, 149n.43, 150n.55,
160n.17; *Titus Andronicus,* 25, 31–34,
46, 49–50, 52–54, 75, 78, 81–83, 98,
145n.9, 149n.43, 150nn.48 and 50;
Troilus and Cressida, 34, 48–50, 52, 97,
107, 145n.3; *Twelfth Night,* 25, 35, 46,
52–53, 55, 75, 83, 97, 99, 107, 145n.3,
148n.30; *Two Gentlemen of Verona,* 36,
53, 75, 85, 99, 147n.13, 149n.43;
Venus and Adonis, 28; *Winter's Tale,
The,* 13, 26, 47, 51–53, 55, 69–72, 75,
78, 80–81, 84–88, 96, 100, 103, 107,
145n.3, 149n.43, 161n.25
Sidney, Sir Philip, 96 *Arcadia,* 42–43,
153n.16; *Astrophil and Stella,* 160n.19
Siegel, Paul, 156n.26
Silberman, Lauren, 161n.26
skepticism, 74, 93–96, 104–7, 134–37
Skulsky, Harold, 162n.36
Skura, Meredith, 13
Slater, Ann Pasternak, 153n.16
Smith, Marion Bodwell, 152n.75
Snuggs, Henry, 147n.15
Snyder, Susan, 123, 152n.2, 166n.7
Soellner, Rolf, 166nn.10 and 12,
167nn.32 and 33, 169n.48
Southwell, Robert, 73–74
sovereignty, 14, 44, 48–49, 51–58,
61–65, 111–16, 122, 124–29, 136, 140,
143
Spenser, Edmund, 16, 87, 89–100,
103–8; *Faerie Queene, The,* 16–17, 89,
93–99, 103–7, 160n.19; *Fowre Hymnes,
The,* 97
Spivack, Bernard, 153n.12
sprecher-magus, 15, 52–55, 63–65, 71,
143, 153n.12
Sprengnether, Madelon, 13
sublimation. *See* psychological functions
superego formation (or collapse). *See*
psychological functions
Summers, Joseph H., 156n.33

Taylor, E. M. M., 167n.32
Taylor, Gary, 27–29, 126, 147n.19
Taylor, Mark, 154n.25
Terence, 13, 24, 31
Thorne, Barry, 148n.21

three-cycle plot (or 2-1-2 act structure).
    See dramaturgy trinitarian psychol-
    ogy, 35, 77, 83, 90, 92, 96, 157n.41
Troublesome Reign of King John, The, 23

vagina dentata or *penis dentata. See* psy-
    chological functions
Verbeke, G., 91, 159n.1, 160n.7
Veszy-Wagner, L., 163n.6

Walker, Roy, 163n.11
Warner, William, 40
Wasson, John, 158n.49
Waters, D. Douglas, 158n.51
Watson, Robert N., 164n.24
Weidhorn, Manfred, 160n.18
Weimann, Robert, 152nn.4 and 6,
    164n.19
Weiss, Paul, 159n.65
Weissinger, R. T., 146n.5
Weller, Barry, 164n.19

Welsford, Enid, 152n.4
West, Robert H., 162nn.39 and 43
wheel, 21, 29, 35, 46–47, 98, 100, 127,
    130, 137–38, 140–44, 168n.46,
    169n.47. *See also* three-cycle plot
Wheeler, Richard P., 13, 145n.3
Whetstone, George, *Promos and Cassan-
    dra,* 23, 38, 41
White, R. S., 80
Wilcher, Robert, 26
Williams, George W., 118–19, 116n.7,
    168n.44
Willichius, Iodocus, *Commentaria,* 26,
    147n.14
Wills, Garry, 168n.35
Wilson, T. Dover, 146n.5
Woolf, Virgina, 83, 85
Wordsworth, William, 84, 87, 164n.20
Wyckham, Glynne, 155n.13

Young, David, 145n.6